SMALL WOOD PROJECTS

SMALL WOOD PROJECTS

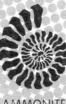

AMMONITE
PRESS

First published 2010 by

AMMONITE PRESS
166 High Street, Lewes,
East Sussex, BN7 1XU

ISBN 978-1-906672-56-0

A catalogue record for this book is available from the
British Library.

Associate Publisher Jonathan Bailey
Production Manager Jim Bulley
Editors Huw Pryce and Ian Penberthy
Managing Editor Richard Wiles
Managing Art Editor Gilda Pacitti
Designers Rebecca Mothersole and Robert Janes

Colour origination by GMC Reprographics
Printed and bound by Hung Hing Co. Ltd.

Show a copy of *Hobbies* to your friends.

Show a copy of *Hobbies* to your friends.

LAST STAND FOR THE

Back in the summer of 1939, **Hobbies Weekly** *carried a momentous article, which in a few words and diagrams, set out the means for converting a radio into a television set. The plans involved a neon bulb connected to the speaker output, viewed through holes in a revolving disc, driven by a belt connected to a small electric motor (made and sold by* **Hobbies***). Sound required a second radio, tuned to the audio frequency.*

The results can hardly have been satisfactory, and very few places in the UK were near enough to a transmitter for it to work at all. Anyone who ever used the motor in question near an AM radio would recognize that the sparks it made would obliterate even a strong signal, wrecking what picture the thing did receive and interfering with the sound. The whole apparatus would be noisy, sprawling and reminiscent of a Heath Robinson invention, but it was a Baird TV set.

By the end of that summer, war had broken out and TV transmissions ceased for the duration. Nevertheless this initial, and remarkable, foray into the future signalled the beginning of the end for Hobbies Ltd, albeit at a high point for *Hobbies Weekly*, which improved in ingenuity and the quality of its modelling projects as the availability of raw materials dwindled. Post-war austerity was to sustain the magazine into the 1950s.

As it had in 1914, war saw the diversion of much of Hobbies Ltd's production to arms manufacture. Defence contracts kept the company alive for two more decades after the war, but when television returned in 1946, it was only a matter of time before cheap, nightly entertainment would convert hobbyists into viewers. The slow decline had begun.

HOME HOBBYIST?

BEGINNING OF THE END

Hobbies Weekly ceased publication in December 1965. The Dereham factory in Norfolk, which once employed hundreds and held millions of yards of timber, that had produced cameras, motors, steam engines, bicycles, tools, boats and weapons, and exported them all over the world, fell silent in 1968. It is now the site of a superstore. The international network of stores and agents was kept on until the stock was sold off and then was closed down. The image of the home hobbyist morphed from that of a busy-fingered innovator into an obsessive anorak, and the world became a poorer, lazier place.

The magazine might, with a little vision, have converted to a monthly, raised its cover price and tapped into the market that continued to nurture other veteran titles such as *The Woodworker, Railway Modeller* and *Practical Wireless*, but the decision was left to concerns keen to extinguish the Hobbies brand and sell off the assets. With the myopia, lack of imagination and will typical of British business in the mid-20th century, a publishing phenomenon with seven decades of archived material was thrown out with the bathwater.

To be fair, by the time of its demise, *Hobbies Weekly* had become a little sad; the quality of the diagrams was a shadow of the clean precision of the 1930s, the projects reflected the fashion for simple, futuristic looking furniture, and the anticipated level of skill of the readership was so diminished as to limit the scope of the projects. A dip into the archive would have

provided useful material, particularly in educating the readership in the ways of joinery and other dying arts. But fretwork was already dead. The mainstay of the Hobbies empire had always been the sale of fretwood and fretwork machines. These heavy, treadle driven tools could make jigsaw puzzles and cut complex shapes, but their original advantage to Hobbies had been in cutting the embellished panels and finials so beloved of Victorian householders, who clearly believed that the more complex the appearance of an item, the greater its value and prestige. This fetish for embellishment combined with a national movement to promote small workshops and artisans, and to foster the preservation of skills and techniques no longer used in Britain's factories and mills, led to the birth of DIY.

CRAFTSMEN UNITE!

William Morris, the man most commonly associated with the Arts and Crafts movement died in 1896, one year after John and Frank Skinner launched *Hobbies Weekly*. Morris, along with a group of artists who called themeselves The Pre-Raphaelite Brotherhood, was concerned that the industrial revolution and the movement of the population from the land to the cities was harming the moral and spiritual life of British working people (and, by extension, all of humanity – the Empire touched the whole world).

A socialist, Morris saw the industrialization, and the systematic simplification of the jobs people did, from craftsman to factory worker, as a waste of human ingenuity and life. He and various of his associates

Give a Fretmachine for Christmas

Nothing could make a handyman happier than to have a Hobbies Fretmachine given him. It provides a factory for him and earns money in his spare time. By keen organisation these machines are sold at really low prices, and repay their outlay quickly and easily. Besides fretwork they come in for ordinary carpentry, fancy woodwork, etc.

There are machines up to £20 but the two illustrated are the most popular. Both are guaranteed, and are supplied ready to use, with instructions, spare saws, designs, spanners, etc. If you do not live near a branch or agent, have one sent from Dereham, by rail, carriage forward

THE GEM 35/-
A wonderful machine for the price. Built with steel frame, a convenient height, and long arms for big work. Polished metal table and parts and fitted with new non-warping metal arms. The machine runs easily and smoothly.

Made in our own Works

THE A1. 50/-
The most popular machine in the world. With cast metal frame to ensure rigidity and steadiness. Long wooden arms, polished metal table with rounded edges, lever spring tension on saw clamps and many other points advantage.

Obtainable from Hobbies Branches in London, Glasgow, Manchester, Birmingham, Leeds, Sheffield, Southampton and Brighton ; also from all leading ironmongers ; or from—
HOBBIES Ltd., DEREHAM, NORFOLK

FURNITURE MAKING WITH THE FRETSAW

formed companies and societies to promote craftsmanship and the link between the maker and the object. Man-made was seen as inherently better than mass-produced, and the act of creation was important to the wellbeing of working people and to society as a whole.

John Henry Skinner started selling fretwork machines and plywood in about 1887, having started out in his uncle's timber yard. The company promoted fretwork as a small business opportunity that could be pursued in people's spare time. He was the first manufacturer of plywood in the Empire, and he identified that the material was ideal for fretwork. Plywood can be made from everyday woods and finished with exotic veneers, which allows the production of good looking, cheap, fretted items of the sort Victorians loved.

TOWN AND GOWN

It is unlikely that Morris and Skinner would have agreed on much. Morris was public school educated and studied at Oxford, while Skinner was from trade; he started out in his uncle's business and ended up owning it. Their two worlds were separated by class, money, education, geography and probably by politics. Skinner's brother, Frank, however, worked in publishing in London.

The Arts and Crafts movement was fascinated by design, not simply of works of art, but of

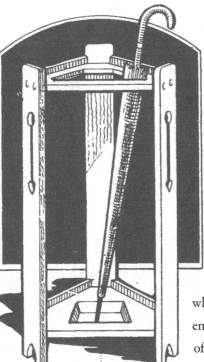

everyday objects. Morris is quoted as saying, 'Have nothing in your house that you do not know to be useful, or believe to be beautiful'. This fascination extended to any produced item, including printed material. Morris (who is now most famous for his wallpaper and furniture) designed several typefaces for his publishing business, the Kelmscott Press, which produced lavishly illustrated and embellished, handmade books as works of art.

Morris's Kelmscott Press took its inspiration from an Arts and Crafts publication, *The Century Guild Hobby Horse*. The *Hobby Horse* drifted out of print in the early 1890s, but during its ten-year run, it published the work of many highly regarded critics, artists and writers, including John Ruskin, Ford Madox Brown, William Michael Rossetti, George Frederic Watts, Edward Burne-Jones and Oscar Wilde. Frank, working in London, can't have missed it or others like it. When the Skinners launched *Hobbies Weekly* in 1895, the influences of the *Hobby Horse* and Kelmscott Press were writ large and are easy to see even now. Article headings were works of art in themselves; the typography was precise and beautifully laid out; illustrations were lavish and detailed.

While *Hobbies Weekly* did not follow the letter of the aim of Arts and Crafts, to restore the dignity of the craftsman in the workplace, it did set out a way for everyday working people of all classes to become craftsmen in their spare time. Morris would probably have approved; something on which he and J. H. Skinner would have agreed was that the Devil finds work for idle hands.

In bringing an idea born to the artistic and intellectual elite to the masses, Hobbies caught a popular wave. Arts and Crafts set British tastes (and those of the Empire and the Anglo-Saxon world) from the martial and heraldic crenellations and vertices of late 19th-century

English Gothic into more free-flowing and organic themes of *fin de siècle* French inspired Art Nouveau. After the First World War, the modernism of the 20th century gave the fretwork patternmakers Art Deco to play with, and they adapted well to the cleaner, geometric lines and curves of the 1920s and 1930s. Fretwork kept up with the styles.

FRETWORK FLOUNDERS

The Second World War left little more room for fretwork than it did for television. Production shifted, as it had in the First World War, from fret machines to bomb racks and missile cones. Hobbies had a good war, emerging in 1945 intact and in profit. Apparent growth continued with share issues and the opening of further Hobbies

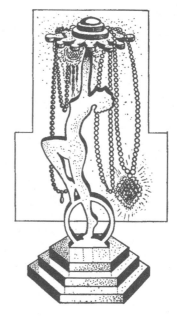

FROM ODDS AND ENDS

The " Blitz " Glass-Top
Ball Puzzle Game

stores in major cities, including one launched as late
as 1959 at Central London Airport Hounslow – now
known as Heathrow.

The Heathrow branch lasted only four years, and the
company only six. The fashion for clean lines, which
saw panelled doors and turned banisters boxed over
with hardboard, had done for the filigree and frippery
of the past hundred years. The Hobbies A1 fret
machine was still sold, up until the final demise of the
company in 1968. The AK47 of the fretwork world, it
had been in production since 1899.

MAGAZINE AND FACTORY

The link between magazine and factory seems a
little unhealthy in the post-monetarist 21st century.
Modern economists would say that the company
sought to corner an unhealthy proportion of the
market. They would be scandalized by the idea of
using the money from defence contracts to underpin
the hobbies side of the business, not for moral reasons,
but because it entailed diverting profits away from
shareholders into a potential loss making
sideline. Also for a general manufacturer of
goods and materials to publish a weekly
magazine would be sheer heresy in these
days of outsourcing to specialists.

Indeed the business died along with
its defence contracts. Without the
additional capital, initially derived from
maintaining contacts made during the
First and Second World Wars, to make
use of surplus capacity at the factory,

Hobbies Ltd could no longer sustain itself. In 1964,
the old board of Hobbies Ltd sold up, pocketing
between them £8,400 in compensation (this would be
worth about £130,000 today).

SAVE FOR VICTORY

The new management set about cutting
out the dead wood. There was a rash
of retirements over the next two years,
of people who knew Hobbies inside
out. The loss of skills and experience,
coupled with the changing culture and
products at Dereham, did not stimulate
magazine sales. *Hobbies Weekly* closed
down in 1965 after circulation fell
below 20,000. In spite of everything,

the company managed to stay in profit to the end and to liquidate in 1968 with enough money to pay its staff the equivalent of a few million pounds to share between them, a decision that could be viewed either as wise or cynical.

In order to keep up with the requirements of the modern arms trade, Hobbies would have needed to retool and redefine itself; it was no longer well enough equipped to compete with younger companies or those forced to refit after the war. As a manufacturer of raw materials for hobbyists, it was not in the business of acquiring high-speed, automated machinery. Time, technology and TV had caught up with Hobbies.

SMALL PROJECTS

During its run of publication, *Hobbies Weekly* changed the world in a multiplicity of small ways. Furniture and ornaments built from projects in the magazine can still be found in British houses, and in other parts of

the world where its influence was felt – from Alberta to Zimbabwe. Hobbyists made a lot of stuff that we assume was factory made, particularly from the smaller projects.

There might well be items from your house, or from your childhood in this book. They may have come from a hobbyist in your family, but the magazine's stated aim was to provide 'Pleasure and Profit'; projects were designed to be made and sold. That stool from your grandma's might've been made in the shed, or bought from a school or Scout troop fete, or even from a shop. While some items might have taken days or weeks to build, many took only a few hours and could be made in batches.

The simplicity and strength of a well-made piece of Hobbies furniture could easily help it outlive its maker. Like larger furniture, toys and games will have fared less well, but it is likely that adaptations of the simpler projects are still made in school workshops in Britain, and even commercially for sale in small toyshops and at craft fairs.

The projects in this book are small, either because they produce small items, or because the items they produce are very simple and easy to make. The wood required for each could usually be bought and delivered in a single package from the Hobbies factory and

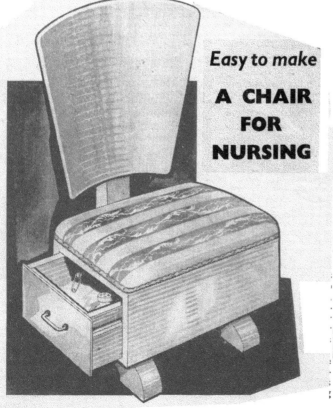

Easy to make
A CHAIR FOR NURSING

warehouses in Dereham when they were published. Often, of course, materials could be improvised or bought locally. The magazine makes no mention of where wood might be gleaned from another source, but people used old tea-chests for fretwood, and for the backs of cupboards and shelves, and they kept bins full of offcuts in the shed.

TEST OF TIME

Some of these projects have stood the test of time and can be made today, others, while still achievable, are less desirable. Some beg the question as to why anyone would attempt to build one in the first place. The Joke Lung Tester, printed in 1937 while TB was still a major killer, and Squaring the Swastika from February 1939 both point to the British having a more robust public sense of humour than the modern media considers appropriate.

While many projects reflect the period in which they were published, (consider the Nursing Chair, or the Blitz Puzzle as anything other than products of their decade and they become almost as tasteless and awkward as each other), others were revived, redrawn and written up over and over. Why waste a good idea when you can recycle every few years? The Child's Cot from 1909 won a prize for the best project made with 2/- worth of wood, the only differences between it and a modern cot are in the size of the mattress and the quality of the joinery.

As a rule of thumb, the older the project, the better the quality of woodwork and the more expertise required. This general relaxation of what *Hobbies Weekly* considered to be the level of skill of the average reader charts the decline of the value of craftsmanship feared by William Morris and his ilk. The projects of the 1960s and the general move away from making complex furniture reflect this. By the end of the 1950s, mass produced furniture was beginning to resemble modern architecture; the utilitarian ethic called for simplicity, lack of embellishment and low build cost.

Why employ a craftsman to make super-strong, invisible dovetails to hold together drawers and carcases when a length of dowelling and a dab of modern glue would do the job for the lifetime of the piece? Furniture was not, of course, expected to last a lifetime. Modern furniture has a life expectancy that can be measured in years rather than decades or centuries. Cabinetmaking, like fretwork before it, was dwindling in significance.

Other projects reflected an inventiveness that extended beyond the realms of common sense. The primitive pedal bin from 1937 is visibly a disaster and must have caused marital stress in many a *Hobbies* reading

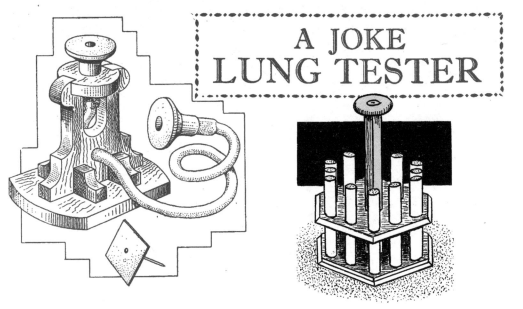

A JOKE LUNG TESTER

in modern pedal bins, but steel rather than wooden rods can be concealed behind and within the bin rather than embracing it like a praying mantis. The wooden car jack, while ingenious and sound in principle, would require nerves of steel and a breathtaking lack of common sense to use (people almost certainly did, and many may still be alive to tell the tale, or possibly not!).

The toy telephone from 1945 was a splendid use for scrap wood, and had the potential to be even heavier than the Bakelite original, giving it a destructive potential close to that of a sock full of lead farm animals. How about wooden roller-skates? Conventional or in-line? A toboggan for use on grass? Sadly there was never a wooden crash-helmet design in the magazine, but first-aid was considered a hobby in its own right.

This collection represents a sample of the hundreds of projects published across the 70-year print run of *Hobbies Weekly*. The results; the product of these projects, varied considerably in their utility, popularity and value (not many of them fulfilled both of Morris's criteria for things you should allow in your house, and many, being neither useful nor beautiful, met either),

but they were aimed at a readership with varying levels of skill and available time.

Many projects were inherently bad, ugly, daft, dangerous, impractical or infeasible, but they got people working, thinking, learning and building stuff. A significant proportion of the things people made became a part of our way of life. This biscuit barrel, that woven-topped stool, the funny limp your grandfather walked with after his grass-tobogganing accident. Hobbies, like its richer older brother Arts and Crafts, still exerts an influence on how we look at the world, and even the way we approach problems and challenges.

If the management of Hobbies Ltd had maintained the drive and initiative of John Henry Skinner and his brother Frank, the daring and ingenuity of its designers, and possibly the loyalty of its workforce, *Hobbies Weekly* might still be with us now. Hobbies Ltd was resurrected by a former Hobbies employee and is still trading under the name. The brand abides, selling craft supplies and kits in Norfolk, near Norwich, but the factory, its employees, its network of shops and its weekly magazine are long gone.

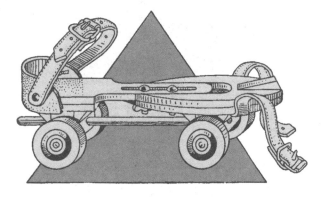

MAKE YOURSELF A PAIR OF ROLLER SKATES!

A Boy's Desk and Stool.

A CHAIR FOR NURSING

So handy for mother

Are We Sitting Comfortably?

OUR BOYS' DEPARTMENT

A Boy's Desk and Stool.

THE desk and stool shown at Fig. 1 will be coveted by all our boy readers, but need not be coveted in vain, as it may be made by any enterprising boy skilled in the use of a few tools. Everyone knows how useful a desk of this kind would be, providing a private place where work or reading could be done without interference, and as the flap is hinged to open the space under will hold quite a number of books or papers.

The work has been kept on simple lines, and the construction is, perhaps, rather out of the ordinary, to enable it to be done with as few tools as possible. Almost any kind of wood is suitable; the legs should be strong, and not of less substance than the sizes quoted, but it should be possible to cut the other parts from packing case wood, such being quite suitable.

The back legs A are 2ft. 5ins. long, and the

FIG. 1.

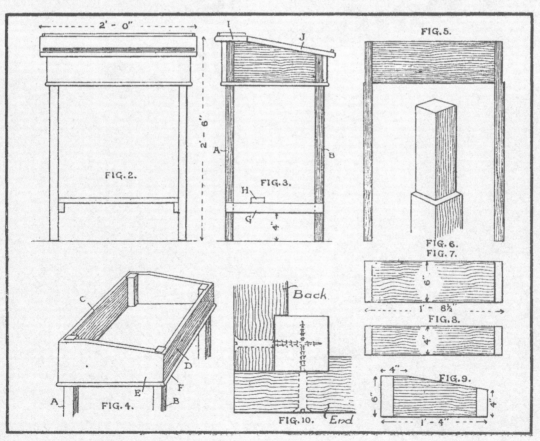

FIG. 2.

FIG. 3.

FIG. 4.

FIG. 5.

FIG. 6.
FIG. 7.

FIG. 8.

FIG. 9.

FIG. 10.

front legs, B, 2ft. 3ins. long by 1½in. square. The back of the desk C (Fig. 4) is shown at Fig. 7, the front, D, at Fig. 8, and one end, E, at Fig. 9, all being cut from 1in. wood. To enable the parts to be strongly fitted together, the legs, back, front, and ends have shoulders ⅓in. deep cut on them. The legs are treated on two sides, as shown at Fig. 6, the shoulders on the back legs being 6ins. long, and on the front 4ins. long. The shoulders on the back and front are 1in. long, and those on the ends are 1½in. long.

In fixing the parts together take the back pair

The bottom rails, G, are 1½in. deep by 1in. thick, screwed in position, and the foot rail, H, which is 2ins. wide, is fixed above.

The top of the desk, I, is 2ft. long by 5ins. wide, the back and end edges are rounded, and it is fixed with screws or nails. The flap J, is also 2ft. long, and is wide enough to overhang about 1in. at the front. It may be necessary to strengthen the flap with cross-battens, and it is hinged to the top with a pair of 1½in. hinges. Small slips about ½in. square are fitted around the back and end edges of the top, and across the front of the

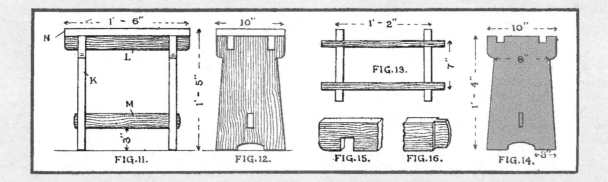

FIG. 11.   FIG. 12.   FIG. 13.   FIG. 15.   FIG. 16.   FIG. 14.

of legs and screw the back to them, as shown at Fig. 5, next screw the front to the front pair of legs in a similar way, and then screw the ends to the front and back legs. The screws are driven through the front, back, and ends, into the legs, and a glance at Fig. 10 will make the fixing quite clear. The screws should be carefully driven to prevent splitting, and the joints should be glued.

The bottom of the desk, F, need not be more than ⅓in. thick, fitted over the legs. The edges should overhang slightly and be rounded, while nails are used for fixing. It will be noticed that the rounded edges will cease at the points where the bottom is fitted over the legs, and small pieces of wood should be fitted from these points to the corners to form an unbroken edge.

flap, as shown at Figs. 1, 2, and 3, to prevent things placed on the desk from slipping off.

If a stool is required one similar to that shown at Figs. 1, 11, and 12, may be easily made. The ends K are cut as shown at Fig. 14, the top rails, L, are 1ft. 6ins. long by 2ins. deep, and the bottom rail, M, is 1ft. 3ins. long, by 2ins. deep. The top rails are notched into the ends, notches being cut as shown at Figs. 14 and 15 to enable the rails and ends to be fitted together as shown at Fig. 13. The bottom rail is tenoned into the ends, as shown at Fig. 16. These parts should be fixed together with glue, and the top, N, which is 1ft. 6ins. by 10ins., is simply nailed in place.

The desk and stool, on completion, could be stained and varnished, or painted.

A FOLDING ARMCHAIR.

pieces, and be ¾-in. wide, this being the thickness for the cross-pieces. In other words, the whole of the ends of the cross-pieces will form the tenons. The mortises will not go right through the wood but to ½-in. deep, this also being the length of the tenons.

The upright bars between the middle and bottom cross-pieces will be ⅜-in. thick, their ends being fitted into corresponding mortises in the cross-pieces, each end extending ½-in. into its mortise. When getting out these upright bars pains should be taken to have each pair exactly alike and the central bar of even

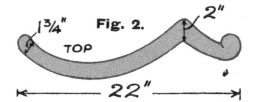

Fig. 2.

1¾" 2" TOP 22"

proportion. The legs, arms and back uprights will be 1in. thick. The edges of these, also the edges of the cross-pieces, will be nicely rounded.

The carpet or plush, the position for which is indicated in Fig. 6, should be of good and strong quality, with nice colour and an attractive pattern. This will be fixed, of course, with its face forward. The arrows suggest where the carpet should be nailed. Brass nails, with fairly broad and attractive heads, will be used, being put an equal distance apart. These nails, however, will not come directly on to the carpet, as this would not give a good finish

IF made as suggested in this article our readers will have an attractive and comfortable chair, it being of the writer's own designing. Fig. 1 shows the pattern of the two uprights for the back, Fig. 2 the shape for the two arms, Fig. 3 the style for the front legs, Fig. 4 the design for the top cross-piece, which at its deepest point should be from 3½ to 4ins. The black portions indicate what is to be cut out, and the fretsaw can be employed for making these cavities, while the round ones can be bored, if care, particularly at the finish, be taken so that the wood does not split. Fig. 5 shows how the top, middle, and bottom cross-pieces respectively, should be curved to give comfort for the back. The middle and bottom cross-pieces will each be 1½ins. deep, that is, from top to bottom. Fig. 6 gives the back complete. The mortises in Fig. 1 should be of the same length as are the ends of the respective cross-

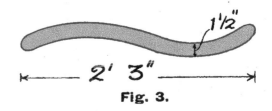

1½" 2' 3" Fig. 3.

Bordering or binding, an inch wide, of a tasty pattern, and contrasting yet harmonious, colour with the colour of the carpet will be laid along the edges and the nails will pass through this and the carpet.

Fig. 7 shows the seat section. The cross-piece at the back which connects with the legs is arranged with its wider way (1½ins.) running in the same direction as the legs, whereas the

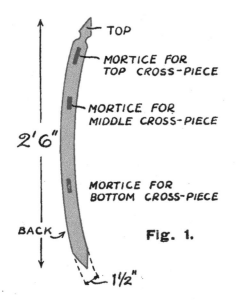

TOP

MORTICE FOR TOP CROSS-PIECE

MORTICE FOR MIDDLE CROSS-PIECE

2'6"

MORTICE FOR BOTTOM CROSS-PIECE

BACK

Fig. 1.

1½"

cross-piece which connects with the front legs has its wider way on the slant with these legs, that is, parallel with the floor when the chair is open. This is so arranged to make comfortable resting for the under part of the legs. Diagram "C" in Fig. 8 which suggests what I mean.

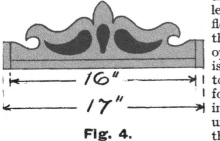

Fig. 4.

The carpet for the seat should be of the same as for the back and will be cut to proper size. Fig. 7 shows that the carpet should be wider at the front than at the back.

After cutting, the edges and sides should be bound with strong braid or binding of suitable colour this being 1 in. wide and will be so sown on that it extends about ⅜-in. under and above. This will prevent fraying of the edges. The carpet for the back should be bound similarly. This carpet must be of that length as makes the seat to open to the right extent for sitting. That is to suggest that it is the carpet which governs how far the seat shall open.

The respective front and back end of the carpet should come well around the respective cross-piece. then be strongly nailed to it. Fig. 8 shows the positions for the mortises to take the tenons of the front and back cross-pieces which connect with the legs diagram "A" giving that for the back diagram "B" that for the front. In other words when the chair is open these cross-pieces should have been so fixed that the seat is parallel with the floor. Diagram "D" shows the hole to be bored near the bottom

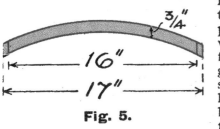

Fig. 5.

of each of the four legs to take the two rods as shown in diagram "E."

These holes should be 2ins. up from the bottom. The rods will be round with ⅝-in. diameter. that at the front when the chair is open being 15¼ins. long, that at the back 17¼ins. long. Each rod

will have its respective end extending ½-in. into each leg.

All the cross-pieces, rods, and upright bars between the middle and bottom cross-pieces of the back, will have their respective ends fitting tightly into the mortises. Very hot glue will be used for the ends and mortises, and when the ends have been driven home carefully they will be nailed from the back. The brads should be strong and of that length that they pass nearly through the back upright and the legs, but not quite. If they came through they would mar the frontal appearance.

The upright bars just mentioned should be fixed before the middle and bottom cross-pieces are secured to the back uprights as they cannot be got in after.

Fig. 9 shows how the lower sections of the chair are riveted to provide the folding effect, the round dots where the rivets are to come. These rivets should be about ¼-in. diameter and about 2¼ins. long. Their heads should be rather rounded and broad, being flat on the inner surface, that is, against which the washer will come. A thin, rather broad washer will come against the head. the bolt then being passed through the hole in the outer leg. Now another washer will be slipped on, the bolt then going through the hole in the inner leg. Next a similar washer will be placed on the end then a heavy weight be rested against the head of the bolt. when the end will be riveted by its being broaded with quick, spreading taps by the hammer. For successful riveting the end of the bolt should

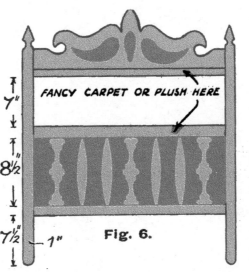

FANCY CARPET OR PLUSH HERE

7"

8½"

7½" 1"

Fig. 6.

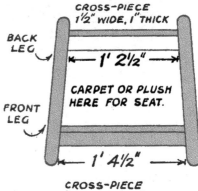

CROSS-PIECE
1½" WIDE, 1" THICK

BACK LEG

1' 2½"

CARPET OR PLUSH HERE FOR SEAT.

FRONT LEG

1' 4½"

CROSS-PIECE
1½" WIDE, 1" THICK.

A FOLDING ARMCHAIR.

extend beyond the washer about 1/16 of an inch. For good folding the holes in the wood and in the washers should be no larger than is necessary for the rivet or bolt to pass through, while riveting ought to be done to that degree where opening and shutting are not too slack neither too tight. Hard wood should be employed in making this chair, and it will be appropriate to select a choice kind. After making, the chair will be finely sandpapered, dusted then finished by French polishing —J.P.B.

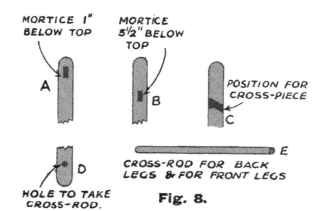

MORTICE 1" BELOW TOP

MORTICE 5½" BELOW TOP

A

B

POSITION FOR CROSS-PIECE

C

D

HOLE TO TAKE CROSS-ROD.

E

CROSS-ROD FOR BACK LEGS & FOR FRONT LEGS

Fig. 8.

⊠⊠ A NURSING CHAIR ⊠⊠

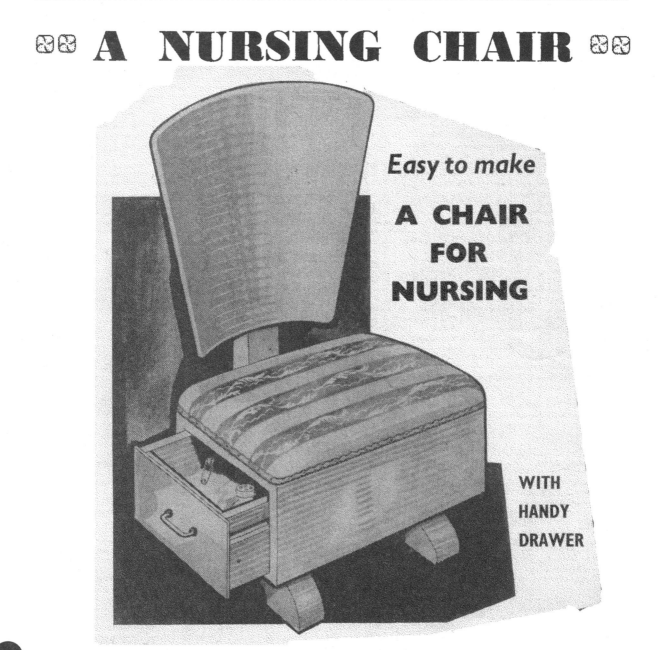

Easy to make

A CHAIR FOR NURSING

WITH HANDY DRAWER

MAKING A NURSING CHAIR

AS a prospective father it would surely be a labour of love to make up this nursing chair in time for the 'great event'. It is so handy, too, for mother's needs; just the right height and complete with a drawer at the side for pins, powder and odds and ends as shown in the illustration on the front page. You would score full marks if you could make it in secret and present it at the psychological moment.

The seat itself is made in the form of a box into which slides the drawer. The back-rest is nicely curved for maximum comfort and the finishing touch is added by the use of suitable padding as shown in the diagrams.

Study the diagrams carefully before commencing work. Essential measurements are given on the front and side views in Fig. 1 which also gives a good idea of the general construction. The back and front (pieces A) of the box seat are of ¾ in. wood, and the top and bottom (pieces B) are ½ in. Pieces B could conveniently be of ½ in. plywood (see Fig. 3).

To commence construction the various pieces should be cut to size ready for assembly. Cut the back-rest C from 2 in. thick wood, the feet D from 1½ in., and the back-rest support F from 1 in. These shapes are shown in the squared diagram in Fig. 2. Enlarge the squares and draw in the shapes square by square.

Screw and glue the back-rest C centrally to the back and similarly fix the feet at the bottom. Screws should be long enough to make a secure joint. Now assemble the seat as seen in Fig. 3. Notice that the piece E is at the open end and piece G at the opposite end. Pieces E and G are both ¾ in. thick.

Screw and glue the shaped support F to the upright C (Fig. 4). These pieces will be halved together as seen in the diagrams. The shaped back is cut from ⅛ in. hardboard or ¼ in. plywood. If the plywood is difficult to bend apply a rag soaked in hot water to the convex side. Do not oversoak or the laminations will part. The back should be screwed and glued in position. Two ¾ in. thick runners are screwed inside the box as shown in Fig. 3.

The drawer is made up from ¾ in. wood. Fig. 5 indicates how the sides I and J are butted on to the back and front (pieces K). The bottom is of ⅛ in. hardboard as is the front M. The front overlaps all round. The runners will of course slide in the gaps between pieces I and J. The drawer can be lined with ⅛ in. hardboard. The drawer handle is Hobbies No. 703, which is a chromium-plated half-round bar 3¼ in. long. It costs 1s. 9d. from Hobbies Ltd, Dereham, Norfolk — postage 4½d.

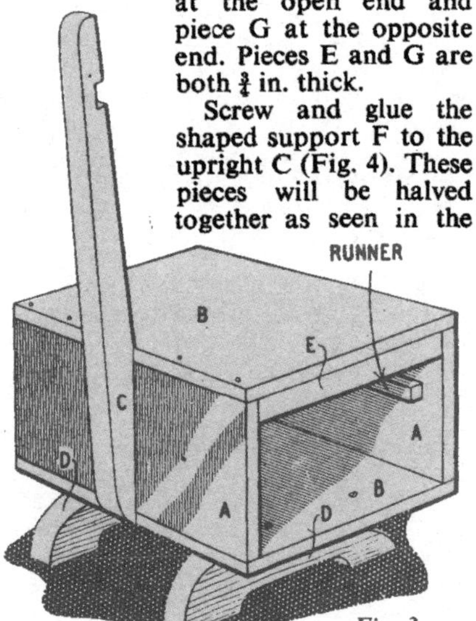

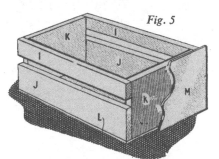
Fig. 3

Fig. 5

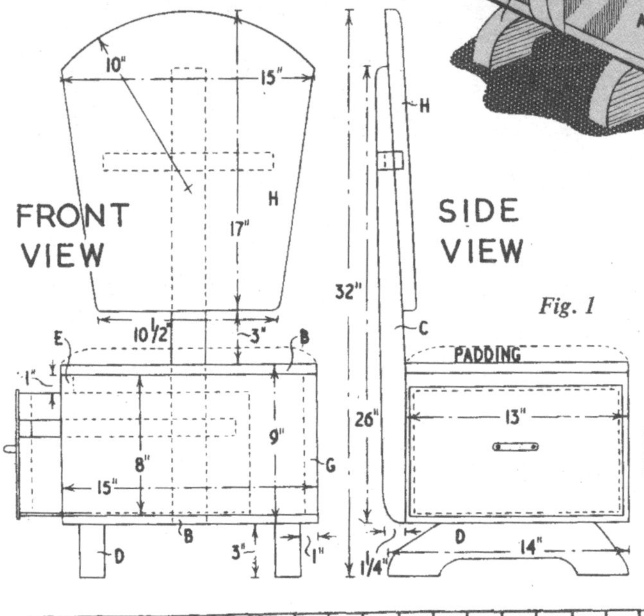

FRONT VIEW

SIDE VIEW

Fig. 1

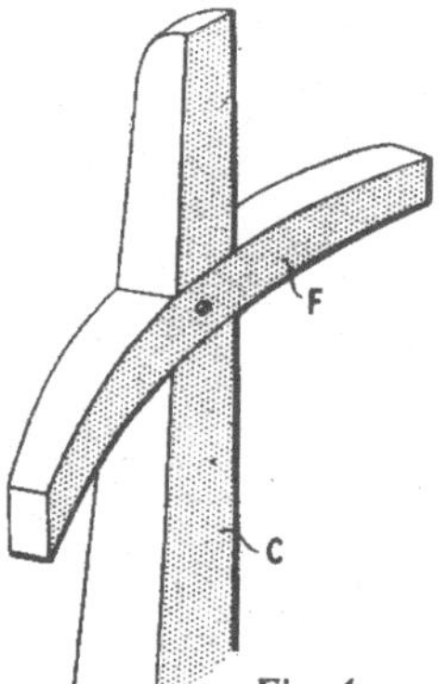

PADDING

Fig. 4

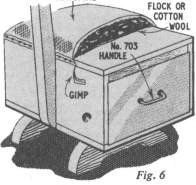
MATERIAL
FLOCK OR COTTON WOOL
No. 703 HANDLE
GIMP
Fig. 6

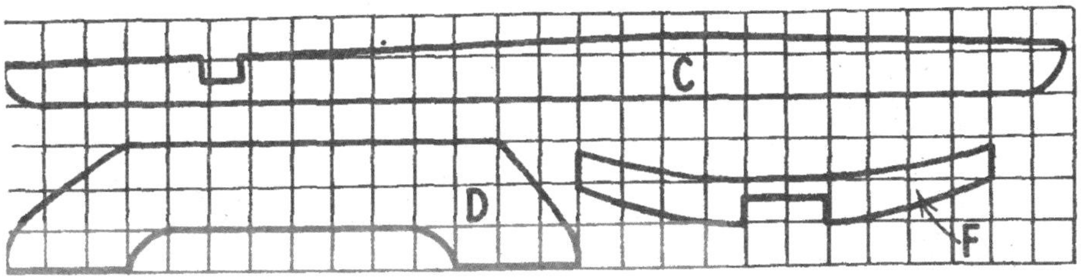

Clean up all round with glasspaper and fill the grain ready for painting. Give two undercoats and rub down with silicon carbide paper used wet. Finish off with one or two finishing coats.

The seat is now padded as shown in Fig. 6. Pin the material all round and then cover with gimp to finish off. The gimp can be held in place with a suitable adhesive. (M.h.

Complete instructions for wood working and weaving a
SEAGRASS-TOP STOOL

OUR illustration here shows a neat little stool with a seat of woven seagrass. This material is very popular and chairs and stools covered with it give a room a cosy appearance, and it is very comfortable to sit upon.

The legs are worked up from 1½in. square wood; oak or beech being suitable. We give the length of the legs here as 12ins., but they may be longer or shorter than this, according to choice. In Fig. 1 is shown the simple shaping of each leg with added measurements for setting out.

The eight rails connecting the legs consist of ½in. hardwood rods cut off in lengths of 11ins. and glued into holes bored ½in. deep to receive the ends. The first thing to do in preparing the legs is to lay all the four pieces, after cutting them to length, side by side on

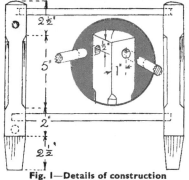

Fig. I—Details of construction

the bench or table, keeping one end hard up against a straight edge or block of wood.

Now set out the distances from the foot end, as shown in Fig. 1, and mark across them all in one operation, using a tee square or a try square for this purpose.

Next draw lines in pencil across the diagonals on the top ends of the legs. These lines form guides for shaping, as shown in the enlarged detail in Fig. 1. Note also the lower extremities of the legs taper off to 1in., this again being set out on all faces of the legs as a guide for cutting.

Rails

Looking again at the detail in Fig. 1 we note the holes for the rods are centred ½in. down from the shaping line at the top, and 1in. from the back edge of each leg. All four of the lower rails are spaced similarly, the plan, Fig. 2, shows the arrangement clearly in a section of the top surface.

The positions of the centres of the rods are again drawn on all four surfaces at one operation as for the general shaping of the legs. With a ½in. diameter twist drill all the holes are made ½in. deep. It might be a good plan, to gain strength, in the general construction of the stool, to arrange the rails as shown on

the left leg of the stool, shown in Fig. 1. Here it will be seen that the rails are set centrally in the width of the leg and are lower on two sides, that is they do not all follow round evenly.

Strength Joint

It is suggested, too, that the ends of the rails might in this case go into the legs a depth of 1in., which is a distinct advantage regarding strength. If the latter course be adopted, the four lower rails will have to be 12ins. long as against 11ins. for the top four.

When boring the holes for the rods see the brace is held perfectly upright, and dip the ends of each rail in glue before driving them in.

Another necessary precaution is to make a shallow V cut along the ends of each rail so surplus glue and air may escape during the process of driving in.

Test the finished frame for squareness and see that equal measurements occur between all the legs so the weaving may be accurately carried out.

The Seagrass Top

The special seagrass for making the seat is obtainable in skeins or hanks and sold by weight. The seagrass is bought in long lengths and several yards should, therefore, be wound off on to a stick previous to commencing to weave. The simplest method of weaving is shown in Fig. 2, which gives a clear plan of the seat.

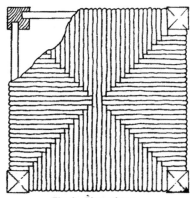

Fig. 2—Plan of top

In the diagram, Fig. 3, is shown exactly how to start and how the interlacing of each strand is made. In the end of the seagrass first make a knot and then, putting in a small staple, fix the seagrass to one of the rails as shown. Now carry the seagrass over rod (A) and under it and over and under (B) to (C).

Here it goes over and under and is brought back over (A) again and under on to (D) where it passes over and under again and is brought up over itself and over rod (C) again and so on to (B) where

it passes over and under again and so over (D).

Close Weaving

At this point we have completed one round and have arrived at the starting point where the interlacing process is repeated. It should be explained, perhaps, that the seagrass is purposely shown very slack and the thickness exaggerated in the diagram, and that in actual weaving, of course, each turn is drawn tightly as possible over the rails.

Each time the seagrass is brought over the rods, too, it must be kept hard up against its neighbour, so that the spaces are completely filled and all strands kept evenly and straight across.

Jointing

When it is necessary to make a join in the seagrass, the knot should be made underneath and, therefore, out of sight. For sake of strength make the well-known reef-knot, shown as an enlarged diagram in Fig. 3.

The legs and the four lower rails should be stained with oak or mahogany stain and afterwards waxed and brushed up or rubbed with soft rag. If it is required to paint the stool, then it should have an undercoating of suitable paint and the finish of enamel or cellulose enamel.

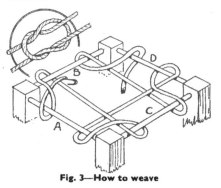

Fig. 3—How to weave

AN ALL-WOOD FOLDING GARDEN CHAIR

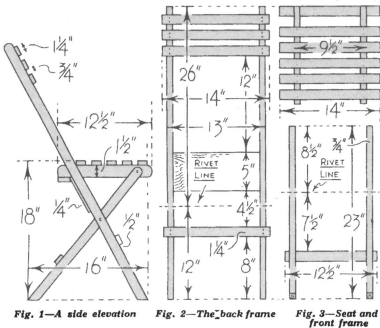

ILLUSTRATED is a novel little chair that folds perfectly flat when not in use and is equally suitable for the house or garden. It is simply constructed, surprisingly rigid, giving a nice support for one's back and making a very comfortable seat, indeed.

The elevation and constructional details will vouch this, and it will be seen that, excepting for a few nails and rivets, it is comprised mainly of wood, this making it light, and convenient to handle. Incidentally, such chairs cost 6/6 in the shops, but you can make this one for about 1/6.

The side elevation at Fig. 1 gives a definite idea of its assembly and shape. To save you the trouble of working to scale to obtain the dimensions, the parts have been separated into three and give the correct measurements concerning each.

At Fig. 2 we show the back frame, the legs being cut from 1¼ins. wide by ¾in. thick whitewood and the grilling laths from 1¼ins. by ½in. or ⅜in. stuff. Of course, any hardwood like birch, beech, ash, or oak would serve ; but if you find this too expensive, pine, chestnut, spruce or deal could be used and—if obtained a little thicker than quoted—with every confidence of making a sound job.

Material to use

To make this chair, the writer went to a local timber yard and ordered a 5ft. length of 5¾in. wide by ⅞in. thick flooring and a 6ft. length of 3½in. wide by ½in. thick sheeting which cost 1/3. He cut the rails from the *planed edges* to full length, cleaned the sawn edges with a smoothing plane and finally cut the rails and legs to the sizes given. He also took care to see that the wood was free

from knots as much as possible and thus saved himself a lot of anxiety.

If you adopt this plan, don't forget to allow for the fact you are working with ⅞in. thick stuff and not ¾in. material as marked in the drawings. And assuming the latter has been decided upon, it will avoid perplexity if instruction is continued as from the beginning.

Therefore, make the back frame as detailed at Fig. 2. Attach with 1½in. nails (either roundhead copper, plain flat, or heel brads) the plywood support, then attend to the cross laths as shown, and drill the rivet holes. Screws such as 1½in. by 10 iron roundheads with suitable washers could be used if you do not feel partial to the rivet method.

Seat and Front Frame

The seat could now be made, the side pieces being 12½ins. long by 1½ins. wide. Attach the laths as shown with nails, omitting the rear lath which is screwed in place after the sides of the seat are attached to the front frame.

The front frame, providing you are using screws instead of 3/16in. copper rivets, should not be drilled where indicated by the dotted line—just mark here with a bradawl. Drill holes, however, at the top or seat end as in Fig. 1. This should be done to give the screws sufficient freedom for movement, i.e., so that the screw threads will eat tightly into the seat rails and not turn with the legs.

A method of preventing their likelihood of working loose is to dip

Fig. 1—A side elevation   **Fig. 2—The back frame**   **Fig. 3—Seat and front frame**

the screw points into water prior to screwing into the wood. This, of course, will cause them to rust in the wood and make them impassive to the knocks of years.

Assembly

To assemble the parts, screw the front frame between the back frame. The heads should screw against a washer, with washers *between* the legs. This would not (unless desired) be necessary with the rivet heads. You must, nevertheless, have a washer between each part and insert on another after the rivet head is pushed through. The projection is then flattened with a sharp cold chisel and the hammer, or the heel of the hammer itself.

Having attached the seat to the front frame legs, allow its rails to rest on the plywood support and look at it sideways to see whether the seat is sitting straight, that is, on a level with the legs. If not— and as it should incline slightly, anyway—cut out small checks in the plywood for the seat rails, then screw the back rail in place.

This procedure completes the work, which can be either varnished, polished, enamelled or just left in its natural state. Level the legs with a length of wood, then cut.

CUTTING LIST

2 back legs, 38ins. by 1¼ins. by ¾in. thick.
2 front legs, 23ins. by 1¼ins. by ¾in. thick.
11 cross laths, 14ins. by 1¼ins. by ¼in. thick.
1 piece plywood, 13ins. by 5ins. by ¼in. thick.
2 seat rails, 12ins. by 1¼ins. by ¾in. thick.
6—1¼in. by 10 roundhead iron screws, with washers.

CHIP CARVING
is quite easy

DECORATIVE
Touches

Lightship Bedside Lamp

A topical piece of carpentry is this attractive
"VICTORY" HALL RACK

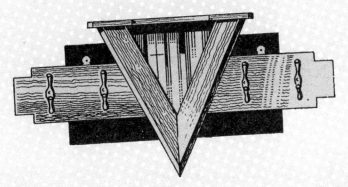

THIS WEEK'S TOY

A BEAD LOOM—A NOVELTY.

THE Bead Loom shown at Fig 1 is an easily-made toy selling at one shilling. It should be packed in a neat cardboard box and supplied together with 150 glass beads in two different colours and two needles. A printed sheet of instructions as well as a few designs should be included,

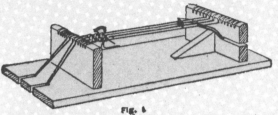

Fig. 1.

the latter being obtainable from the British Toy Association at a small cost.

In the original loom the wood is beech, but this is not essential, any hardwood will do. Two thicknesses are needed, 5-16in. and ¼in. The wood must be planed and finished smooth with glasspaper, and as there is such a small amount of work in the article, it is quite worth while spending a little extra time in getting a good finish. The base should be cut from ¼in. to a width of 3⅛in. and length of 9¼in. and the ends rubbed smooth with glasspaper.

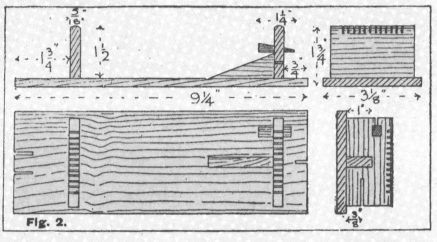

Fig. 2.

Tenon or circular saw cuts should be made in the ends, two at one end and one at the other. With a circular saw this is only a matter of setting the gauge, but if the sawing is done by hand it will be necessary to use a sawing board as shown at Fig 3. The board should be placed in the bench vice with about a dozen pieces of wood on it, or it can be supported against a table and the wood held in position with a G cramp. In both cases the sawcuts are only ⅜in. deep, the single cut is in the middle and the two cuts are ¼in. each side of the centre. This completes the preparation of the base pieces, and it will be seen that there is very little work in them.

Both the uprights are the same in every particular and are cut from 5-16in. wood, but as the top edge has to be slightly rounded,

it will be necessary to prepare the wood in strips before cutting it into the correct lengths. The width of the strips should be 1½in., and when sufficient material has been prepared one edge should be slightly rounded with a plane and finished with glasspaper. The amount of curve is only slight, as will be seen from the full size detail at Fig. 4. The wood should now be cut off into lengths of 2¾in. the ends being neatly glasspapered and left neat and fairly smooth.

The next stage in the operations is to make the saw cuts as shown in the full size detail at Fig 5. It will be seen that there are twelve sawcuts, each ⅛in. apart. This is another case where the use of a small circular saw would be of great help, particularly as several pieces could be held together on the bench. If sawn with a tenon saw it will be necessary to use a similar arrangement to that suggested for sawing the ends of the bottom pieces. When one is doing a large number of parts similar to these uprights, it pays to make the board, particularly as such a piece of apparatus takes very little time to make and may be made from any odd material. The width of the sawcuts should not be more than ⅛in., and may with advantage be a little less. The whole width of the twelve sawcuts with the spaces in between should not be more than 1⅞in. or 2in. The depth of the

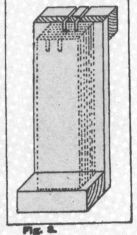

Fig. 3.

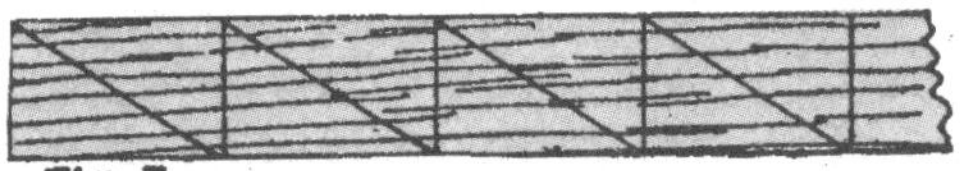

Fig. 7.

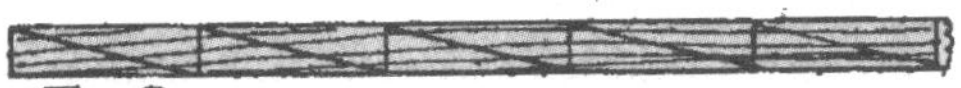

Fig. 8.

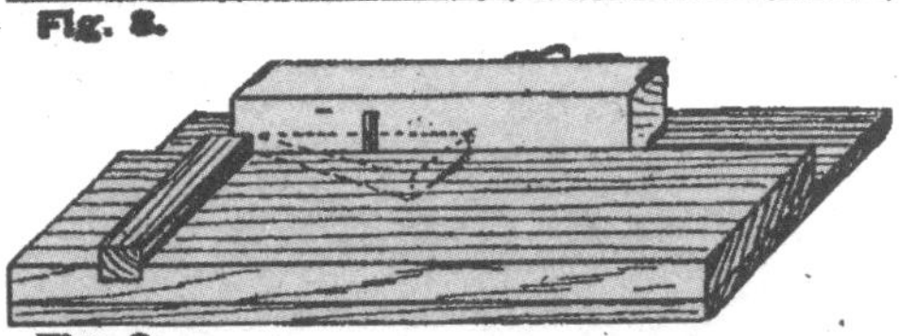

Fig. 9.

cuts should be $\frac{1}{8}$in. and for the sake of neatness they should all be taken to the same level. This certainly will not be easy at first if the sawing is done by hand, but with a circular saw this difficulty will be entirely removed. It has already been mentioned in a previous article that a small treadle circular saw will be found one of the most useful machines a toymaker could invest in. Strips of wood can be cut to the same width without any trouble, and one is sure that they are all alike, and in making sawcuts such as required in this toy, there is nothing to equal it.

One of the end pieces is quite plain, but the other should be provided with the two sawcuts as shown at Fig 5. On one side the sawcut is $\frac{3}{8}$in. up from the bottom and $\frac{3}{4}$in. along, on the other it is 1in. up and $\frac{1}{2}$in. along. Before the latter cut is made it will be necessary to make a $\frac{1}{4}$in. hole as shown at Fig. 6, the centre being $\frac{3}{8}$in. along from the outside edge. After the saw cut has been made, the round hole should be squared with a $\frac{1}{4}$in. chisel, this is easily done by three or four cuts with a sharp chisel. The top edge of this hole should be bevelled slightly to take the wedge as shown.

When a sufficient number of these parts has been made, we have still two parts to make, the bracket supporting the last upright and the wedge. Both parts are cut in a similar manner and are finished in the same way. For the brackets some strips of 1in. by 5-16in. should be marked out as shown at Fig. 7, and for the wedges strips of $\frac{3}{8}$in. by $\frac{1}{4}$in. wood should be marked as indicated at Fig. 8. The strips are easily cut across and then the pieces may be trimmed smooth on the sawn edge with a sharp plane, using a shuting board as shown at Fig. 9. This type of planing board is very useful for planing thin wood, it is easily made and used with an ordinary jack plane.

The operations leading to the preparation of the parts ready for assembling are as follows: Sawing.—1. Strips $3\frac{1}{4}$in. and $\frac{1}{2}$in. wide from $\frac{1}{4}$in. planed wood, or $\frac{3}{8}$in. unplaned. 2. Strips $1\frac{5}{8}$in. and 1in. wide from 5-16in. planed or $\frac{3}{8}$in. unplaned. Planing.—1. The $3\frac{1}{4}$in. to $3\frac{1}{8}$in., the $\frac{1}{2}$in. to $\frac{3}{8}$in., the $1\frac{5}{8}$in. to $1\frac{1}{2}$in. with the top

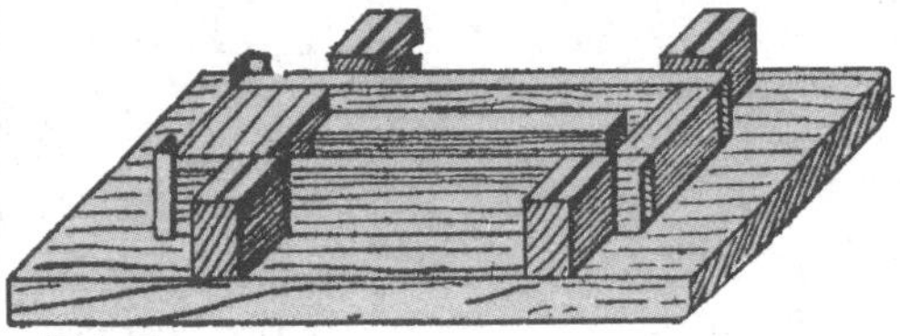

Fig. 10.

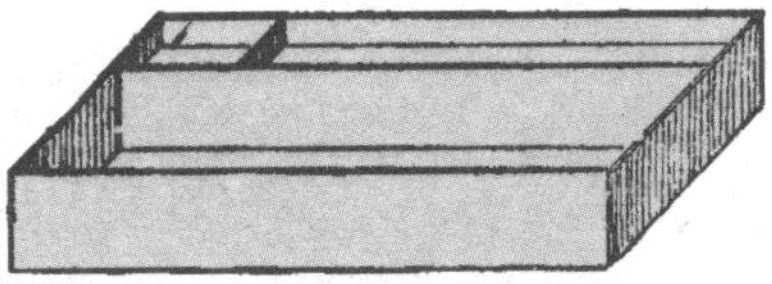

Fig. 11.

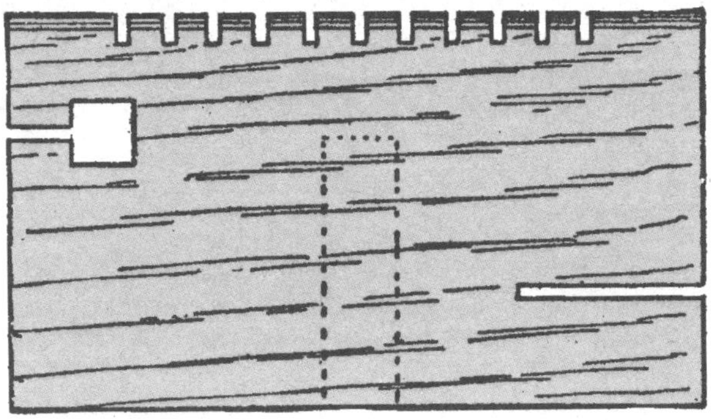

Fig. 5.

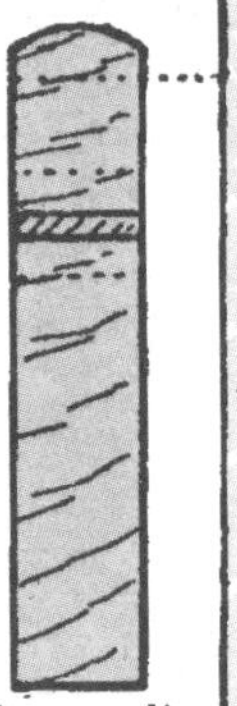

Fig. 4.

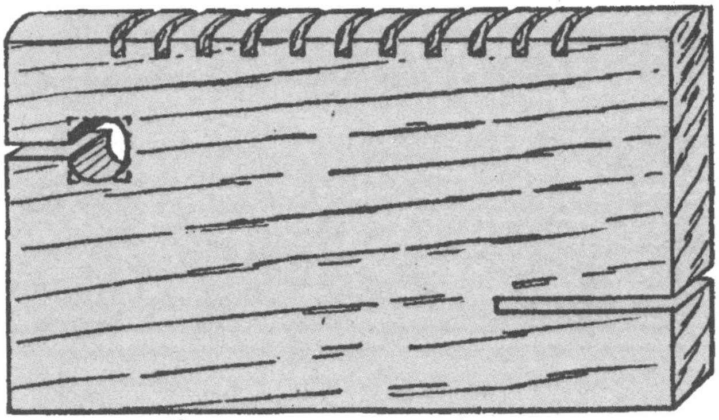

Fig. 6.

edge rounded and the 1½in. strips to 1in. Grooving.—1. The bottom piece cut down at each end ½in. deep, the uprights cut as directed ½in. deep on top, and one half the number bored ½in. and then grooved with the saw as shown. Brackets and wedges cut across and finished on the planing board.

A block should now be prepared for nailing on the uprights, as shown at Fig. 10. The middle block should be 6½in. by 1½in. by 1in., the end blocks should be 1¾in. long, 1½in. high and 1¾in. and ¾in. respectively. The end blocks are nailed to 9½in. by 1½in. by 5-16in. pieces, and the whole should be nailed to a base so that there is a space of 5-16in. at each end of the middle block. Corner pieces of tin should be nailed at the top corners as shown. The object of these corner pieces is to give the exact position of the bottom piece and when the four side blocks of 1¾in. by 1in. are nailed on, marked in the centre as shown, it will be possible to drive the nails in without any difficulty and with the certain assurance that they will be in the centre of the upright pieces.

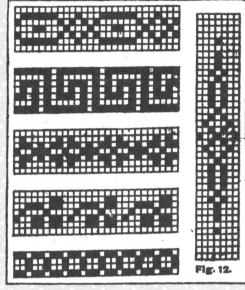

Fig. 12.

To assemble the parts the following order should be followed. First take one of each upright and place in the grooves in the back, the plain one to be in the groove next the narrow end block. The edges of the uprights should now be coated with glue and then the base may be placed in position, the end with the two sawcuts being placed at the end where the plain upright is. Wire nails ⅝in. long should be driven in each upright. The two stages of assembling the above parts is quite straightforward and will carry the work to the stage preparatory to gluing in the bracket. Both sides of the right angle should be coated with glue and the bracket pressed into the angle against the upright as indicated. When the glue has set, the work should be prepared for packing by fastening on some threads in the following manner. Cut off two 30in. lengths of thread, double them and place in the two cuts at the end of the base. Separate them and place in the sawcuts in the tops of the uprights and then, gathering the ends together, pass them through the the long slot, carry them across the top of the

bracket, into the square opening, round again through the slot, into the opening again and slip the wedge in position and tighten up. A few beads should be woven on to show the action of the loom, this is quite simple and may be gathered from the directions printed below.

The box should measure 9½in. by 4½in. by 1¾in. inside measurements, a partition should be made on one side to hold the needles and beads and should be raised up so that the depth of the partitions is ¾in. The box is shown at Fig. 11 and may be purchased from any cardboard box-maker at a low cost per gross. Particulars of price and names of firms supplying these boxes may be obtained from the Secretaries of the British Toy Association.

The needles are No. 5, and two should be wrapped in a piece of white paper, another being left in the actual piece of commenced work. The following directions should be supplied with the box. In order to continue the commenced design, string on three beads for one row in the colours of the pattern. Place the beads *under* the stretched threads so that each bead is enclosed by two threads, place the finger under the beads, bring the needle over the outside thread and pass it through the beads on top of the threads. This will bring the thread attached to the needle to the first position again. Three beads should be threaded on again, the thread carried below the stretched threads and the operation continued as before. The stretched threads form the warp and the thread in the needle the weft. When the space has been filled up, the end threads should be tied in couples close to the beads to complete the weaving. Larger designs using up all the grooves may be done in the same way.

Additional designs are shown at Fig. 12 and may be obtained together with the above printed directions ready for pasting on the outside of the boxes.

This loom is a registered design and may only be made for sale by members of the British Toy Association The whole price ready boxed should be 6s. 9d. per dozen, a price which allows of a good margin of profit.

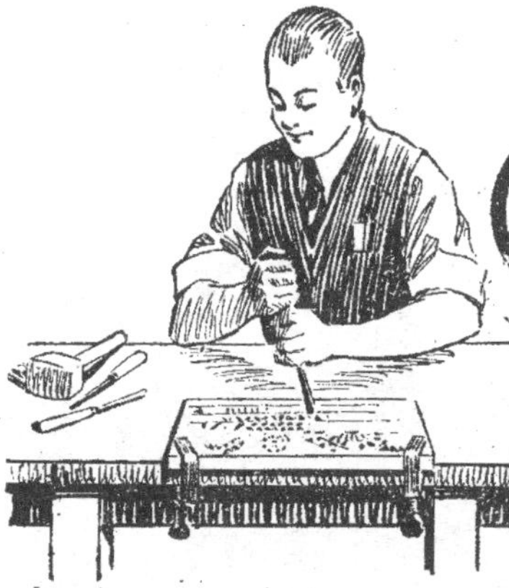

CHIP CARVING
is quite easy

THE Cabinet Photo Frame shown, is an inexpensive and ornamental piece of work for the carver to put in hand. The frame requires very little constructional work, and the carving is quite simple, being executed with the same kind of cut throughout.

The Material.

Oak of ¼in. thickness is the most suitable wood to use, a piece 8in. long by 6¼in. wide being required for the front of the frame ; a piece 7in. long by 5in. wide for the back, another 5in. long by 1½in. wide for the strut, and small slips to form the grooves between the front and back of the frame. The whole of the parts may be easily cut from a square foot of wood. Light oak costs 1s., or figured oak 1s. 4d. In addition, a photo-frame glass (No. 5804), size 6½in. by 4⅛in., price 3d., and photo-strut hinge (No. 5364), price 1½d., are required, from Hobbies Ltd., to complete the frame.

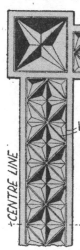

Fig. 1. How the corners are shaped.

CENTRE LINE

VEINED LINES

CENTRE LINE

The Front of the Frame.

The front of the frame measures exactly 8in. high by 6¼in. wide. The corners are shaped as shown at Fig. 1, and the opening is 5½in. high by 3¾in. wide. The portion of the frame shown at Fig. 1 is large enough for us to make out on the wood, and from this both the shape and the carving pattern may be copied for the complete rectangle. The pattern may be copied with the aid of a pair of compasses and a rule, the lines being firmly marked with a dark lead pencil. The main lines of the carving pattern should be veined, the veining being done with a small veiner or V-shaped chisel, or with two sloping cuts from an ordinary chip carving knife as shown at Fig. 2. The carving is executed by cutting a series of pockets similar in shape to that shown at Fig. 3. In doing this the carving knife or chisel is inserted at the

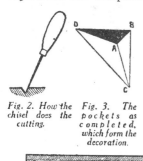

Fig. 2. How the chisel does the cutting.

Fig. 3. The pockets as completed, which form the decoration.

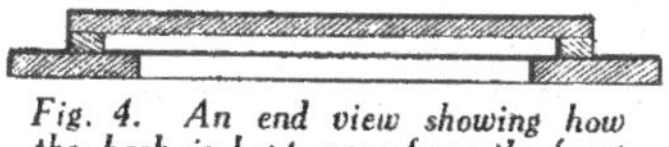

Fig. 4. An end view showing how the back is kept away from the front by strips on each side.

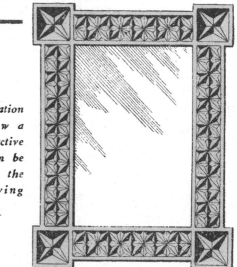

centre A, and vertical cuts are made from the centre to the corners B, C, and D. The cuts should be ⅛in. deep at the centre, and should rise to the surface at the corners, the carved pocket being formed by chipping out the wood from the outlines B—C, C—D. D—B to the centre A. The opening in the frame should not be cut until after the carving is finished.

The Back of the Frame.

The back of the frame is now cut to its size—7in. long by 5in. wide, and three strips, two being 7in. long and one 5in. long by ⅜in. wide, are prepared. The back and strips are screwed behind the front of the frame, as shown by the sectional drawing at Fig. 4 and the back

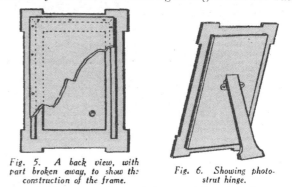

Fig. 5. A back view, with part broken away, to show the construction of the frame.

Fig. 6. Showing photo-strut hinge.

view of Fig. 5, to form the groove for the glass and photo. To finish the frame the strut must be prepared and hinged to the back. It is 5in. long by 1½in. wide, and it is shaped and hinged to the back (as shown at Fig. 6), with the special photo hinge (No. 5364) obtainable from Hobbies Ltd.

A topical piece of carpentry is this attractive
"VICTORY" HALL RACK

A RATHER unorthodox, but modern style of hall rack (for hats and coats) is shown, oak being used throughout the construction. Ordinary metal fittings may be used, but in case of difficulty in obtaining these, modern-shaped wooden brackets can be easily made.

The design of this 3ft. long rack is, of course, based on the "V" sign. The latter forms the framing for the mirror; wood used is fairly wide so its significant shape is obvious at a glance. While plain oak should be used, a good job is possible with deal flooring which is more readily obtainable.

The Construction

Cut the back piece to length and shape its ends with a tenon saw. Use, if possible, ¾in. thick stuff, this also applying to the 3ins. wide mirror framing pieces. The latter is ploughed to take a ¼in. mirror plate or thinner stuff.

To find the correct size and shape of the triangle, rule a central line across the back board. Tick off, at the top edge, marks 3ins. from the centre line (see constructional details). The back board is then trenched ¼in.

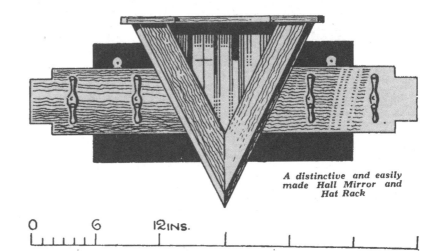

A distinctive and easily made Hall Mirror and Hat Rack

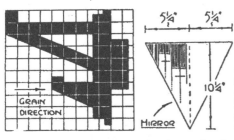

Wooden bracket shapes, plotted in ½ in. squares   *Approximate size of Mirror*

deep by 3ins. wide to accept the mirror frame pieces.

Mirror pieces are mitred by placing one in position on the back board and ruling (by judgement) the mitre line, working from the vertical centre line on the back board. Cut off the waste from both framing pieces and true up the joint by alternate fitting and trimming. Sufficient waste is allowed in the length of the framing pieces for fitting purposes (see Cutting List).

Mirror Backing

The back board serves as backing to the mirror. An additional 4ins. wide by ¼in. backing is needed, however, same being fitted in a suitable recess cut in the back framing pieces, as detailed. Back view of the frame shows additional backing fixed in position, glue and ¼in. by 4ins. flathead iron screws being used.

The completed frame is glued to the back board trenching and held with suitable flathead screws driven in from the reverse side. It is advisable to do this prior to fitting and attaching the additional backing strip.

The Wooden Brackets

If the wooden hat-and-coat brackets are used, the back board must be mortised for these prior to fitting the mirror framework. The shape of the brackets is plotted in ½in. squares; note that the grain runs horizontally. Use ½in. plain oak, by the way, and cut the shape with a coarse fretsaw.

The pediment is cut from ½in. material and serves a double purpose, i.e., forms a serif to the letter "V" and helps to keep the mirror down in its grooves. It should, therefore, only be *screwed* down to the ends of the framing.

The Mirror

Approximate dimensions of the mirror are shown. The best course is to make a cardboard template and take it along to a local glass merchant; this is safer than stating sizes. Plate glass, which is ¼in. thick, is suggested, but thinner glass, such as 15-oz. stuff, could be incorporated, the ¼in. grove (if ploughed) being suitably packed by adding a backing of cardboard.

Finishing Details

If plain oak is used, the work should be polished oak. The back board could be done lighter in shade than the mirror framing so both contrast. If deal is used, the work can be stained and polished to any particular finish, such as oak, mahogany, rosewood, walnut,

etc. The wooden brackets should be done the same colour as the mirror framing.

Fit two brass screw plates to the back board, as suggested in the elevation. Wall should be plugged for fixing plates with screws. An extra hook, such as for a hat, or coat, if metal fittings are used, could be

screwed over the mitre joint in the mirror frame, or a key hook could be screwed on, this also serving to hold a coat brush.

Incidentally, the mirror framing may be bevelled ½in. at the sides, as shown in the elevation. A smaller rack could be made, this having hooks—one at each side of the mirror frame—for a hat and coat brush.

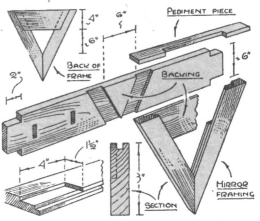

Showing constructional detail of woodwork

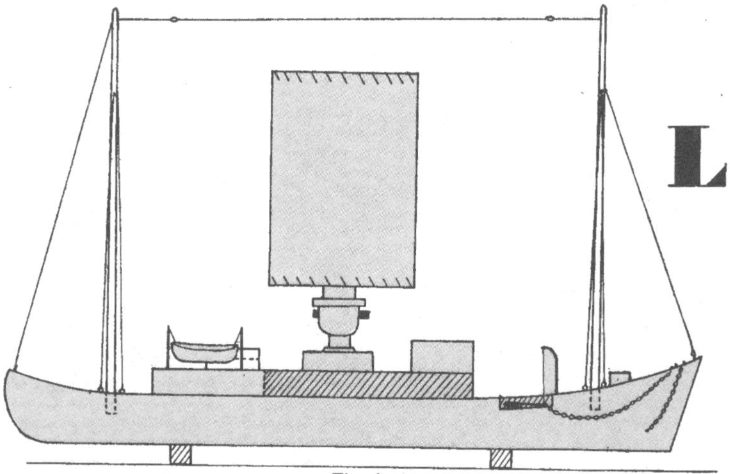

Fig. 1

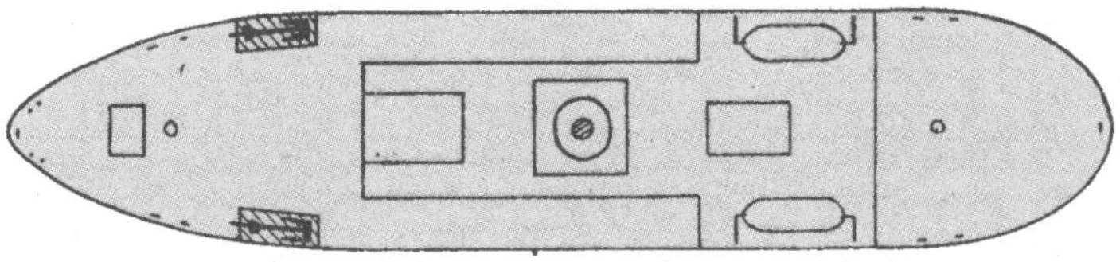

Fig. 2

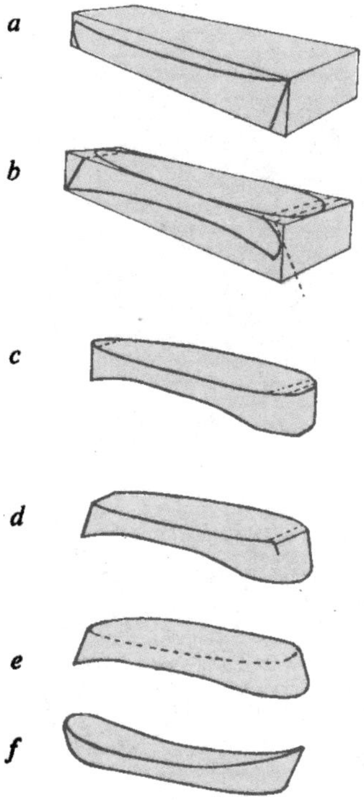

A BOY'S bedside lamp makes a useful present, and in the form of a lightship it will add to the fascination. With a view to aptness in design, being primarily a lamp shade, the detail is simplified. The beauty lies in the long sweeping curves of the hull, and being made from a solid block of wood, its sturdiness is assured.

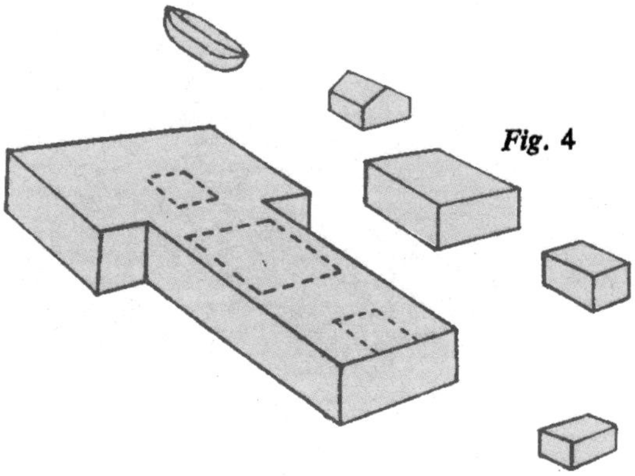

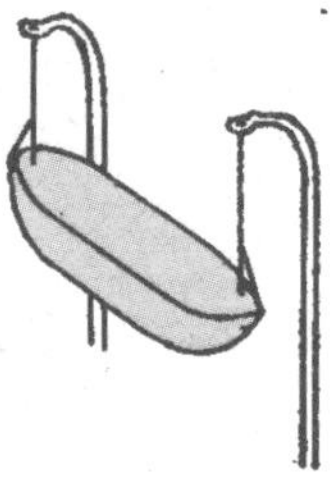

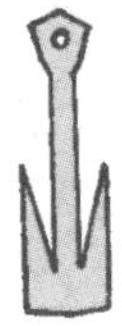

Important Part

The cutting out of the hull is the longest part, but on the accuracy and finish of this, mainly depends the effect, so it is as well to take time over it. Various tools help to make the work easier, particularly a spokeshave for obtaining the curves of the hull, but this is not essential, and saws and glasspaper work wonders.

The Hull

A block of wood 18ins. by 2½ins. deep by 3½ins. wide is obtained and the shape of the hull is marked on the side (Fig. 3a). It will be noticed that only the top part of the hull is made; the flat base represents the level of the water line. Across the width of the base, a mark is made where the line representing the front of the bows will cut the base. A second line will also be marked on the base, where the straight saw-cut will be made for the shape of the stern. A third line should also be marked where the bottom curve of the stern reaches the base. The plan of the hull is also traced on the base (Fig. 3b).

The excess wood at the ends of the block are cut off square, allowing for glasspapering to a fine surface. The deck is cut out according to the tracing on the side of the vessel, and the plan of the hull is cut round, according to the tracing on the base (Fig. 3c). This will also cut away the shape of the bows and

a

b

c

d

e

f

Fig. 3

Fig. 4

Fig. 5

Fig. 6

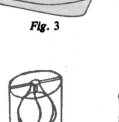

a   *b*

Fig. 7

THE IDEAL
LAMP FOR A
BOY'S ROOM

stern traced on the side of the block, but with the aid of the marks that have been made on the base, the sloping lines of the bows and stern can be sawn and shaped (Fig. 3d).

Superstructure

For the superstructure a piece of wood is cut 7¾ins. long by 3½ins. wide by ⅝in. thick, out of which two pieces are cut from each side, ¾in. into the block and for 5ins. of its length. This leaves a thick T-shape. It is fixed 3½ins. from the stern with the wide part nearest the stern. Above this another small section is added, the top of this sloping to the sides. It is 1¼ins. long, ¾in. wide and ½in. high in the middle line from which the top slopes. This is fixed where the narrow part of the T-shape broadens out. At the end of the narrow part, another piece is glued on top, 1½ins. long, 1in. wide, and ¾in. thick. A small block ¾in. wide by ½in. by ¼in. deep, can be placed in front of the foremast to break up the area (Fig. 4). Two thin pieces of wood 2ins. long will be needed for the aerial.

Two masts are made 9½ins. high of ¼in. diameter dowelling, tapering to the top. The stern mast is slotted into a hole bored 2½ins. from the stern, and the foremast 2½ins. from the bows. Small holes are drilled in the masts to take the rigging and aerial. 2ins. from the top of the foremast a small hole is drilled from side to side to take the side rigging. ⅛in. above this a hole is drilled from front to back to take a line from the bows. ¼in. from the top, a hole is drilled from front to back of the mast to take the aerial wire. Through the mast at the stern a hole is made 2ins. from the top, from side to side, to take the rigging from the sides of the deck. ¼in. from the top a front to back hole is required to take a line from the stern, also the aerial wire.

Out of the deck two niches are cut, 1¼ins. long, ½in. wide and ¼in. deep on either side of the deck, the front of the niches being 3½ins. from the bows. In these niches the anchors rest. The anchors may be cut out of wood, or obtained ready-made from a model shop, with two short lengths of chain. Two davits are made from which a strand of thin wire is joined to the anchor. A short pin can be inserted to hold the anchor in its niche. Small pieces of wire or pins are inserted in the deck near the bows. Through these the chain runs from the anchor, then drops over the side to be inserted in the hull.

Two lifeboats are shaped, 1½ins. long, ⅝in. wide and ½in. deep. Four pieces of thick but bendable wire are cut for the davits. The wire is rounded and in the

end of each is flattened and a small hole is bored. Four small holes are drilled in the superstructure to receive the davits. The lifeboats have a small hole drilled at each end, and are hung from the davits by very thin wire (Fig. 5).

A centre square is made, which also fits on the T-shape. This is 1¾ins. square and ½in. deep. On this the lighting is fixed. Two strips or 'feet' are made 2½ins. by ½in. by ½in. for fixing on the bottom of the hull, to raise it off the ground to allow the lamp wire to go under the hull to the light plug.

All the wooden parts may be varnished before assembling, or stained, another coat being applied after gluing together. Or the boat when assembled may be painted, but if good wood is used, varnishing will make a nicer finish for a lamp shade. Feet, hull and superstructure are marked for position, glasspapered, and glued.

A hole is bored through the superstructure and hull, through which the lamp wire is threaded. This can be done before gluing together, but it is necessary to make sure they are in line. A screw-on fitting is fixed to the centre square of the superstructure, and a lamp shade is easily made on a frame of the type which clips on to the top of the electric light bulb.

The Shade

The best type of shade is a simple round one, similar to the lamp of the lightship, but it will have to be bigger in proportion. If a candle-shaped bulb is used, the frame used can be of the type held to the fitting by a ring below (Fig. 7). A very effective shade is made by using two circular wires, 3½ins. in diameter, and a plain piece of parchment, 11½ins. by 4½ins. At top and bottom a series of small holes is pierced ⅜in. apart. The parchment is folded round the wires, the slight overlap being marked. It is then taken off, curved round in a circle and glued. Thin wire is then threaded through the holes, so holding the rings in position top and bottom of the shade. A brass or copper coloured wire of the type sometimes used for ship rigging is quite effective. It gives a more appropriate finish than if coloured ribbons or thread are used.

THE IDEAL LAMP FOR A BOY'S ROOM

For the rigging ten screw eyes, ½in. in length are needed. On the deck, and near the edge, two are placed on either side of the masts. The ninth and tenth screw eyes are fixed, one at the bows, the other in the centre of the stern. Rigging cord may be used, but thin wire made of several very fine strands is easier to thread through the necessarily small holes drilled in the masts. First the side rigging is put in place. Thread a length of it through one screw eye at the side and twist the end round to hold firmly. Run it up through the side hole in the mast, and down the other side to the opposite screw eye. Repeat so that there are double lines through each mast. Then a line is run from the screw eye in the bows, up to the hole just above the side rigging, and fix so that the foremast is upright when the wire is taut.

The aerial is wired through the hole in the mast, looped round the ends of the cross stays and cut of such a length that ensures both masts being upright when the wire is taut. Finally a line is taken from the top of the stern mast to the screw eye on the stern. This line pulls the whole into position, giving firmness to the masts and rigging. (D.Y.G.)

MODEL AEROPLANES

KITES & KITE FLYING

THE HOME AVIATOR

AEROPLANES AND HOW TO FLY THEM

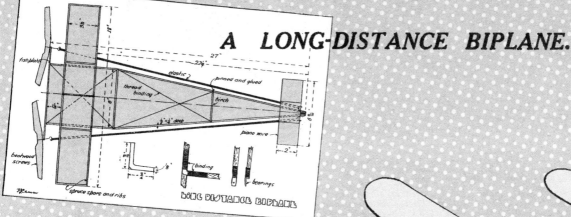

A LONG-DISTANCE BIPLANE.

fish plate
elastic
pinned and glued
thread binding
birch
beechwood screws
piano wire
binding
bearings
spruce spars and ribs
LONG DISTANCE BIPLANE

An interesting way to make a
GLIDER RELEASE

CARVING A PROPELLER

By R. H. Warring

PROPELLERS for model aircraft are usually carved from balsa. Choose hard or medium-hard grade, with a straight grain, for the block. Soft or light block is suitable only for folding propellers. Recommended wood density is 12lbs. per

be 3ins. or 4ins. to get the required amount of blade area. A considerable proportion of the carved blade is trimmed away in the final stage, so a lot

After the squared blocks are marked out they are cut to shape to produce propeller blanks ready for carving (B and D). The diagonal layout leaves an untapered blank (B) and the quartered layout a more complicated blank. Both, however, are equally easy to carve. For

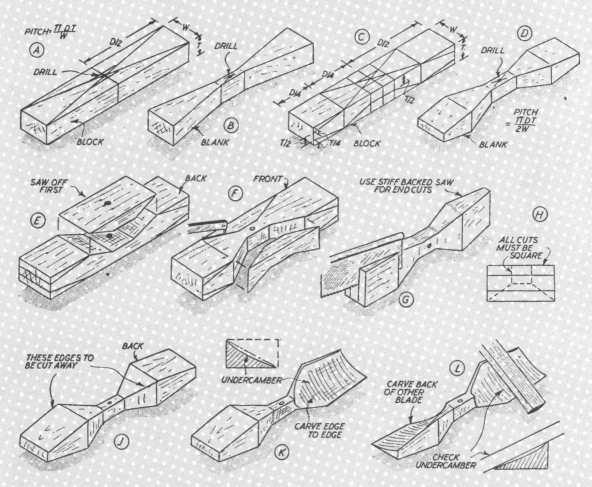

cubic foot. Hardwoods are not recommended for they are more difficult to carve, somewhat prone to splitting, and generally too heavy.

There are two ways of marking out a propeller for carving. The starting-point in each case is a squared-up block of balsa in which the pitch of the propeller is fixed by the width and thickness dimensions (W and T respectively). The diagonal method of marking out (A) is simplest, but used mainly for small propellers. It can be used for larger sizes, but the W dimension may have to

of wood is wasted. The quartered layout (C) is more usual for propellers over 12ins. in diameter.

The pitch is calculated from D, W and T, according to the formulas shown. Thus for a required pitch, the other dimensions can be adjusted to suit. Diameter size (D) is usually fixed by the design. W is usually about one-tenth of the diameter for the 'quartered' layout and about one-sixth of the diameter for the diagonal layout, although it can be smaller if only a small blade area is required.

the remainder of the description we will assume that a 'quartered' propeller blank is being used.

If the block is marked out as in (C), the various cuts can be made in the following order, which will avoid removing parts of the layout. First cut away the back piece (E) using a fretsaw or a similar tool. This leaves the markings on the front face undisturbed, so turn the block face up and cut away the two side pieces from the hub (F). The end cuts can then be made with a stiff-backed saw to complete the cutting out of the blank (G).

It is very important that all the cuts be truly square, as the outline edges of the blank act as carving lines in shaping the rest of the propeller. Check that you have cut square (H) and correct, if necessary. It is a good plan to drill the hub hole *before* starting to cut the blank, when the block is still square. It can, however, be drilled at this stage if you prefer.

make sure that you have got the same amount of undercamber on each blade.

Carving the underside edge to edge fixes the pitch angle of the blade along its whole length, so do this job accurately and finish by sanding down smooth. Carve right up to the edges, but leave the hub section still square for finishing off later. This need not be such an efficient part of the propeller in any

thick edges at several points along the blade. These must now be sanded down to the back of the blades, i.e. all the wood removed from the *front* of the blades, so as not to disturb the pitch angles established in the original carving. Then smooth down the whole propeller with glasspaper, carving and rounding the hub to blend into the blade roots (Q).

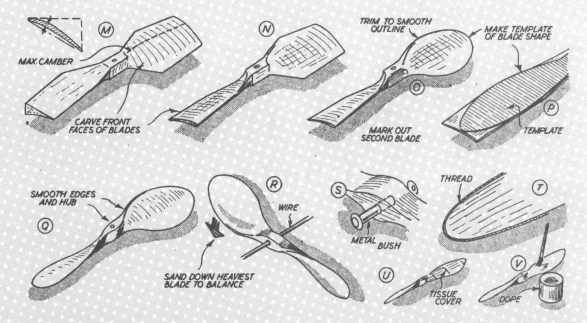

The blank should now be laid face down as in (J). The edges to be cut away are shown on this diagram, and it is important to carve these and not the opposite edges; otherwise you will end up with an 'opposite hand' propeller. The rule is, for a normal propeller, carve away the right-hand edge of the blank, facing away from you.

Carving is done from edge to edge (K) using a sharp knife. A cobbler's knife or a small kitchen knife is excellent for this job, and easier to handle than a modelling knife. A razor blade is an unsatisfactory tool for carving propellers.

As the blade is formed from edge to edge, scoop away wood from the centre, so that the final surface has a certain amount of undercamber. You will find it difficult to work in undercamber right up to the hub, so let the section flatten out and become slightly convex here, so as not to weaken the blade unduly. The majority of the blade, however, should have a small, but definite amount of undercamber.

The second blade is carved in the same way, simply turning the block round, end to end. The undercamber can be checked by laying a straight edge across the blank (L). Use this check to

case and does not need a very good aerofoil section.

Having finished the backs of the blades properly, turn the blank over and carve the top or front faces (M). This reduces the blades to an aerofoil section. For a good propeller, the point of maximum thickness and camber should come at about one-third of the width of the blade, all along its length. It will not hurt to get it a little forward of this, but never farther aft. The rear portion of the blade sections should be thinned right down, and the leading edge finished fairly sharp. The actual thickness of the blade should taper from a maximum at the hub down to about $\frac{1}{8}$ in. at the tip. The taper should be gradual and uniform, which will ensure that the propeller is as strong as possible.

Card Template

The propeller as carved so far will look something like (N). Do not bother to sand the front faces of the blades smooth yet, but mark on the outline required, and cut one blade to this shape (O). Make a copy of this shape on stiff paper or card, cut out, and pin or hold against the second blade (P). Mark round the template, and cut the second blade to an identical outline shape.

The result is that you have produced

The propeller must now be checked for balance. Push a length of wire through the hole in the centre of the hub and see if the propeller will balance level. If not, you can usually feel where wood should be removed from the heavier blade. Sand down the heaviest blade until the propeller will balance, but take care not to distort the aerofoil section or sand right through at the relatively thin tips.

All balsa propellers should be fitted with a metal bush. A screwed bush can be used, locked in place with a nut, or a bush can be made from brass tube, with washers soldered to each end (S). The bush should be a push-fit through the hub hole and should be securely anchored in place.

Final treatment of the propeller is then largely a matter of preference. Many people leave the propeller at this stage, others prefer to strengthen and waterproof the blades, or finish them with a gloss. The whole propeller can be covered with tissue to strengthen, and doped, or just given several coats of dope, sanding down smooth between each coat. A final polish with metal polish will then bring up the finish.

The edges of the blade are the most vulnerable part of a thin propeller, and

Carving a Propeller

these can be protected by cementing thread around the propeller outline (T). This is quite easy to do, and the protection afforded is well worth while, if you have spent a long time working the blades down to a nice thin aerofoil section.

Tissue covering (U) can be used with or without thread protection for the edge. Ordinary lightweight tissue can be used, applied with tissue paste or dope. If paste is used, a coat of dope over the top is necessary. If the tissue is put on with dope, further coats of dope are optional.

A plain doped finish has the virtue of making the propeller waterproof, so that it will not pick up moisture when the model lands in damp grass, etc. It adds very little strength. For a shiny finish, the final coat should be of high gloss or paper varnish. If a coloured effect is required, use a translucent colour dope, or a wood dye, but not pigmented colour dope, as this would add too much weight.

FOR LESS THAN A SHILLING

You Can Make This Delta Wing Glider

THE paper dart has grown up into a full size aeroplane, and the triangular or delta wing shape is now used on many of our latest and fastest fighter aircraft. For less than a shilling you can make a thrilling glider model to test for yourself the advantages of this peculiar wing shape.

Wings, tail and fin are cut from $\frac{1}{8}$in. sheet balsa. You will need a 19in. length, 3ins. wide. Cut this into three pieces, 9ins., 6ins. and 4ins. long. Trim one end of the 9in. length to make part 2, as shown. A diagonal cut across the 6in. length makes parts 1 and 3. Mark and cut out the fin and tail from the remaining piece, as shown. You will find a sharp knife or a razor blade ideal for cutting balsa.

Now cement the three wing parts, 1, 2 and 3, together over a flat surface and leave to dry. Use balsa cement for sticking as this dries in a few minutes. Now notch a 1in. length of 12in. by $\frac{1}{8}$in. balsa as shown, and round off the bottom. Similarly shape the fuselage top from a 10$\frac{1}{2}$in. length of $\frac{1}{2}$in. by $\frac{1}{8}$in. balsa.

Cement the bottom strip under the centre of the wings and then add the fuselage top. Finally cement on the fin, making sure that this is upright; and the tail across the top of the fin.

To fly, hold the bottom of the fuselage under the centre of the wings and throw the model gently forwards, slightly nose down. Aim at a point about six or seven paces in front of you. You will probably have to add a certain amount of weight to the nose of the fuselage to obtain proper balance. Stick a small blob of plasticine in place and add more, as necessary, until the model glides straight and level instead of nosing up and stalling. If the model dives, on the other hand, reduce weight.   (R.H.W.)

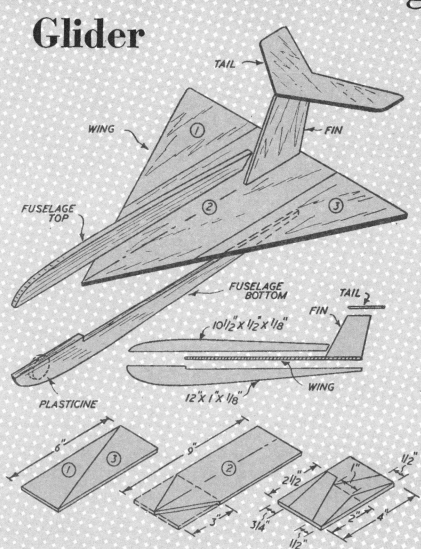

TAIL

WING

FIN

FUSELAGE TOP

FUSELAGE BOTTOM

TAIL

FIN

WING

$10\frac{1}{2}" \times \frac{1}{2}" \times \frac{1}{8}"$

$12" \times 1" \times \frac{1}{8}"$

PLASTICINE

6"

9"

2$\frac{1}{2}$

3"

3/4"

$\frac{1}{2}$

1"

2"

$\frac{1}{2}$"

4"

Learn all about the art of making
KITES AND KITE FLYING

KITE flying has always had a fascination for both old and young alike. The joy of seeing a kite rise gracefully in the air, like a living thing, is much greater, however, when the kite is of one's own construction.

There are several kinds of kites, but this article is confined to the flat kind, or one-plane kites. These must be flown with a tail, which is as essential as a bird's tail, and which, if properly made, adds to the beauty of the kite.

The only tools needed are a good sharp knife and a fretsaw. Paste and liquid glue will be needed and possibly, for small curves, some No. 20 iron wire.

The sticks can be made from orange crate boards or thin picture backing wood. Where large curves are required, drain-pipe canes can be used. Light string or twine—the best is grocer's twine—is used for binding the wood together.

Suitable Paper

For covering the frame use plain or coloured crêpe paper if the surface is small, and tissue paper if the surface is large. The best is bank paper, which can be obtained, either plain or coloured, from a local printer and is known as 11lb. Bank.

For the tail use crêpe paper, but if the kite is extra large, rag is best. Two or three kinds of paints will be necessary for the man or animal kites in order to make them more realistic.

There is no end to the designs of kites that can be made after having once acquired the ' knack ' of construction. For this purpose the construction of the ordinary two-stick will be given.

You will require two sticks, one 27ins. long by ½in. by ¼in. for the centre and another 24ins. long by ½in. by ¼in. for the cross piece. Scrape the ends of the two sticks and make them about ¼in. square. Then, parallel to the flat sides, make a notch or slit at the end of each stick.

The Frame

On the longest stick make a mark about 8ins. from one end and place the shorter stick across this, an equal distance each side. Secure together with string and a dab of liquid glue.

Make sure the sticks are quite square, and then bind the ends to prevent splitting where the notch has been made. Do not, however, pull too tight or you may break the stick.

When you have done this, frame the kite with string. Start from the top and fasten to save the string from slipping. Then place the string between the slits and pull taut, but be careful not to bend the sticks.

Covering

The frame is now ready for papering. Choose the colour you desire and lay this on a flat surface and put the frame over it. Cut the paper, leaving a 1in. margin all round. The pieces cut from

RUBBER RING

THICK LINES = KITE STICKS
DOTTED LINES = STRING

The ordinary flat type showing rubber bridle

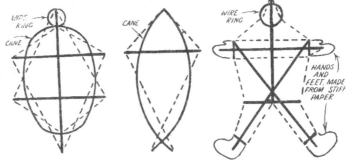

Shapes for the five—six and eight-pointed star

No. 20 WIRE CIRCLE

The five-pointed star with wire circle covered with paper

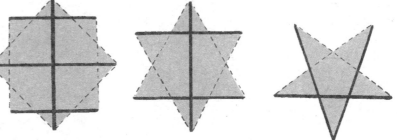

WIRE RING

CANE

CANE

WIRE RING

HANDS AND FEET MADE FROM STIFF PAPER

How to make the shapes for a Tortoise, Fish and a Clown Kite the sides will be enough to make a splice at the bottom.

Make a margin of paste, press the frame well down on the paper and fold the paper over the string and press. When pasting down be careful you do not pull the string out of place.

The kite is now complete and ready for the bridle and string for flying. This should be placed on the paper side, and when tied, should be three feet from top to bottom. Fasten the string at the top and thread it through the bottom, leaving 9 ins. over.

No Darting

To stop the kite from darting or being torn away in a sudden gust of wind, insert a rubber band. Cut the string at the bottom 9 ins. up and fasten the short end to the rubber band so it is 4ins. from the bottom of the kite when tied.

Now fasten the top string to the other end of the rubber band, and adjust so the whole length of the string from top to bottom, is 31ins. The remaining short end of the string that has been threaded through, should be fastened 2ins. above the rubber band on the long string.

Fastening the horizontal string requires a little patience. Fix the string at one side first, then make a hook of a piece of wire and hold the vertical string taut, but do not stretch the rubber band. Make a knot where the two strings cross—which must be exactly over the intersection of the two sticks. Secure with a little liquid glue.

The other side can now be fastened. Where the two strings cross tie a little piece of string for towing.

For this size kite you will require a tail 15 feet long. Tails can be made from crêpe paper placed at intervals of one foot, but the better tail should be made from thin rag one to two inches wide.

Shaped Kites

If you have made the ordinary kite successfully and have gained some experience, attention can be given to Star Kites. The construction is similar to the ordinary kites and the proportion can be according to personal requirements.

The diagrams of the 5, 6, and 8 pointed stars show you where to place the string and sticks for the frame.

The Star kites can be improved by placing a circle of No. 20 wire round the frame, between the slits and this can be whipped with coloured wool or paper for effect.

Should a circle be added, the tail will need to be 6 feet longer.

Frogs, tortoises, fish, animals and people can all be shaped into kites by means of sticks, cane and wire. The diagrams give an idea of the construction of some of these and with a little imagination a number of others can be made. None of these, however, should be less than 2 feet long.

To fly a kite use an open space as far away as possible from houses, buildings and trees. Stand with your back to the wind. Should the kite drop, do not drop it along the ground. The flying string can be of various kinds, but wrapping twine

is as good as any for larger kites, and carpet thread for the lighter kind.

Some kites fly better in one wind than another, but the flying capacity will be improved if you have fixed the elastic bridle band properly.

Should the kite not rise, or having risen, darts, it is because of too much wind or too little. If too much wind the darting can be overcome by adding more tail. Some kites, it must be remembered, rise better than others. Such differences as weight, paper, rigidity and size affect a kite's performance and can only be overcome by experience.

Causes of Bad Flying

A word or two on the causes of bad flying and how to adjust may help the reader to make a successful flight. If the bridle is too low, the kite will go round and round in circles, being too top heavy. If too high, the kite will lie flat and only fly in a light breeze.

When the kite darts too much to one side, the cause may be that the string on that side is shorter than it should be. The towing point should be altered and both sides made equal.

Kites which are "foxy" can sometimes be overcome by shifting the towing point farther away from the kite. Should this be necessary, alter a little at a time and only the top end of the vertical string.

Experience will show how much tail will be required. If too long, it may make the kite rise slowly, but it must be remembered that when aloft the wind may be stronger and the extra tail necessary.

Care after Flight

In conclusion after a flight, do not wind the kite in too quickly and if possible use a reel. Care should be taken as the kite nears the ground, since a sudden dart may end in disaster. When the kite has been finally landed, roll up the tail carefully to prevent damage and to prevent it from becoming tangled. Place it in a bag, and fasten it to the end of the kite.

A Real Piece of Fretwork

THIS splendid article was made from the Hobbies Century Clock design published nearly 45 years ago, and evidently still in demand. The photograph was sent in by A. Waterhouse of Kersal, Salford, who must be congratulated on his ability. Note the Clock and the Dresden China figure.

An interesting way to make a
GLIDER RELEASE from KITE

IN the article we had recently on Kites, mention was made of a method by which a small balsa glider could be released from a kite line. The glider which is described here, while intended mainly for this kind of release, will also give excellent flights from hand launching or catapulting. The construction is all balsa.

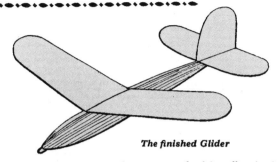

The finished Glider

Construction

The first step is to draw the plans out full size and care should be taken to see that the shapes of the wing and tailplane tips are accurate.

It is a good plan to draw only one half of the wing and tailplane and then fold the paper over with a sheet of carbon paper between and re-draw, so that the two halves are exact duplicates.

The fuselage or body of the glider is cut with a razor blade or fretsaw from ⅛in. sheet balsa to the shape shown in the side view. The bottom is glasspapered to a knife edge as shown in the front view.

The Wings

Next the two wing halves, which are ⅛in. sheet, may be cut to shape. The outline having been cut, it is now necessary with the aid of rough and medium glasspaper to get them to the shape shown in Fig. 2. Note that the wood is brought to

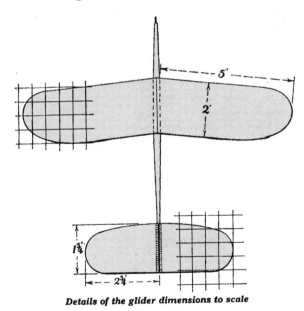

Details of the glider dimensions to scale

a knife edge at each tip as shown in the front view.

The next step is to bevel the ends of the two wing halves in such a manner that they may be glued to each other again as shown in the front view with each tip raised to a height of 2ins.

It is essential that a firm joint be made, and it should therefore be given a coat of glue. This will, when it hardens, form a tough skin effectively sealing the joint.

Next the top of the body should be slotted in the position shown, and the wing glued into place. When doing this care should be taken to see that the wing tips are raised to the same height at each side.

Toil Surfaces

The tailplane and fin are cut from 1/32in. sheet balsa. The tailplane is first glued to the top of the body, and when the glue has dried the fin is added on top. At each side of the junction of the fin and tailplane a short length of ⅛in. sq. balsa should be added as there is not sufficient gluing surface to hold the fin upright otherwise.

The construction of the glider now being complete the nose weight may be added. This takes the form of a headless nail, bent as shown in the side view of the glider, and pushed into place.

Besides acting as a weight this also serves as an attachment for the glider release explained later in this article.

Quite Smooth

The next step is very important. All the component parts of the glider must be cleaned thoroughly. For this purpose several sheets of glasspaper must be purchased, including one sheet as fine as can be obtained, for finishing.

The fuselage may be papered smooth without the aid of a block, but for the wing and tail surfaces a glasspaper block should be used.

Each wing half must be placed on a table or bench individually and papered, and the resulting sawdust should be allowed to remain on the wood.

Next we need a can of ordinary model aeroplane dope, and with a wide brush the wing may be given a coat of this dope and left to dry. The dope, mixing with the sawdust, fills in the pores of the balsa wood.

Doping in Colour

This process may then be repeated, smoothing and doping alternately, but using finer grades of paper each time.

When this has been done six or seven times the balsa will assume a glass-like smoothness. If desired, the final two coats may be of coloured dope without any detriment to the model.

The body may be treated with dope in the same manner, but the tailplane and fin not more than twice, or, as they are only 1/32in. thick in the first instance, they may become too thin and consequently very weak.

The small lengths of balsa at the joint of the fin and tailplane may also be smoothed with a piece of fine glasspaper wrapped round a pencil bringing the joint to the shape shown in Fig. 1.

Incidentally the more care taken in the papering and doping and the smoother the glider becomes, the better will be the performance of the finished model.

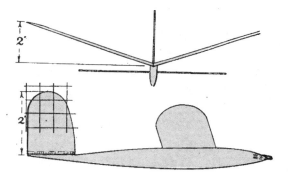

The glider may be tested by hand launching into the wind. It should not be thrown forward violently, but just launched gently and slightly downward. If it stalls, that is, tries to climb, hesitates and then dives, the nose of the glider requires more weight. This may be remedied very easily by adding a little modelling clay.

Any sharp turning tendency apart from a very gentle turn (which is, of course, desirable), may be corrected by breathing on the trailing edge of the fin and warping in the desired direction.

Once the model glides correctly, that is, steadily and in a right-hand circle, full hand launched flights may be tried.

Launching

For this kind of flight the glider must be gripped between the index finger and thumb, and held sideways as if it were banking to the right. It should now be thrown upwards, as if one were bowling a cricket ball sidehand. It should not travel upwards in a straight line or the excessive speed will cause it to loop, but in a right-hand upward spiral and it will then level out at the top of the climb.

A little practice with this kind of launch soon brings proficiency and surprising heights can be attained. If difficulty is experienced in gripping the smooth fuselage firmly, two small pieces of glasspaper, glued in place one on each side will afford a good grip.

If catapult launching is desired, a slot should be cut in the bottom of the fuselage just forward of the wing, but this slot must be reinforced by a small piece of thin aluminium or the elastic of the catapult will split the soft balsa.

Returning again to the kite release gear mentioned at the beginning of this article we will now see how this operates.

In the first instance, the kite must be flying steadily and strongly before we commence operations.

Once there are a few hundred yards of line out and the kite is flying steadily, we must attach another length of twine about one yard long to the kite line, and to the bottom of this length must be tied a ring of wire about ½in. diameter.

A Second Line

We must now obtain a further ball of twine about 600 yards in length, and pass one end through the ring, and then as the kite line is paid out the ring will travel upwards pulling the second line with it.

The second line is not actually tied to the ring, but only passed through it so that when the ring has travelled 300 yards upwards the two ends of the second length may be joined.

We must now "anchor" the kite to a railing or a peg thrust into the ground and walk out towards the kite until the second length of twine stretches vertically upwards to the wire ring.

We next require the little component shown in Fig. 3. This is made from a length of 18s. gauge

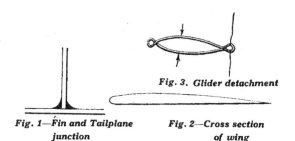

Fig. 3. Glider detachment

Fig. 1—Fin and Tailplane   Fig. 2—Cross section
           junction   of wing

piano wire. The pincers end of this clip fit into the nail at the nose of the glider and the other end is fastened to the twine running through the ring.

We are now ready to operate the release. With the glider clipped into position, it only remains to pull one side of the twine, which, running through the ring, operates like a pulley and the slider is thus towed up into the air.

The Slip

When it reaches the ring it naturally has to pass through and in doing so the sides of the wire ring press against the clips at the points marked with arrows. This pressure causes the jaws of the slips to part and, of course, releases the glider.

It is now an easy matter to pull the line until the clip again comes to the bottom in preparation for another flight.

The length of twine mentioned can, of course, be varied. Indeed the glider could be towed up into the clouds if desired, but of course, it should not be released too high or it may fly too far away or run into a thermal current when the duration of flight would be unlimited.

A LONG-DISTANCE BIPLANE.

SEVERAL designs for monoplanes have been given in this series, both of the tractor and canard variety. The designs here given show a different type —a twin-screw canard biplane.

The main framework, or fuselage, should be made first of rectangular cross section, ⅛in. deep by ⅛in. wide, and cut from straight-grained birch. At a point about ¾in. from the front ends they are to be slightly bent, and 6½ins. from the near end they are to be bent to the same angle, but in the reverse direction, as shown in the plan view.

The propeller-bearing crossbar is 8¾ins. long and 3-16in. square, and is secured to the frame members by means of right-angular fishplates, also shown in detail. The cross-bar is slightly tapered off each end to receive the brass bearings, the taper to be of such an angle that it is at right angles to the skein of rubber. Two other light cross-bars span the frame or fuselage, and these should be of birch 3-16in. wide by 1-16in. thick. They are bradded on in the

positions shown in the plan, but before nailing right down the joint is glued, and a strong thread passed round the nail or brad. This thread is to be used to stiffen the framework by bracing it diagonally. The brad is then driven well home and clinched underneath the frame. The two main members at the front are bound together (glue being interposed in the joint); a piece of wire is then passed through the fuselage and bent to form two hooks (one on each side of the spar—see plan view), to which the elastic skeins are secured.

The main planes are rectangular, measuring 18in. span by 3½in. chord, and the spars and ribs forming the framework for them are 5-16in. wide by 16in. spruce. Four stanchions are secured to the fuselage before covering the planes and secured by pinning, glueing and lashing.

These stanchions incline towards the top, to allow the upper or head main plane to rest upon their top ends, whilst the lower main plane fits into suitable saw cuts made in them,

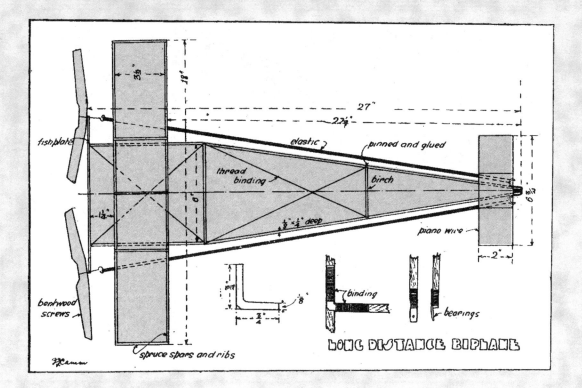

LONG DISTANCE BIPLANE

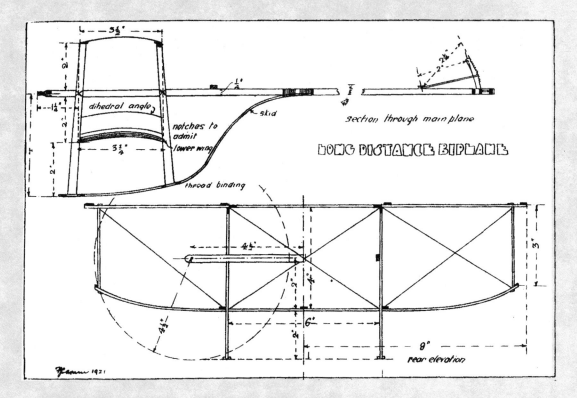

section through main plane

LONG DISTANCE BIPLANE

rear elevation

as shown in the side elevation. The top plane is secured to the stanchions by means of fishplates. The cane skids ($\frac{1}{4}$in. by 1-16in. section) tie the stanchions in place at their lower ends, and so hold the lower main plane into its saw cuts by friction.

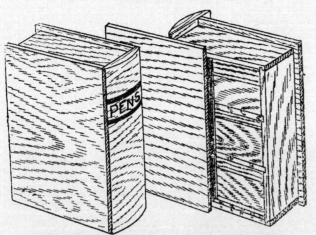

PUZZLE BOOK FOR PENS

How to make
A DART BOARD

Rainy
AFTERNOONS

GAME OF NINE PINS

THE PUZZLE CUBE

WOODWORK - PUZZLE.=V.

PUZZLE BOX FOR PENS. -

THE woodworker, with a taste for small work, will find the puzzle box illustrated at Fig. 1 very interesting. It may, of course, be made to a larger scale, but the dimensions given are those which look well when the box is completed.

The box should be made from ⅛in. thick fretwood, with two small pieces, 3-16in. thick. The wood should be hard and close-grained, owing to the small tongues and grooves entering into the construction; Birch, Mahogany or Rosewood will be very suitable, particularly the latter.

It will be seen at Fig. 1 that to open the box the back is pushed along, and when far enough the lid is pushed open; three divisions are suggested, but this part of the work may be altered to suit individual taste.

Commence work by cutting out the pieces for the sides of box, shown at A, B, and C, Fig. 2. We shall require one piece exactly 2⅝in. by 13-16in. by ⅛in., and two, 1⅞in. by 13-16in. by ⅛in. one 2⅝in. by 11-16in. by ⅛in. The two short lengths, which may be sawn off longer than required, should be grooved out as shown at Fig. 3, one groove 1-16in. wide, and deep, to be cut out from one end 1-16in. away. Another groove the same size should be cut 1⅜in. away from this, and then ⅛in. away cut out a 3-32in. wide groove, 1-16in. deep; but this is only 11-16in. long, and stops ⅛in. from the top edge. A notch, 1-16in. deep and ⅛in. along should be cut out as shown, and also the long groove 1-16in. wide and deep, 1-16in. away from the edge. Make the two

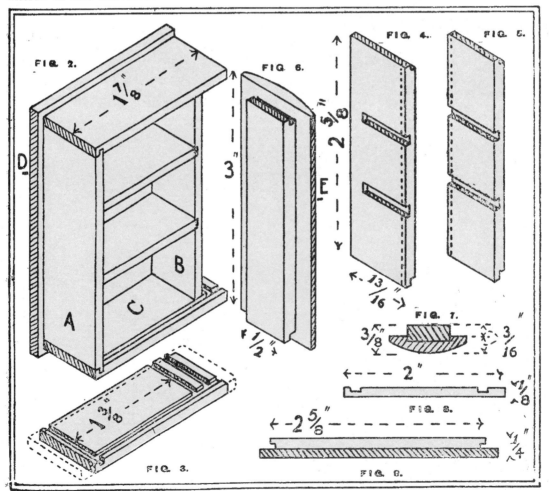

FIG. 1.

FIG. 2.

FIG. 6.

FIG. 4.

FIG. 5.

FIG. 7.

FIG. 8.

FIG. 3.

FIG. 8.

pieces to pair, and then cut out the tongued sides, as shown at Figs. 4 and 5. The former representing the outside piece is grooved with ⅛in. grooves, 1-16in. deep, stopped ⅛in. from the top edge, the length being equally divided. The tongues on the end should be 1-16in. each way. The divisions, 1½in. by 11-16in. by ⅛in. should be cut and fitted, and the frame glued up.

The back, Fig. 6, may now be made. This is a 3in. length of wood, 1in. wide, and 3-16in. thick, rounded to 1-16in. on the edges; it should be noticed, however, that the grain runs across, so that it really is only 1in. long, but 3in. wide. At the back of this piece a piece is let in as shown in the section on E, Fig. 7. This piece should be 2⅝in. long, ½in. wide, and ¼in. thick. At the ends a 3-16in. thick and 1-16in. deep tongue should be cut out, and then the back let in 1-16in. deep; the recess in the back being 2½in. by ½in. by 1-16in. It will be advisable to cut out the recess before the back is rounded, and when the pieces are glued to shape it up, the grain of each piece resuming opposite.

The back should now be fitted into the groove and adjusted carefully with a fine flat file until it moves without any play.

One of the outsides may now be prepared, a piece about 2½in. long and 3½in. wide being trued up, and then the box laid on it, and the sides marked out, so they may be grooved out to take them in 1-16in., as shown by the dotted lines at Figs. 3, 4 and 5, the section across D being shown at Fig. 8. A considerable amount of careful work will be required for this part of the work, but it is necessary to hold the parts tightly together. When the grooving is done plane the piece up to 2in. long and 3in. wide, and ⅛in. thick (the grain being in the direction shown at Fig. 1), and then place in the back, and glue up the box, and side, taking care that the glue does not run into the grooves of the sliding back.

We are now ready to make the lid, and this is a piece of wood, 2in. long, 3in. wide, and ⅛in. thick, glued on to another piece, placed at right angles, to the grain, as shown in the section, Fig. 9. The under piece should be 2⅝in. long, 1¾in. wide, with a tongue 1-16in. each way top and bottom. The two pieces may be glued together, as shown in the section, or the underpiece may be let in about 1-32in. to make it more secure. Fit in the lid by pushing down the back.

FROM ODDS AND ENDS

The "Blitz" Glass-Top Ball Puzzle Game

R EADERS will be familiar with the type of puzzle consisting of a shallow box containing a small metal ball which has to be manoeuvred over a specified course without falling through any of the holes in the bottom.

The topical example shown here represents a badly blitzed district. The player is supposed to be ambulance driver, and the ball represents the ambulance. This has to be piloted safely from the First-Aid Post to the Bombed Factory and thence to the Hospital.

The holes in the base, which have to be avoided, represent bomb craters.

Three pieces of fretwood, size 5¾ins. by 3¼ins. are required. One is a plain rectangle used for the base (A), shown in the cut-away view. Another forms the false bottom (B). This has a number of holes cut in it as shown by the black circles in the diagram.

It also has a narrow rectangular opening ¼in. by 1½in. at one end, so that a sloping runway can be glued

into position leading up to the First Aid Post. This allows the ball to be brought back into play from the lower chamber after it has fallen through one of the holes.

The third piece of wood is cut up into the various shapes shown by the

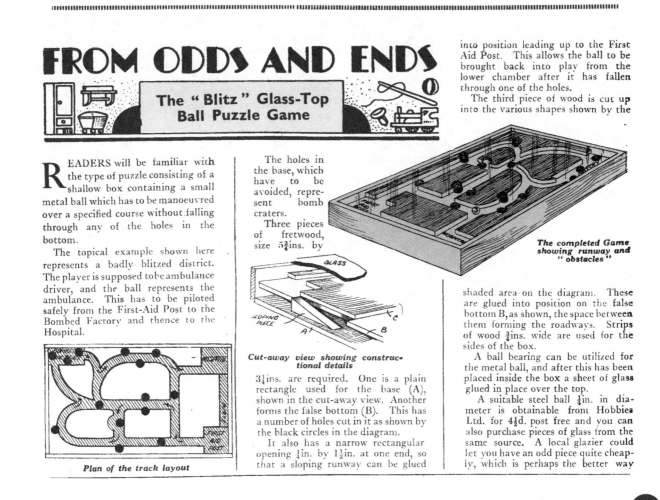

The completed Game showing runway and "obstacles"

Cut-away view showing constructional details

Plan of the track layout

shaded area on the diagram. These are glued into position on the false bottom B, as shown, the space between them forming the roadways. Strips of wood ⅜ins. wide are used for the sides of the box.

A ball bearing can be utilized for the metal ball, and after this has been placed inside the box a sheet of glass glued in place over the top.

A suitable steel ball ¼in. in diameter is obtainable from Hobbies Ltd. for 4½d. post free and you can also purchase pieces of glass from the same source. A local glazier could let you have an odd piece quite cheaply, which is perhaps the better way

How to make
A DART BOARD

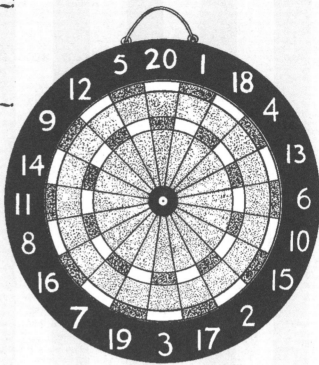

IN view of the popularity of the game of darts, and the absorbing interest which it now holds in many places, it is only right we should offer the handyman reader the opportunity of making a suitable board. Shop-bought ones can be had for anything up to 25/- but the home worker who reads this article should be able to complete one for a very few shillings.

The main cost depends on what he has to pay for the circle of elm which forms the board itself. If you have a timber yard locally, see the merchant and ask him if he will cut you off a piece suitable, and how much it would be. The usual price is about 2/6.

The Wood and Wire

The wood must be cut through the trunk, and not, as is usual in boards, lengthwise to the grain. The object is to get a piece 1½ins. thick and 16ins. in diameter. If the tree is a sound one, the heart will be in the centre of this circle of wood. The timber merchant can cut it off for you flat both sides, but you may have to shape the edges round and smooth each face down with glasspaper.

To get the outer circle you can put a thin nail in the centre, then loop a piece of string to provide an 8ins. radius circle. Get the loop the right length, and with the pencil at the opposite end to the nail, make a mark lightly round the diameter required. This method of marking the circles

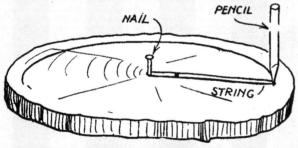

NAIL   PENCIL   STRING

Fig. 1—Drawing the circle

can be utilised also for the smaller ones if you have not a set of compasses large enough. Do not, however, drive the nail in to make an unsightly hole in the middle, and when the work is done, draw it out and fill the hole in again as much as possible. The method of drawing the circle is plainly seen at Fig. 1.

Shape up the edge and keep it at rightangles to the surface of the board.

Wiring

Next comes the wiring, and for this you can obtain the special dart board wire which is of 17 gauge, and sufficiently pliable to turn into the shapes required. You could probably obtain the wire in a coil, but it is essential to have it in fairly long lengths for the various circles.

For the outer ring, for instance, you require two pieces at least about 2ft. 6ins. long, and for the inner ring two pieces 2ft. long. The outer and inner bulls take another piece 9ins. long, whilst there are 20 radial arms which require 6½ins. each. All these lengths allow for turning and wastage.

The wires are held in position by staples at certain points, and these can be cut from another length of, say, 12in. or one can utilise the waste wire from the longer lengths mentioned. The actual positions of the wires are given on the diagram at Fig. 2.

The Circles

The two rings of wires are ⅜in. apart, the outer one being 6in. radius, the next 5⅝ins. then the inner circle 3⅝ins. with the next ring 3¼ins. The larger bull has a radius of ⅝in. and the smaller one ¼in. These six circles of wood are fixed first.

Mark the circles in pencil on the actual wood, then drive in about a dozen small nails lightly in a position just inside the actual line so that when the wire is laid round outside them it is on the line itself. The end of the wire is filed to a point, turned down about ¼in. and driven into the wood, the other circle coming up to it as close as possible. The join should be made under the position of one of the radial arms to be less conspicuous.

It is advisable to mark out in pencil the position of the radial arms before actually putting down any of the wire. An easy method is to mark off with a pair of compasses a distance of 1⅞ins. right round the outer circle. Then run a pencil line from that point through towards the centre, but stopping short at the outer bull.

The wire should be kept free from kinks or

turns but should be curved round to the various circles evenly and gracefully. The final result should be as near a perfect circle in every case as possible, and a little patience in this direction will soon bring about the desired result. Fix one end of the wire into the board first, but do not cut the other end off until you are sure its length is sufficient. Remember, too, to allow an extra piece to turn down and fix into the board. If you

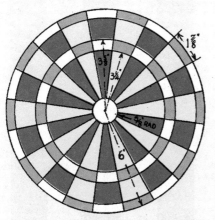

Fig. 2—How the board is marked

are handy at soldering the turned ends can be fixed together. Or a better plan, if you can, is to sweat the ends together. Fix one end of the ring in position and then carry the rest round the pencil line fixing temporarily with staples here and there.

The whole of the radial arms stretch outwards from the centre bull. In every case they pass over the circles and are fixed with the ends driven into the wood in a similar way. Each piece should be cut off 6ins. long with the ends filed. The inner end is driven into the wood $\frac{1}{8}$in. inside the outer bull, is then carried outwards and fixed into the board about $\frac{1}{4}$in. beyond the outer circle.

The turning in every case can be done with a small pair of flat nosed pliers, the wire being held and turned sharply to form a correct rightangle as seen in Fig. 3. The whole of the wire is beaten down as much as possible to the wood, and fixing staples are added to each arm. These little staples can be cut from the actual wire used or can be the specially small staples obtainable from an ironmonger.

One is put over the arm half way on the "double" line, and the other is put just inside the inner circle of the outermost ring.

These staples should be $\frac{1}{4}$in. long and driven well into the wood to form a sufficient anchor for the parts.

Numbering and Painting

Next comes the actual numbering and painting. The numbers are shown in the diagram and can be painted on or made the correct shape in wire. The keen handyman can make quite a good job of the latter, and make shapely numbers which must, of course, be stapled down in one or two places to fix them firmly.

Two other methods are to paint them on or to use the transfer numbers obtainable from Hobbies, Ltd. In every case the remainder of the board must be painted first, and this is the next job.

The outer rim upon which the numbers are, is black, then every alternate space between the narrow scoring ring is a different shade, using two colours right through. Red and green, red and brown or red and blue can be used, flat paint or enamel being applied according to taste. Notice, as seen in the finished drawing, that if the outer rim is painted red the similar space on the inner ring will be painted blue or whatever the second colour happens to be. The inner bull can be black with the outer one red.

The wider space between the two rings can be a lighter shade than the rest. The edge of the board can be painted black, whilst a loop of wire or thick string should be put in at the top by means of two small eyelets.

The actual darts themselves can be obtained from most stores or toy shops, and one should obtain those with the correct balance, and not just the cheap ones which will not always function properly.

How to Play

The game, of course, can be played by any number and scoring is usually done backwards. If two play the idea is to score 101, if you play in pairs or teams against each other, then the game should be proportionately higher. Before anyone can score, however, it is necessary to get a "double." That is, the scorer counts double if the dart lands between the two outer rings of wire. Having once obtained this "double" the score goes on in the usual way.

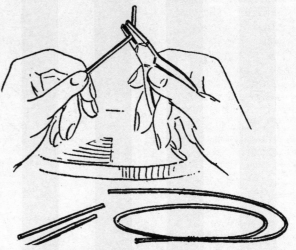

Fig. 3—How the wire is turned with pliers

A good plan is to have a board and a piece of chalk handy and score as you go along. Put down the 101 first, then subtract the numbers of each score. This makes it easier because at the end you must go out on a "double," and get the exact score. That is, if you have only 9 to get out, then you must get say a single three to allow you to get a double three (six) to get out. Or if you want say 15 for a game, you can score say a five then a double five to get out.

If, however, you only want say four (you must have an even number, of course) to get out, and your dart lands on five or anything over four, you miss your turn and are not allowed to play again until your opponent has done so.

GAME OF NINE PINS.

ALTHOUGH the game of Nine Pins is very ancient, it has always been popular, but to be played in the original way it requires rather more space than most of us have to spare. The table game described in this article is very interesting and requires some degree of skill. The game will especially appeal to our boy readers, and it is one which anyone of average intelligence may make quite easily at little cost. As shown at Fig. 1, the game consists of a square board with dwarf sides, the nine pins are set up on a square stand in the centre of the board, and in playing the game, as many of the pins as possible must be knocked down with the ball which is attached by a string to the upright rod at one corner of the board. Every pin knocked down counts one point, and games may be played for 50 or 100 up, the ball being swung once, twice, or three times by each player in turn.

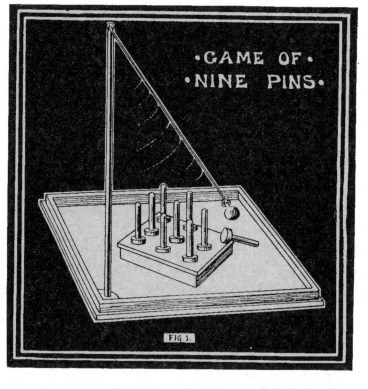

FIG 1.

1½ins. wide for the corner block; two 3ft. lengths of ½-in. dowel rod; and a No. 22 Turned Ball Foot 1¼ins. diameter. All the material mentioned may be obtained from Hobbies Ltd., prices being shown in the Catalogue.

Making the Game.

The plywood for the board is cut quite square, the narrow sides are prepared with square edges, and are fitted around the board to stand ¼-in. in from the edges, as shown at Figs. 2 and 3. Glue is used to fix the sides to the board, pins are driven through the board into the sides, and the corners are also pinned. The sides of the stand are cut and nailed up to measure 8½ins. each way, as shown at Fig. 4, and the plywood top is pinned to the sides. The stand is fixed exactly in the centre of the board, as shown at Fig. 3, pins being driven through the board into the sides of the stand.

The corner block into which the long upright rod fits could be cut from two thicknesses of the ½-in. fretwood glued together. The block is shaped as shown at Fig. 5, a hole exactly ½-in. diameter is bored through it, and it is fixed in a corner of the board with glue and pins. The rod is 2ft. 3ins. long, it should fit firmly into the block, and the top end is neatly

The Material.

To make the game we shall require a piece of ¼-in. plywood 1ft. 8ins. square for the board, and another piece 9ins. square for the stand; four pieces of ½-in. fretwood 1ft. 8ins. long by 1in. wide for the sides of the board, four pieces 9ins. long by 1¾ins. wide for the sides of the stand, a strip 1ft. long by 1¼ins. wide to cut the bases of the nine pins, a piece 3ins. long by

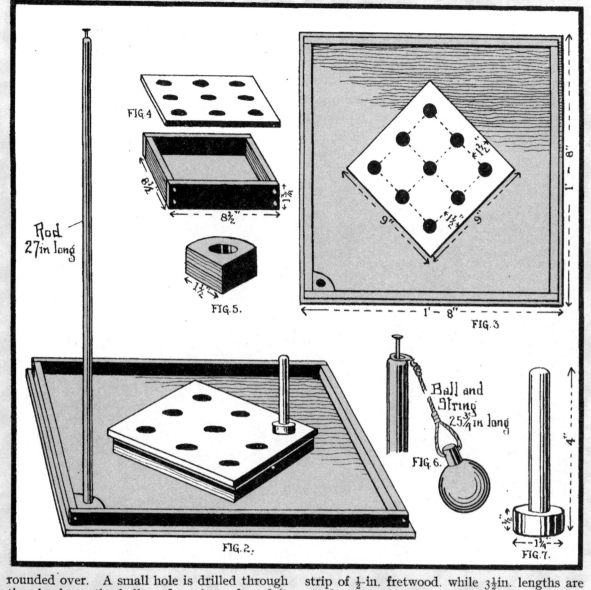

FIG. 4

Rod
27 in long

8¾

1¾

8½"

FIG. 5.

1½

1' 8"

1½

9"

9"

1½

FIG. 3.

FIG. 2.

Ball and
String
25¾ in long

FIG. 6.

4"

½

1¼

FIG. 7.

rounded over. A small hole is drilled through the shank on the ball, and a piece of cord is looped through the hole. Another loop is formed at the top end of the cord, and this fits over a small nail driven into the top end of the rod, as shown at Fig. 6. The length over the cord and ball should measure 2ft. 1¾ins. This allows the ball to just clear the narrow sides of the bottom when it is hung on the rod.

The nine pins are made as shown at Fig. 7. The bases are cut 1¼ins. diameter from the strip of ½-in. fretwood. while 3½in. lengths are cut from the dowel rod to form the pins. The bases are fixed to the pins with glue and small nails, and the top ends of the pins are rounded over.

On completion, the playing board and stand could be varnished, round spots could be painted on the stand to clearly mark the position for standing the pins, as shown at Fig. 3, and the pins could be painted a bright colour.

GRAMOPHONE CHRISTMAS CARDS.

As Christmas Greetings by Gramophone will undoubtedly appeal to quite a host of our readers we would direct attention to the excellent sets of three in dainty boxes for 2/6 issued by Messrs. Raphael Tuck & Sons, Ltd., Raphael House, London. These RECORD CHRISTMAS CARDS, it may be noted, can be sent through the post without fear of damage, whilst the surface of the records themselves, which are made of entirely non-inflammable material, cannot be scratched except by the most violent usage. The selections are most pleasing.

Entertain yourself and your friends by making these
TWO WOOD PUZZLES

HERE are two wood puzzles, quite simple to make and finish, but which will prove fascinating to solve and of interest to hand round at a party, or to visiting friends. Cut all parts carefully and finish nicely.

That shown at Fig. 1 is handed to a friend on some flat surface, say the back of a book or piece of card. The puzzle is made up of four pieces. He is also handed the extra small square "A" and asked to rearrange the pieces and form another square, but this time including the extra piece.

This at first seems impossible, but it can be done and the solution is clearly shown in Fig. 2. The size of the original square is 4ins. by 4ins.

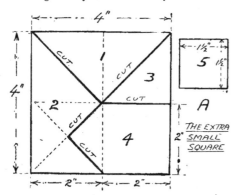

Fig. 1—Cutting the puzzle

and by drawing in the construction lines shown dotted, the placing of the main cuts can be readily determined, all being on the half or diagonal lines.

Use Plywood

Three-plywood should be used and the pieces painted black on both sides, as it makes it more difficult if it is not known which side up the sections ought to go.

The Baffling Mosaic forms the second puzzle, having just about the right degree of hardness. Eight strips of material are handed to the solver, each 1in. by 2ins. and upon which are depicted sections of a coloured mosaic pattern.

These pieces, when put together, in many different ways, will always form a square but the problem is to make up the square with all the adjoining colours agreeing. That is to say, a half yellow fitting with a half yellow to make the complete diamond—a green with a green, and so on.

Marking Out

To make the puzzle, on a section of 3-ply wood draw out a square with 4in. sides, marking these at the inch positions. Then complete the "lattice' work by drawing diagonal lines from these points as Fig. 3. Now with

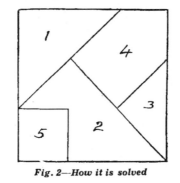

Fig. 2—How it is solved

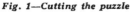

Fig. 4—The puzzle marked

Fig. 5—The Holder

any four colours you have to hand, paint the squares as shown; the colours indicated only being suggested for their brightness.

Note that the squares do not follow in absolute perfect sequence over the whole area. The paint should be put on with some care and a second or even third coat given if necessary to secure depth and vividness.

Symmetrical Strips

After this, cut the square into eight strips as Fig. 4. The cuts are all quite symmetrical and not hard to do, being simply a matter of first quartering the square and then halving the pieces so formed.

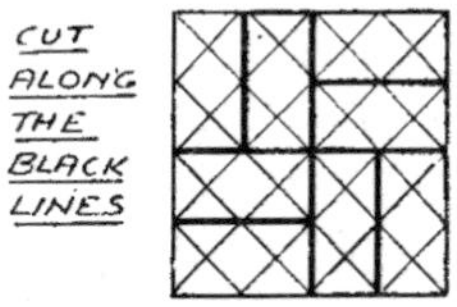

Now make the simple tray as Fig. 5. This consists of a base 5ins. by 5ins. and the walls of the same thickness wood as the puzzle itself. The wall is made up of four trapezium-shaped strips (A) ½in. wide and sides of 5ins. and 4ins. respectively. These are secured to the base by glue and one or two fine sprigs, filing off any which project too far.

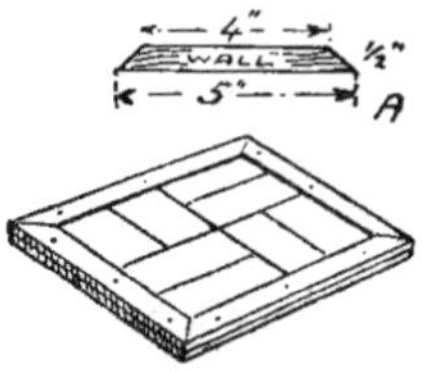

If being given as a present a lid may be fitted to the tray, a simple cloth hinge being used with a cloth fastener.

Instructions should also be neatly printed on white paper with indian ink and pasted to the base. The tray can be given a coat of stain or left plain as desired.

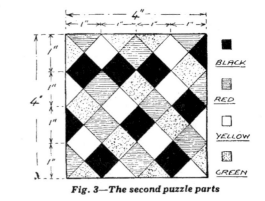

Fig. 3—The second puzzle parts

Here's fun to provide for yourself and friends
TWO SIMPLE PUZZLES

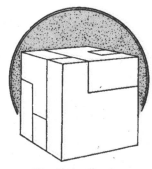

The Cube Puzzle

SOME of those odd scraps of fretwood which accumulated might be used to make the two interesting and popular old puzzles illustrated.

For the first one, some ½in. thick wood will be needed, and it must be exactly ½in. thick, which it will be if planed fretwood is bought. The parts required are shown full size on the inside back cover of this issue.

Paste parts 1 to 6 on to the wood, and cut them out accurately with either tenon saw or fretsaw. It is important that the edges of these pieces should be square, with their face sides—if they are not, an ill-formed cube will result.

If you use a handsaw, not having the good fortune to own a fretsawing machine, and are not too confident in your skill to ensure a truly vertical cut (remember the wood is ½in. thick!) then cut the parts to shape with a tenon saw.

Finish off all of them to smoothness with the finest glasspaper, and do not rub too much, or the thickness of the wood will be reduced and make a good fit together impossible.

The Fifteen Puzzle

The second cube puzzle is, in the present instance, a misnomer, as flat squares are used instead of cubes. The original puzzle consists of cubes however, so let the name stand. It is perhaps better known as The Fifteen Puzzle.

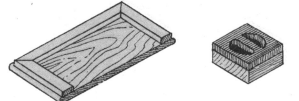

Fig. 1—Cut-away detail of tray.   Fig. 2—A number cube

The fretted design should be pasted down to a piece of thin wood (1/16in. overlay wood for

choice) and be carefully cut out.

Cut a second piece to the outline only, and in ⅛in. wood, and glue the two together. If you can, use different woods of contrasting colour, the numbers will then show up plainer.

The Fifteen Puzzle

Now divide into squares by sawing through the white lines, so the finished squares will then appear as in Fig. 2.

The Tray Holder

For the tray, to hold the squares, cut out the parts 7 and 8. Glue the rim pieces 8 to bottom piece 7, where shown by the dotted lines, to form the tray, as in detail at Fig. 1.

Give the square and tray a clean up. If the squares are a tight fit in the tray, then glasspaper their edges until they all fit snug, but by no means loosely.

Finish off the puzzle with a rubbing with french polish or a coat or two of pale glaze.

Place the squares in the tray in numerical order—o to 15.

What to Do

Remove the square o, then shift the remaining squares until their order is reversed, to read 15 to 1. The squares must not be lifted out of the tray (except the o square), but shifted about in the tray — that constitutes the puzzle.

Those who might like to carry this puzzle about with them to amuse their friends, can make a second tray and hinge it to the first to make a lid. The squares will then not fall out, but be held in a shallow box.

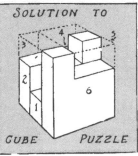

SOLUTION TO CUBE PUZZLE

Keep your friends intrigued by making the

ARMOURED CAR PUZZLE

IT cannot be said that this armoured car is on the secret list, but what, to the uninitiated is 'hush-hush', is the way in which it is assembled. It consists of a number of wooden parts, all interlocked. The secret is rather subtle and by no means obvious, especially if the parts are well made and accurately fitting.

A first glance at the diagrams may give the impression that everything is terribly complicated, but, actually, the mass of dimensions only serves to make things easier. The joints involved—lapped halvings—are the simplest of joints to make.

It is possible to make the model twice the size indicated, and if the puzzle is intended to be given to children as a plaything, it is as well to make it as strong as possible. On the other hand, it can be made **half** the size given. Though stripwood is specified, plastics may be used, especially for the Connectors (part 4) which tend to be a bit delicate.

Base Grooves

The base (1) is 9-ins. by $1\frac{1}{2}$ins. by $\frac{3}{4}$in., one part being required. On the top face cut grooves $\frac{3}{4}$in. wide and $\frac{1}{4}$in. deep, starting 2in. from one end and $1\frac{1}{2}$ins. from the other. These grooves are then divided into three $\frac{1}{4}$in. divisions and the outer thirds chopped away. As with all other joints, they must be dead accurate and nicely smoothed with glasspaper, wrapping the paper round a suitable stick and using like a file.

Two of the sides (part 2) are required but it is most important to note that these parts must be 'handed' (see Fig. 2).

If cut alike (as 2 in Fig. 1) they would not have outside vertical grooves as in Fig. 2. They are cut from 8-in. lengths of $1\frac{1}{4}$in. by $\frac{3}{4}$in. stuff. On the wide side, cut two $\frac{3}{4}$in. grooves, $\frac{1}{2}$in. deep as shown, starting $1\frac{1}{2}$ins. from one end and 1in. from the other. As an extension of these grooves on the inner side, cut a $\frac{1}{4}$in. by $\frac{1}{4}$in. groove right across.

Parallel with these is another groove, also right across, $1\frac{1}{2}$in. wide and $\frac{1}{2}$in. deep on the under side. At right angles to this (i.e. on the other wide side), make a groove $1\frac{1}{2}$ins. wide and $\frac{1}{4}$in. deep. Chop off the corner, as shown in the sketch, and this part is finished.

Four uprights (part 3) are required, cut from $\frac{3}{4}$in. square stripwood, $2\frac{3}{4}$in. long. The grooves are $\frac{1}{4}$in. deep. The corner can either be rounded off or chopped off straight (as seen in the assembly drawing). It is an advantage to clamp these pieces together and trim them up together so that they are all alike.

Two connectors (part 4) are required of $\frac{1}{2}$in. square stripwood, and are shaped somewhat like dumbells except that *the rounded part is not central* (see 4a). This rounded part is $\frac{1}{4}$in. diameter. As will be explained shortly, the whole puzzle depends on this part.

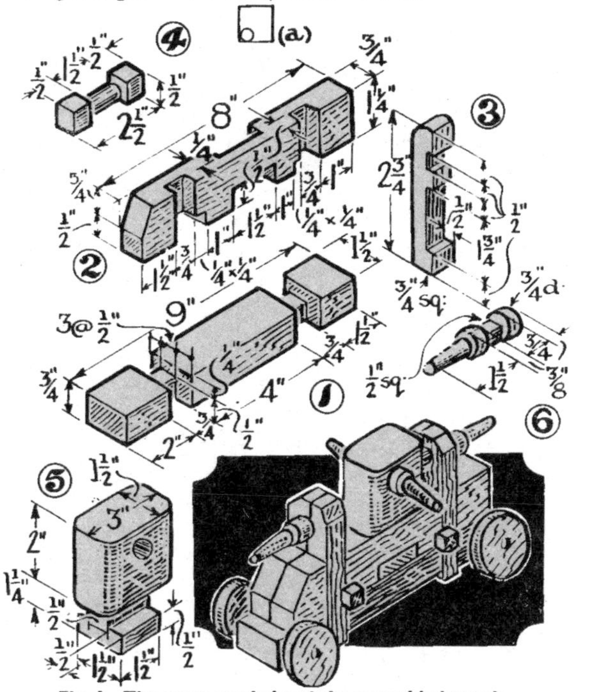

Fig. 1—The parts needed and the assembled puzzle

As the middle part is rather delicate, it may be a good idea to make this part from plastic or even of metal but in this case, the guns (part 6) and the wheels had best be made of plastic or metal too, so as not to draw undue attention to the connectors.

One turret (part 5) is required shaped from a piece of 3in. by $1\frac{1}{2}$in. section wood, $3\frac{1}{4}$ins. long. By studying the assembly drawing and also the side pieces (part 2), one can see how the inverted T-shape of the bottom of the turret interlocks. A $\frac{3}{8}$in. diameter hole is bored for the guns.

The guns (part 6) are either turned in a lathe or whittled down from $\frac{3}{4}$in. diameter dowel. It will be seen that in the case of the fore and aft guns, the square part is gripped between a pair of uprights (parts 3). The guns for the turret are not dimensioned separately but they are in one piece, at either end of a piece of $\frac{3}{8}$in. dowel. This part does not interlock and is simply pushed in, friction tight, in the hole in the turret.

The wheels are not interlocking either, but are simply cut from $\frac{1}{8}$in. plywood and screwed on with round-headed screws. It would not be much extra trouble to interlock these and the turret guns, but there is no point in describing a too-complicated model.

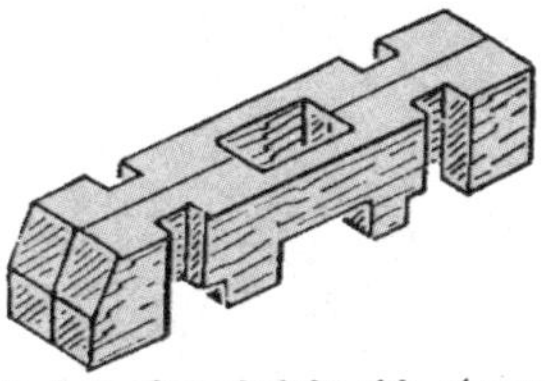

Fig. 2—Left and right side pieces

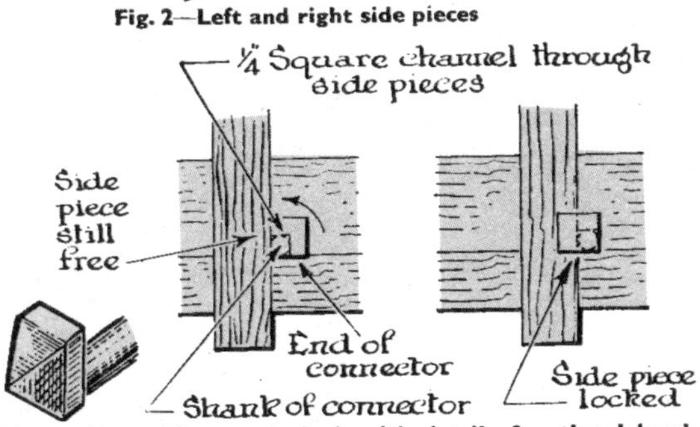

Fig. 3—How sides are locked, with detail of optional head shape

Lay the two side pieces together as in Fig. 2 but with the turret piece clipped between them. (Incidentally in fitting together, minor adjustments will probably have to be made.) Turn the base the other way up to that shown in the drawing. Stand the three parts just assembled upon it, slipping in the two connectors. Keep the square heads of these turned so that the vertical channels are clear and then press on the uprights.

Before these are right 'home' however, slip in the fore and aft guns. The connector heads are then turned and the whole job is locked together. The turret guns are simply pushed through the hole.

In showing 'how it is done', the turret guns are pushed out and, by implication, the would-be solver is led to believe that the connectors are pushed through. Even if, as is likely, he finds that they turn a little, he may attribute this to a little looseness in fitting and it does not immediately occur to him to give the heads a turn through a half circle.

The small sketch (Fig. 3) shows how the heads may be tapered off so as to afford very little finger grip. Apart from the interest in this model, it is an excellent excercise in cutting and fitting.

HOW THE AMATEUR RIFLEMAN MAKES A TARGET

CIGARETTE SERVER

HEALTH AND SAFETY

EVERY FIRST AID DEPOT WILL BE GRATEFUL FOR A BANDAGE WINDER

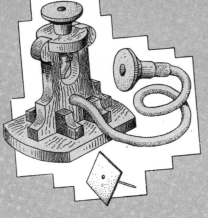

A JOKE LUNG TESTER

A MODERN SMOKER'S COMPANION STAND

A PIPE REST

Every first aid depot will be grateful for
A BANDAGE WINDER

WITH so many first-aid classes functioning all over the country and using roller bandage, we are sure that this design for a wrapping frame for this kind of bandage will be found of interest.

With it the long strips of material, which often get into rather a tangle, can be quickly and neatly rolled up after use, thus saving much time and making them more presentable for storing, and incidentally putting them in better condition for use at the next class.

The frame, though small, is made of fairly heavy wood to help sturdiness and in use is clamped to the edge of a table. The base is 9ins. by 4ins. and ½in. thick, and can be of any piece of not too soft wood, while the ends are 8¾ins. by 3ins. (also ½in.) and the top 9ins. by 3ins. of ¼in. material.

Size Adjustment

Section (a) is a sliding piece and is adjustable to the size of bandage being wound. It is built up of the two sides (b) 8¼ins. by 2½ins. and ¼in. thick and two blocks (d) 2½ins. by 1in. by ½in., these being set ½in. in from the ends.

A rectangle (e) of 1/8th wood is let into the one side as indicated to give neater rolling. It is 4ins. by 2ins. This sliding section moves on the two strips (f) which are of ½in. square section and 8ins. long.

When all these parts are ready, together with two 8½in. lengths of ¼in. diameter dowelling, they

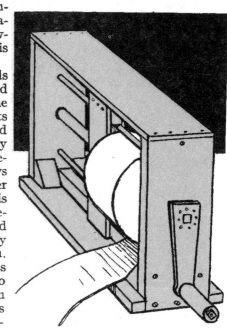

can be assembled; the diagrams showing how this is done.

The ends are recessed (x) into the base (at its ends) and secured by three one-inch screws and the lower strip (f) is fitted between and held by several ¾in. screws through to the base with their heads slightly countersunk, also two screws into the extremities, through the main end pieces.

Greater strength is given by the triangular corner blocks (g), the two lengths of dowelling being simply let in by boring two ¼in. holes at position 2ins. from top and bottom; the pieces being slipped into place when assembling.

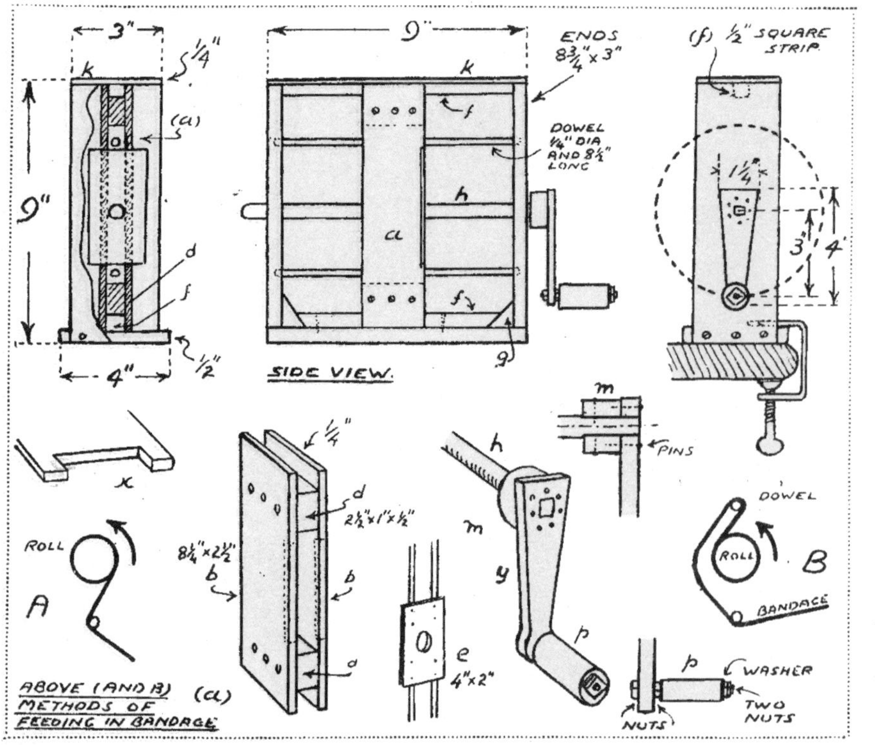

The top, with the upper strip (f) fastened down the centre, is laid over the upper ends of the side-pieces and secured with ¾in. screws.

The sliding section (a) is now fitted on to the frame, the second side only being screwed into position after the first is in position between the (f) strips. Care must be taken to get good fitting of the piece as a whole, which should slide comfortably from end to end of the frame without binding at any point.

On the other hand it must not be too loose on the guiding strips and should hold by friction at the point to which it is adjusted.

The Handle

Finally comes the central spindle (h) and handle. This part must be made to with‑

(Figure labels, lower diagram:)
3" ¼" k (a) 9" d f 4" ½"
ENDS 8¾" x 3" (f) ½" SQUARE STRIP
DOWEL ¼" DIA AND 8½" LONG
SIDE VIEW. 1¼" 3" 4"
ROLL A 8¼" x 2½" b d 2½"x1"x½" b a
ABOVE (AND B) (a) METHODS OF FEEDING IN BANDAGE
m PINS DOWEL ROLL B BANDAGE
h m y p e 4" x 2" p WASHER TWO NUTS NUTS

stand fairly rough usage, and to this end the crank (y) must be firmly attached to the centre rod. To get the necessary sturdiness the one end of the spindle (which is a $10\frac{1}{2}$in. length of $\frac{1}{2}$in. diameter dowelling) is slightly flattened at each side and a piece of thick plywood (m) with a suitable hole cut out of the centre is tapped on the end.

This block can be left as a rectangle or cut to polygon shape, but to make the neatest job it should be cut or turned to a cylindrical collar.

A quarter-inch of the spindle is left protruding (for the crank) which is of $\frac{1}{4}$in. plywood dimensioned as shown, a hole being cut at the top centre to take the spindle end. Make the hole rather less than the spindle so that the crank has to be finally tapped into place.

Fixed to a Table

Once together, spindle, crank and block are made finally secure by several fine model-maker's pins driven in horizontally and a couple going through radially into the spindle from the block.

The handle grip (p) can be bought or built up of a $2\frac{1}{2}$in. double threaded bolt held to the crank by two nuts taken tightly home over small washers, and a loose cover which is kept from coming off by two nuts at the further end ; the second nut being to lock the first. A washer is placed between these nuts and the cover also.

For using, the frame is clamped to the edge of a table by a suitably-sized clamp. The bandage is fed in over the dowels in either of the two ways shown in the bottom diagrams and is " started " on the spindle by just giving a turn or two.

Passing over the dowels helps to straighten it out, it also gives a little friction and prevents the rolling from being too loose.

The central spindle it will be noted is not fastened at its further end and the finished roll is removed by simply withdrawing the spindle after giving a couple of turns backwards (while holding the roll) to loosen the centre.

HOBBIES.

How the amateur rifleman can make
A SAFETY TARGET

MOST of us, especially the youngsters, like to get hold of a gun and have a " pot " at something now and then. In the country, of course, there is nothing to prevent us. Sparrows abound in the farmyards and the farmers are only too glad to be rid of them.

In the town it is different. After about ten minutes' shooting you will probably have the next-door neighbour round, asking you to pay up for a broken window or a dead chicken.

Even apart from direct hits, there is always the danger of a " ricochet " injuring a passer-by.

Air Gun Bullet Catcher

We have designed a bullet catcher, shown in these pages, which will answer the purpose of the town dweller admirably. It will take two targets and entirely eliminates the risk of ricocheting bullets. When two are shooting, each can use a target, and compare the scores afterwards.

Targets can be bought from most local iron-mongers, who usually stock guns and their accessories.

The box is designed to hang on a wall, and is made up of ½in. wood. The kind of wood does not really matter, and the choice is therefore left to the reader. Figs. 1 and 2, show sufficient of the construction to enable you to confidently start work.

The front is a piece 16½ins. long and 9ins. wide and has an opening measuring 13½ins. by 6ins. cut in with a fretsaw.

Armoured Inside

The box is simply two pieces 16½ins. by 8ins. and two pieces 8ins. by 8ins. butted together as shown. Screws should be used in preference to glue or nails, since the box will have to stand a good deal of knocking about.

The front can now be screwed securely in place and the back cut out. As will be seen in the diagrams, the back is not shaped and is simply a piece of ½-in. wood measuring 16½ins. by 11ins.

The " armour " inside consists of a piece of ⅛in. sheet iron bent round to cover the top, bottom, and back. The sides are not quite so important, and can be covered with 1/16in. sheet.

It would do quite well if you opened up several tins and used about two thicknesses for the sides. After the sides have been covered and the back and top covering slid in, the back can be screwed permanently in place.

Hang and Use

To hang the box up, two brass hangers (No. 6176) are employed. They cost only 1d. each and are fixed by two small screws. The shape of these hangers enables you to lift the " catcher " down and put it up again quite easily when next required.

To use, you must pin two targets over the opening and, shooting two at a time, fire your number of shots and then compare scores.

You must bear in mind that the measurements given here cannot be strictly adhered to, since the size of the targets vary. It is best to find out first what size you can obtain and then make your box accordingly.

An Electric Indicator

It will add considerably to the enjoyment of the shooting if you have something to tell you definitely when you have scored a bull.

Figs. 3 and 4 show you how this can be arranged while still using the same size box. You will see

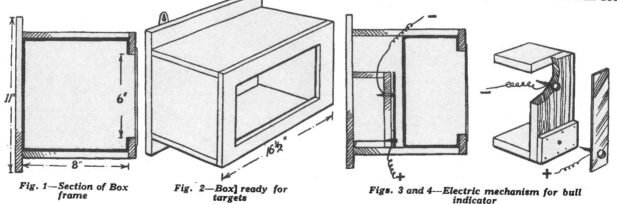

Fig. 1—Section of Box frame

Fig. 2—Box] ready for targets

Figs. 3 and 4—Electric mechanism for bull indicator

that the ⅛in. metal sheet does not go so far back and that a connecting gadget is fixed behind it. First of all however, you must bore a hole in the ½in. iron exactly behind the bull. The hole must be slightly larger than the bull, since those bullets which only cut the bull are counted.

Naturally, since you are using two targets, you will need one hole behind each target and a separate connecting and wiring scheme for each.

For each target a spring switch is made as suggested in Fig. 4. Three pieces of ½in. wood are built up with an eighth inch piece pinned on as shown.

A round head screw is driven through about level with the bull of the target and to this, from the back, is attached a wire leading to one pole of the battery. Next is required a strip of brass or iron which has a certain amount of spring in it.

This is fixed, by means of 1¼in. or 1in. round head screw as shown on Fig. 4. A wire fixed to this screw leads to the bulb holder and from there to the other pole of the battery. For these connections it is advisable to use rubber covered wire, since this is less liable to result in a " short." Fig. 3 shows the position of the spring switch in place.

The "Bull" Action

When the bullet pierces the bull, it travels through the hole in the sheet iron and strikes the upright strip of brass. A connection is thus made with the round head screw causing the bulb to flash its message.

The simplest method of wiring is to use two batteries and two bulbs. Each target and indicator can be independent of the other.

Wood of suitable thickness can be obtained from Hobbies Ltd. at reasonable prices, whilst other materials such as covered wire, bulb holders batteries, etc., can be obtained at your local stores.

It is a good idea to mark out your range and place a post at the position from which you will shoot. The wire should now be led from the targets to the post where they can be connected to the bulbs mounted on a suitable piece of board.

Ordinary pocket-lamp batteries will suffice and last a long time especially if different voltage bulbs are used. When the batteries are new and strongest it is best to use a 3.5 volt bulb, but when they begin to noticeably run down, this can be substituted for a 2.5 This will brighten the light considerably and enable the batteries to be used for a much longer period.

Finishing Hints

We suggest that for better effect the bulbs might be painted red or green according to taste.

The bullet catcher too will have to be painted since the sun is bound to cause a certain amount of warping. Black is the most suitable colour, since the targets are usually printed on a white ground.

When painting, do not let any of it run into the box or it will stop the working of the spring switch.

There is the possibility that you have no suitable wall on which to hang your targets. In this case you must make the backing of 1in. thick oak or beech.

Large Backboard

A backing board about 4ft. by 3ft. should be large enough to catch any " misfires." The boards should be screwed to battens and then fixed at a convenient height to two 2in. by 2in. posts. The targets can now be hung on this as on a wall.

All these precautions are a waste of time if you are careless with a gun, so take this word of warning to heart.

Whenever you are using a gun, loaded or unloaded, always keep the muzzle pointing upwards or downwards. Never swing it round in wild circles.

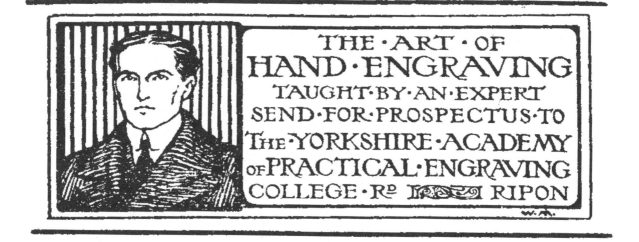

Here is another type of easy-to-make table

CIGARETTE SERVER

IN a previous article instructions were given for a simple cigarette 'server', for use at parties or on dinner tables, or indeed anywhere when guests are expected to help themselves. Here are details of a rather more elaborate server which will hold twelve standard-sized cigarettes.

A piece of $\frac{1}{4}$in. material is required first on which two circles each of 2in. diameter can be scribed. Inside both the circles the six-sided figure shown is drawn, this being obtained by placing the leg of the compass, which is still set at the 2ins. at any point on the circumference and by swinging in both directions making two marks (on the circumference)—one on either side.

Move the compass leg to one of these points—it does not matter which—and swing again, continuing thus right round the circle. If correctly done the circumference should divide exactly into six equal parts. Join the points so found by straight lines and the desired shape is secured.

Two Hexagon

The six-sided shapes are then scribed out, the one as (A) and the other as (B), Fig. 2. On both shapes lightly mark in the radii from the six points to the centres and put in the line (a) which is a $\frac{1}{4}$in. from the points, along the radii, that is a shade less from the outside edges.

On the second piece (B), the one that is going to be the upper level, mark the points (b), a $\frac{1}{4}$in. more along the radii. The holes which are to take the cigarettes are of $\frac{3}{16}$in. radius and points $\frac{3}{16}$in. further still along the radii give the centres of the corner ones, and these can be drawn in.

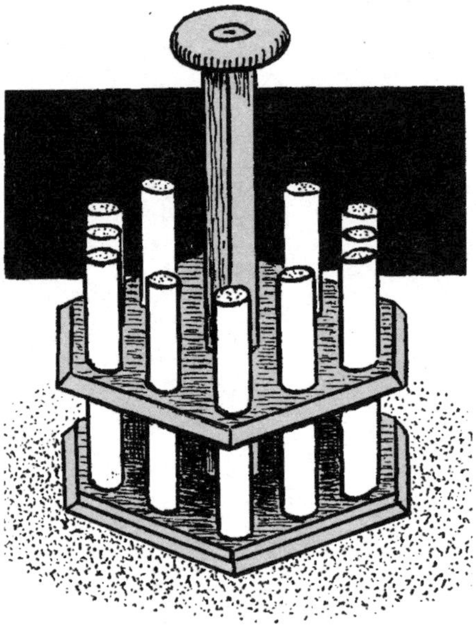

Fig. 1—A completed stand for 12 cigarettes

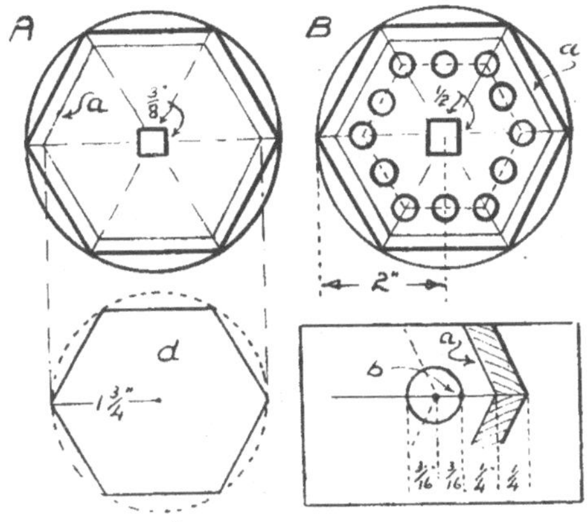

Fig. 2—How to make the shapes

Now join the centres of these six corner holes and you get the centre-line for the intermediate openings which lie mid-way along the flat sides. The centres of these secured, they also can now be marked in.

Next required is the second base-piece (d). This is from a thin section of material, $\frac{1}{8}$in. or $\frac{3}{16}$in. thick. The shape is obtained by drawing a circle of $1\frac{3}{4}$ins. radius, marking off the circumference as above in radii lengths, and again joining up the points found.

Temporarily fasten this piece to the top (B) with two or three fine sprigs and aligning it to the line (a). Carefully bore down through the two sections at each hole position. A standard cigarette is just $\frac{3}{8}$in. diameter so the apertures are first taken out to this measurement and then eased off with a round file or glasspaper wrapped round a thin pencil or skewer, till a nice comfortable fit is secured for the standard 'smoke'.

The Base

When all is ready separate the pieces and bevel the edges of the top and under sections (A) and (B) as far as the first line (a). This will give a pleasing slope. After this secure (d) to the base-piece (A) with glue, putting under pressure while drying takes place. See to it that the edges of (d) nicely meet the top of the bevel, glasspapering a little if necessary to obtain this end.

A base having twelve circular depressions has now been made and at this junction check to see that all these are quite free from unwanted bits of glue, etc., as at the best they only just grip the ends of the cigarettes.

Now take a $\frac{1}{2}$in. square opening out of the centre of (B) and another of $\frac{3}{8}$in. sides from the middle of the base. These are for the handle (G) (Fig. 3). It would be nice if this latter could be turned on a lathe at the top to some pleasing shape, but in lieu of this finish, a square-section length of wood with a 'button' on top will do quite well.

In either case the lower end (g) is taken to a square section of $\frac{3}{8}$in. sides for $\frac{3}{8}$in. up, and to a $\frac{1}{2}$in. section for the next $1\frac{3}{8}$ins. up. If a square section handle is being used throughout, this section can be retained to the top, otherwise any turned part would start here. The length of the handle is $5\frac{1}{4}$ins.

Handle Piece

The top of the handle is completed with any of the circular 'buttons' that can be obtained at dealers in wood fittings. It should not be too large—about $1\frac{1}{4}$ins. doing nicely. The button is secured to the top of the handle with a round-headed chromium screw, a chromium washer being put between the head and wood to give a bright finish.

Assembly of the three main parts can now be effected. If well cut this will not be difficult as the square hole should grip the upright fairly tightly and at a true right-angles. This ideal is not always obtained, but it is essential that the main pieces are perfectly horizontal and at an accurate ninety degrees to the upright. To this end two blocks of wood of the same thickness should be slipped between the pieces as gluing and drying proceeds,

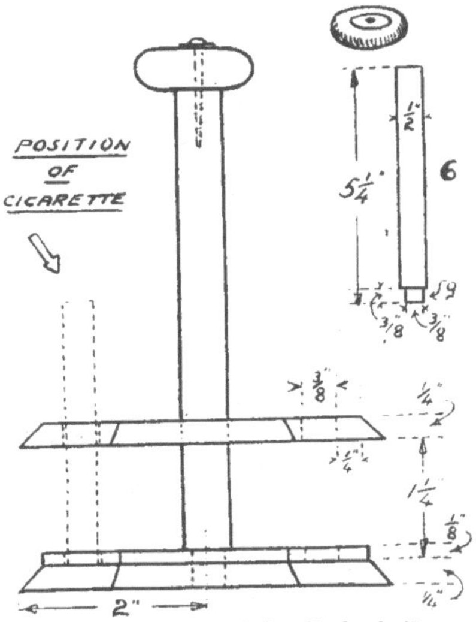

Fig. 3—Section and detail of spindle

the upright being checked with a set square.

As with the first server described, finish can be with stain or stain and polish, or if good wood has been used a plain finish could be adopted. A too-dark livery should definitely be avoided, anything to do with cigarettes for some reason always looking better in a fairly light setting.

Thin baize should finally be glued to the underside of the base to give safety on even the most highly polished surface. The server as given is designed for the standard cigarette.

A MODERN SMOKER'S COMPANION STAND

HERE is an ideal item of furniture to have by the side of an easy chair during that quiet hour with a book and pipe. The table part is handy for accommodating various things such as a cup of coffee, tobacco jar, cigarette casket or writing materials.

The piece may be carried out in oak or mahogany or, for the sake of economy, birch plywood and one of the softer woods may be used. In the latter case, stain of almost any shade may be chosen.

A start is made with the shaped piece and Figs. 1 and 2 give an idea of its construction. The long pieces are 1in. by 2ins. in section. Eight blocks of the same material are glued between them and the whole thing shaped later. If this part is marked out full size on paper, the approximate lengths of the short pieces can be ascertained.

The Main Stand

Starting with the longer leg, the first block is glued and nailed to it. A second block is fixed to the first and so on until the other leg is fixed to the rest of the structure. When the glue is thoroughly set, the lower end of the work is made perfectly square and true.

The surfaces may need a little attention with a block plane before the shape is marked out. A fretsaw is the best tool for cutting it out. If the work is laid flat on the bench and vertical cuts

made through the thickness of the wood, splitting will be avoided. A spokeshave or file and glasspaper will produce a smooth finish. As will be seen at Fig. 2, the outer edges are also shaped near the bottom.

The base is a piece of ⅝in. wood, 15ins. by 8ins. with bevelled edges. This is supported on feet, details of which are given at Fig. 3. Two pieces of 1in. by 1½in. stripwood each 10ins. long are required. The top edges are bevelled at each end, and blocks 1¾ins. by 1¾ins. by ⅜in. thick are fixed underneath so as to leave an overhang of ⅛in. at the sides and end. The feet are fixed with glue and a couple of 1½in. screws driven from underneath into each.

Fitting the Legs

At this point the legs are prepared to receive the top. A 9in. batten of ⅞in. by 2½in. material has a mortise or socket cut half way through its centre to take the top of the shorter leg as shewn at Fig. 4.

The lower edges of this piece are bevelled and holes are bored for screws to fix the table top. Incidentally these holes should be enlarged into long ovals to allow for swelling and shrinkage of the top. The batten is glued and screwed to the top of the shorter leg, making sure that it is level.

The table top is cut from ⅝in. solid wood or ½in. plywood. A piece 20ins. by 10ins. has a semicircle marked out at one end. A fretsaw is the ideal tool for the cutting out. The edges are finished off by rounding them slightly with a spokeshave and glasspaper.

Top and Base

The table top is laid on the batten and the position of the notch on the longer leg for its reception is marked out. A piece ⅜in. deep is cut away at this point. In addition, a notch is cut in the edge of the top. This will allow the back edge of the top to lie flush with the back of the leg. The top is glued and screwed through the leg but it is merely screwed to the batten.

Having proceeded so far, the base may be

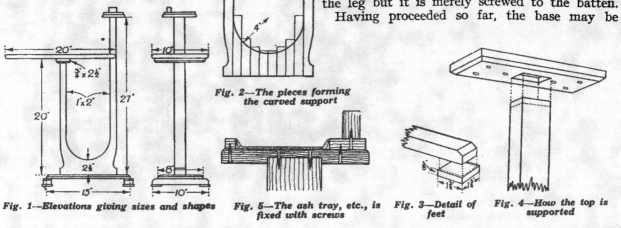

Fig. 1—Elevations giving sizes and shapes

Fig. 2—The pieces forming the curved support

Fig. 5—The ash tray, etc., is fixed with screws

Fig. 3—Detail of feet

Fig. 4—How the top is supported

fixed, and three long screws from the underside will provide ample fixing. The ash tray and match holder now remains to be made.

As the size and shape of the metal or china ash tray will determine the size of the block of wood, the tray should be obtained first. A piece of ½in. wood is used with an overlay of ⅜in. material having an opening cut in it to form a recess for the tray. The upper piece stands in by ¼in. all round as shewn in section at Fig. 5. The matchbox holder is merely a block of wood, 1⅜ins. by ⅝in. by 1in. high, fixed near one end.

As a finish stain of an appropriate shade followed by " Hobbies Waxine " gives a very durable surface from which those inevitable marks caused by hard wear are removed easily. For a more brilliant result the reader will be wise to choose Hobbies " Lightning Polish."

A PIPE REST

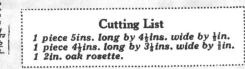

THE artistic pipe rest illustrated, is just the thing for a smoker friend to rest his pipe when working at the table or desk. The base of the article is made in wood ½in. thick and a piece is cut to size 5ins. by 4½ins. as indicated in Fig. 1. Take a distance of ½in. from the end and ½in. from either side, and then carefully cut the two slots 1in. by ⅜in. as shown.

Now measure a distance of 2ins. from the other end, and taking a centre line ⅞in. from either side mark off squares of ¼in. as indicated, and then draw the shape of the cavity for the pipe bowl to rest in. These cavities for the pipe bowl should be made about ⅜in. deep at the broad end, and they are quite easily cut out by means of a gouge.

The support end for the pipe stem is indicated in Fig. 2, and this is made in wood ⅜in. thick. First cut the wood 4½ins. long by 3⅛ins. wide. On a centre line a

distance of 1⅛ins. from the top scribe a circle of 2¼ins. in diameter.

The bottom edge is carefully marked off for the two tenons which are cut 1in. wide by ½in. deep as shown, and should be a good fit in the slots cut in the base. The curved shape on the ends are readily marked off by dividing the surface into ¼in. squares and then neatly cut out.

The support end when made is fixed into the base and the wood is then made nice and smooth. Strips of 3/16in. half round ball beading are fixed round the edges, and 2in. oak rosette is fixed on the front as shown in Fig. 1, also the position for this is indicated by the dotted circle in Fig. 2. The pipe rest is now finished by giving it a good coat of stain.

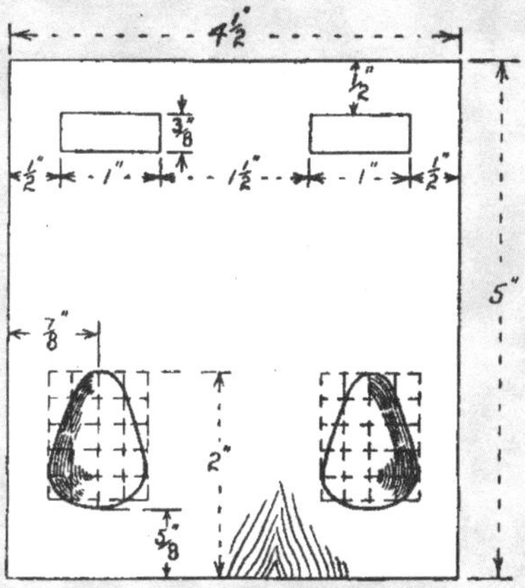

Fig. 1—Details of the base 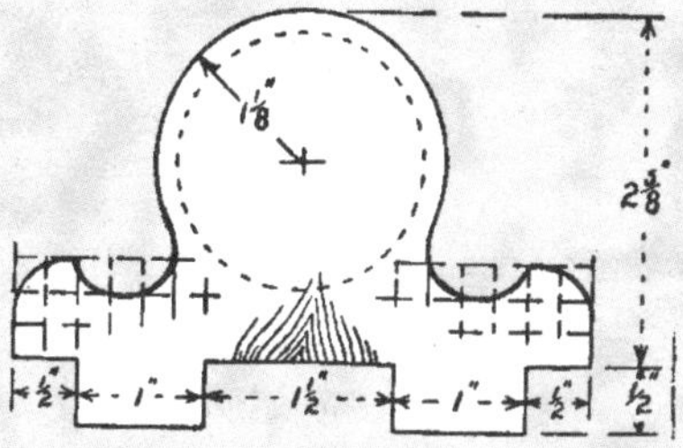   Fig. 2—The end support piece

Cutting List
1 piece 5ins. long by 4½ins. wide by ½in.
1 piece 4½ins. long by 3⅛ins. wide by ⅜in.
1 2in. oak rosette.

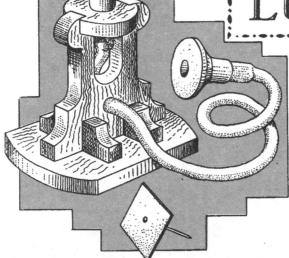

A JOKE LUNG TESTER

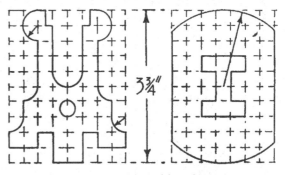

THIS queer, surgical-looking device never fails to arouse one's curiosity, and of course, when informed that it is nothing more than a lung tester—well, we are very anxious to show the owner there is nothing weak about our lungs, and tell him so.

"O.K.," he grins, picking up the small square of card through which a pin projects, "I bet you anything you like you can't blow this tiny piece of card from here"—it is placed point foremost on the top spool of the strange device—"inside two minutes."

"Sez you," we challenge, picking up the mouthpiece. "Well, just watch—I'll have it off in a second!"

Taking a deep, deep breath, we blow lustily until all the air is expelled from our powerful lungs, and then we wonder why the card remains impassive to our efforts and why our friend is almost bursting with silent mirth.

The Joke

Not to be outdone, we try again, puffing and blowing until we are red in the face—and still the card won't move! It merely revolves in an agitated manner and absolutely refuses to budge.

Yet, it should do so, because the air-line is quite free, and the pin is not stuck in the wood, but simply rests in the spool to keep the card in place. What is the reason—what's the mystery?

Our chortling friend, or rather, practical-joker knows, and explains that it is due to the consequent escape of air which has a suction power rather like a vacuum. Thus, the harder we blow, the stronger the suction, and the more impossible it is to remove the card. No wonder we couldn't shift it!

The Construction

The idea, you will see, is simplicity itself, but in order to make it more effective, we have designed a novel sort of apparatus that makes it look more

like a medical or surgical appliance. If you wish to "test" the vacuum power now, an ordinary spool and the pinned card would serve.

As you will doubtless want to make the structure suggested, we will proceed with the construction. The wood used could be ⅜in. stuff marked out to the ⅜in. squared outlines given in Figs. 1 and 2. On the other hand, if you have nothing available except ½in. wood, then you can draw up ½in. squares and follow the outlines accordingly, or if it should happen to be 5/16in. thick, use 5/16in. squares and so on.

Before cutting the hole in the upright, it is advisable to obtain the rubber tubing and find its diameter. Any local druggist or chemist or rubber appliance store should be able to supply you with this tubing which should be 12ins. long by ⅜in. in diameter.

The Tubing

If you have a chemistry outfit, the tubing supplied with it (for use with the Bunsen burner) might serve as, if of the right diameter, you will *not* destroy it in any way.

Having cut out the upright, base and two support pieces (see Fig. 2), glue the latter to the base mortises, then insert the upright. The circular cap, which is also cut from ⅜in. wood, is fitted and glued to the top as in the illustration. The arrows given in the outlines indicate, of course, how the compasses can be utilized.

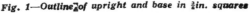

Fig. 1—Outline of upright and base in ⅜in. squares

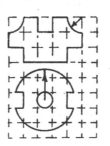

Fig. 2—Support pieces

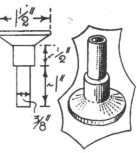

Fig. 3—Details of the spool

Joke Lung Tester

The head and mouthpiece fitments are made from two cotton reels or wire (S.W.G.) spools. The latter, if you can obtain them, are the most suitable to use in respect to the measurements given at Fig. 3. With the reels, you may not be able to cut a ⅜in. shank as depicted owing to the diameter of the bobbin-pin hole.

To proceed with the spools, at least, remove one flange, then divide the " stem " and saw a shoulder neatly around it, the waste being removed with a penknife or rasp. You will require two made identical, and having got them made, insert one to the upright cap and—if found necessary—apply a smearing of tube glue.

Insert the tubing through the upright hole and over the stem projection of the head spool, the mouth-piece going to the other end. The hole in same should be widened with a countersink bit, but this is not highly essential; do not interfere with the head spool hole in any way.

Should the tubing be ½in. in diameter, and consequently, somewhat loose over the stems, a piece of galvanized wire or twine tied tightly around will prevent any escape of air.

This completes the " apparatus " and as a finish the wood could be varnished or enamelled. When polished ebony black, with Hobbies Lighting Polish, there is a " professional touch " about the article and victims are not so apt to treat the whole with a critical, if not a caustic eye. It would help matters (or should we say, the delusion?) better if the head and mouth-piece were enamelled bright red or green.

In conclusion, let the victims place the square of card on the head spool themselves, otherwise they might, after a breathless struggle, think you had stuck the pin point into some part of the spool. We should add, too, that one should look no further for victims than in one's own family or make use of intimate friends who possess a good pair of healthy lungs.

MATERIAL LIST

1 piece wood	...	...	4ins. by 4ins. by ⅛in. thick.
1 piece wood	...	...	4ins. by 3ins. by ⅛in. thick.
1 piece wood	...	...	3ins. by 2½ins. by ⅛in. thick.
2 cotton reels.			
1 piece rubber tubing		...	12ins. by ⅜in. in diam.

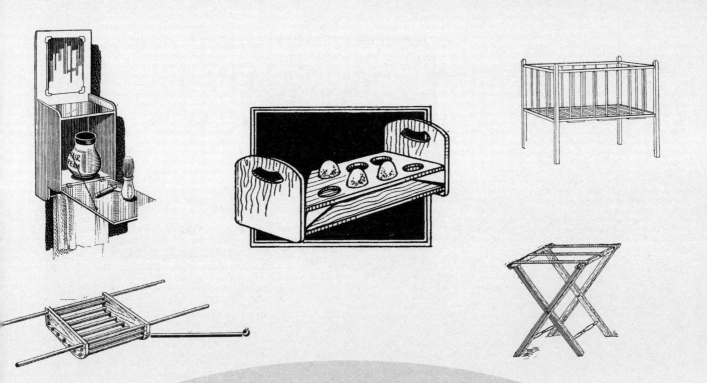

HOME IMPROVEMENTS

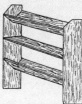

A CONVENIENT BOOK-REST

A SMALL SHAVING CABINET

A SIMPLE BATH RACK

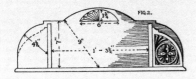

A SIMPLE BATH RACK

Any boy can make it

MOST houses could find a use for the simple bath rack shown herewith, and in consequence any handyman with woodwork tools should set to work to make it. Such an article does not take much in time or wood, and the whole requirements in materials can be purchased for about 1s. 6d. The rack, which rests across the bath and holds sponges and flannels, is

An everyday article made for a few pence, by anyone with a few carpentry or fretwork tools.

composed of a number of pieces of round rod, known as dowel rod, held by two pieces of wood which form the ends of the basket. These two pieces are cut from ½in. wood—plain deal, or oak, or sycamore being equally suitable. Each piece measures 8in. long and 3in. wide, and can therefore be cut from a single board 8in. by 6in.

The Rods required.

The other requirements are lengths of ½in. dowel rod, and all of it can be cut from five of the 3ft. lengths in which it is supplied (at 2d. a length) by Hobbies, Ltd. The length of the completed article as shown is 2ft. 3in., which is wide enough for a full-size bath. If, however, it is a smaller one, the rack can be proportionately shorter. The measurement of the bath (about half way down its length) should, therefore, be taken before commencing work. Providing the bath is full size, two rods 2ft. 3in. will be required for the longest supports. The actual basket rods can be made the same length, however, whatever the size of the bath. We shall require nine pieces measuring 10in.—that is, three cut from each of three 3ft. lengths.

Marking off the Wood.

Cut off all the lengths of dowelling as stated, and then rub down with sandpaper to take off any projecting shivers. Next prepare the two basket ends by marking on them the curve in the bottom corners and the eleven holes for the rods. The diagram at Fig. 1 shows how to set out the work. The corner curve has a radius of 1½in., and the holes have their centre on a line ½in.

from the bottom edge and the two ends. The holes are 1in. apart, but the one nearest each of the round corners is ⅝in. from the edge to form the shape. Having marked out the wood, the curve is cut with a fretsaw or bowsaw, and the holes drilled with a brace and ½in. bit. Remember to drill the hole from one side only until the bit point is peeping through. Then turn the wood over, use the hole for the centre and drill the hole from that side. Thus you will get clean holes without broken edges.

Finish with White Enamel.

To fix the parts, find the centre of both long pieces of rod, measure off 5in. either way. Make a pencil mark, and slide on the pieces of wood so the outside face is just against the pencil mark. Glue in place, and run a fine nail through into the dowel to further fix it. Put the nine 10in. lengths through the remaining holes, and fix with glue. See that the ends of the rods are flush with the rest of the wood by sandpapering all the

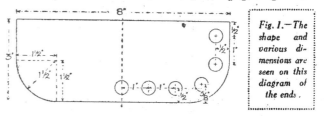

Fig. 1.—The shape and various dimensions are seen on this diagram of the ends.

ends level. The rack is now complete, and can be left with the wood in its natural state, or treated with an even coat of white enamel, which will withstand the heat and steam of the bath water.

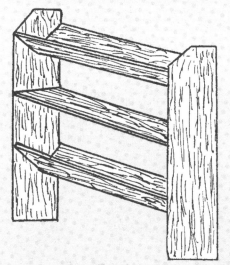

FIG. 1.

A BOOK-REST of the trough variety is a useful addition in any home or office. The article shown in Figure 1 herewith is of very simple form, and can be made by the veriest beginner in woodcraft. It may be made in any kind of wood—oak, deal, or even mahogany—according to preference.

For the end uprights, cut two pieces of wood 7ins. wide, 31ins. long, and ¾-in. thick, making sure that the wood is free from knots and similar blemishes. At the top of each upright, make a mark 5ins. from the back edge; make another mark 3½ins. from the top at the front edge; and draw a straight line between the two points, which should be 4ins. long. Then remove the corners with a straight saw-cut, as shown in Figure 2. The wood should be well planed on both sides and along all the edges.

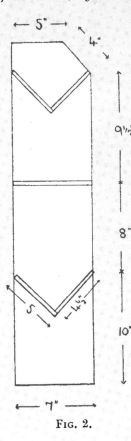

FIG. 2.

The troughs and shelf may be of any desired length, preferably about 30ins., and are ½-in. thick. The back portions of the troughs are 5ins. wide, and the front portions 4½ins., the width of the middle shelf being, of course, 7ins. Make sure that all the horizontal members are identical in length, and are cut absolutely on the square, and then have them nicely planed.

The various parts should now be stained and polished in any desired manner, and can then be mounted.

The position of the cross pieces is clearly shown in Figure 2, and the various dimensions given. They are fixed to the uprights by means of screws.

The holes for the reception of the screws should be countersunk to permit of the heads being screwed below the level of the wood. The gaps remaining may be filled in with plastic wood or putty, and afterwards stained.

An alternative method of supporting the troughs and the middle shelf, which gives a very pleasing effect, is to mount them on supports made from Hobbies stripwood. The supports are attached to the side members with a few brads and a little glue, the shelves being afterwards glued into position.

After receiving a final polish, the book-rest will be ready for service in the library or elsewhere.—T.J.B.

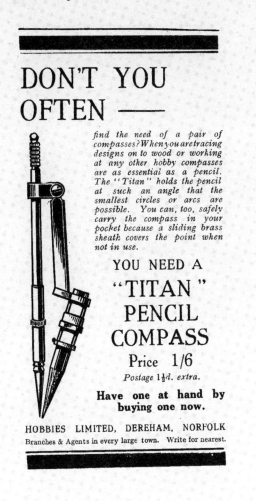

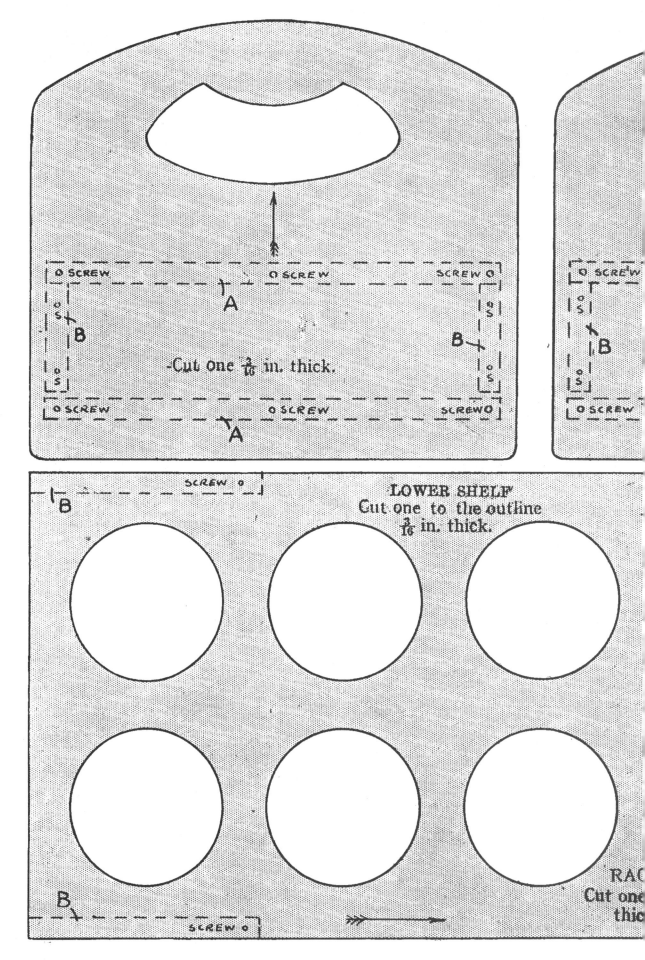

O SCREW O SCREW SCREW O

A

B

-Cut one ³⁄₁₆ in. thick.

B

O SCREW O SCREW SCREWO

A

O SCREW

O SCREW

B

O SCREW

B

SCREW O

LOWER SHELF
Cut one to the outline
³⁄₁₆ in. thick.

B

SCREW O

RAC
Cut one
thic

EGG RACK

ELEMENTARY

The ⇒———→ indicates direction of grain
of wood

For this design we can supply a
panel of wood "B," Price 10d.,
postage 6d. extra.

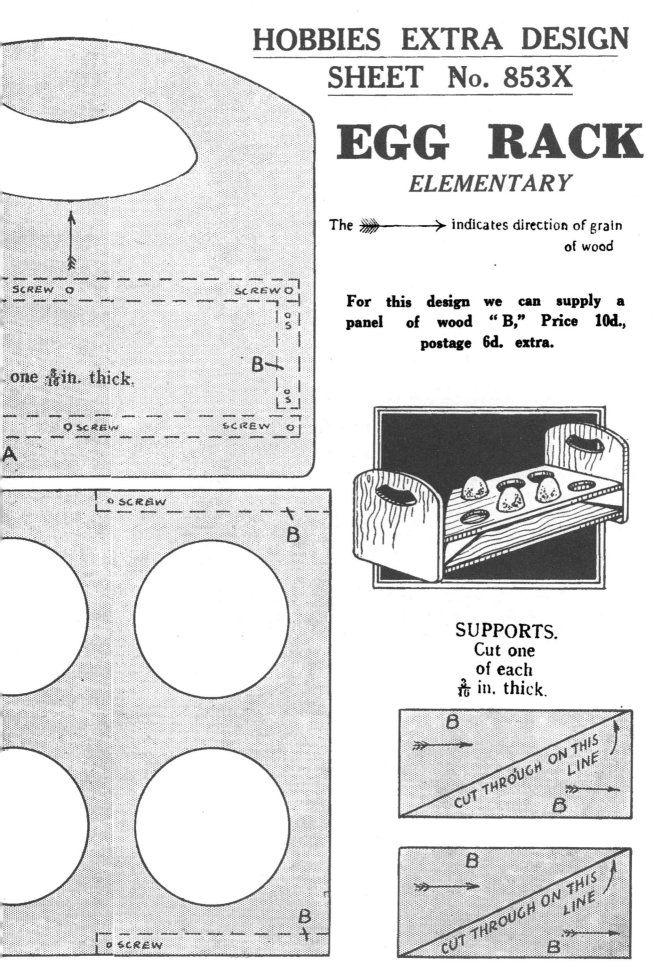

SCREW O   SCREW O

one $\frac{3}{16}$ in. thick.

B

O SCREW   SCREW O

A

O SCREW

B

B

SUPPORTS.
Cut one
of each
$\frac{3}{16}$ in. thick.

B
CUT THROUGH ON THIS LINE
B

B
CUT THROUGH ON THIS LINE
B

CHIP CARVING.

BOOK STAND.

THE carved book stand shown at Fig. 1 is of a new and pleasing design, and is intended to be placed on a side table. There are three compartments for the books, one at the front and one at each end, and this arrangement will be found to greatly add to the effectiveness of the stand. The carver who is not a skilled cabinet-maker will welcome this design because the stand may be easily made even by an amateur. A very creditable job will result by simply cutting the parts to shape, and gluing and screwing or nailing them together, or if trouble is taken to cut shallow trenched joints the work will be even more satisfactory.

The Material.

Fretwood of ½-in. thickness should be used, Oak, Satin Walnut, or Mahogany being selected with the view of making the stand to harmonize with existing furnishings. The parts required are a back 2ft. 1½ins. long by 9ins. wide, bottom 2ft. 2½ins. long by 7ins. wide, two ends 6½ins. long by 6ins. wide, and two fronts 6ins. long by 4½ins. wide. This cuts into about 4 sq. ft., and current prices of the woods mentioned above will be found in Hobbies' Catalogue.

Construction.

The back should be set out to the dimensions and particulars shown at Figs. 2 and 3. The bottom is cut with straight and square edges as shown at Fig. 4. The ends are shown at Fig. 5, and a full-size pattern for the fronts is shown at Fig. 6. A fretsaw fitted with one of Hobbies' special heavy saw blades should be used to cut the parts to shape. If trenched joints are to be used they will be cut between the ends and back, and between the front and ends as

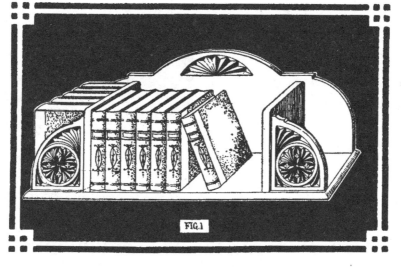

FIG. 1

shown at Fig. 4, the bottom being simply screwed to the bottom edges of the back, ends, and fronts. The trenches may be cut with a fine saw and chisel; they are just ⅛-in. deep, and an extra width of ⅛-in. must be allowed on the ends and front. In fitting up the parts, the ends are fitted into the back, the fronts into the ends, and the bottom, which has its front and end edges neatly rounded over, is fitted below.

Carving.

The centre of the back and the faces of the two fronts are carved. The carving for the fronts may be traced from the full-size pattern, Fig. 6, the traced lines being afterwards firmly marked with a dark pencil. Before the carving is started the principle lines should be veined as shown in the pattern, this being done either with the chip carving knife or a V-chisel. Starting with the circular piece of carving, the four lozenge shapes are cut by making vertical incisions A—B, A—C, A—D, and chipping out the waste wood from the lines C—B, D—B, to the centre line A—B. In carving the remaining parts, vertical incisions E—F, E—G, E—H, are made, and the waste wood is chipped out from the lines F—G, G—H, H—F, to the centre E. The illustration, Fig. 7 will make this operation quite clear. Owing to lack of space it has been impossible to give a full-size pattern for the carving on the back, but it may be easily set out from Fig. 2, and the carving is carried out in a manner similar to that just described.

In fitting up the parts, the ends are glued to the back, and screwed or pinned through, the fronts are glued and pinned to the ends, and the bottom is glued and screwed below.

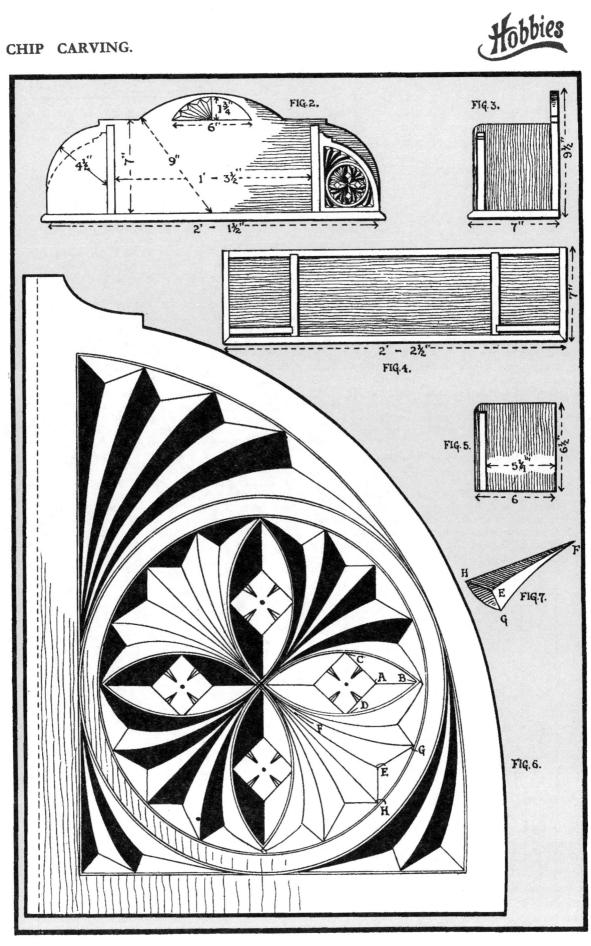

FIG. 2.

FIG. 3.

FIG. 4.

FIG. 5.

FIG. 7.

FIG. 6.

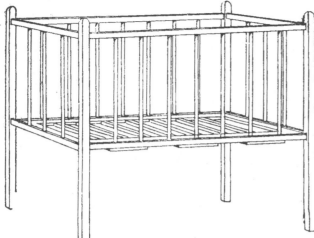

A CHILD'S COT. COST 2s.

Six pieces of 1¼in. by ¾in. by 34½in. long for the sides;

Four pieces of 1¼in. by ¾in. by 35in. for end uprights;

Four pieces of 1¼in. by ¾in. by 18in. for the cross-bars of the ends.

From each of two of the 12 foot lengths cut three of the 34½in. pieces, and two of the 18in. pieces; and from the remaining length cut four 35in. pieces.

The round wood is all to be cut up into 17in. lengths, 16½in. of which appear white; the bar is let into the frame ¼in. top and bottom.

Having cut up the various lengths, they will be assembled as shown on the diagram. The position of the round vertical bars will be marked, and then a ¾in. bit will be employed to take out a circular hole ¼in. deep in the framing bars, into which the end of each round vertical bar is to be driven.

The slots and tongues to enable the cot to be taken to pieces are made up of three-ply wood from an old tea-chest, and fixed, as indicated, on the diagram. If it is not required that the cot be taken to pieces, the slots and tongues may be dispensed with and the frame screwed together.

In fixing all the parts of the independent sections, screws should be used. For fixing the vertical bars, drive screws from the top of horizontal framing bar down into the vertical, and in the case of the lower horizontal bar drive screws from underneath.

THE child's cot, which we here reproduce, was the subject which took the first prize in our late Carpentry Competition.

It will be recalled that the prizes were offered for the most useful and unique article made out of two shillings' worth of wood. The receipt of the timber merchant who supplied the wood was sent by Mr. Legg, and, all things considered, a complete cot at a total cost of two shillings merited the place of honour which it attained on our recent prize list.

The wood required is as follows :—

30ft. 0¾in. diameter round.

36ft. 1¼in. by ¾in.

The round material was obtained in 10ft. lengths, and the 1¼ by ¾ in 12ft. lengths. In addition to the above, some strong lathes are required for the bottom, and these may be obtained by utilising part of a sugar box. Cut the wood as follows :—

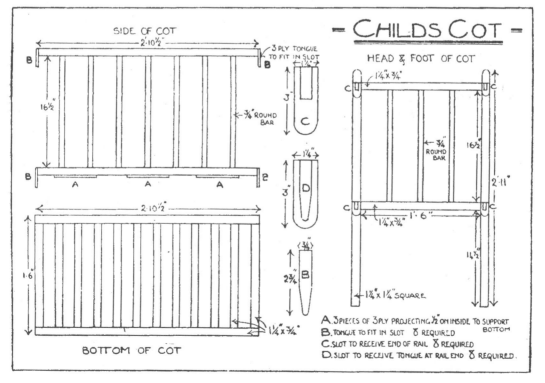

SIDE OF COT

2·10½"

16½"

¾" ROUND BAR

3 PLY TONGUE TO FIT IN SLOT

J

C

D

B

2·10½"

1·6"

BOTTOM OF COT

1¼" x ¾"

— CHILDS COT =

HEAD & FOOT OF COT

1¼" x ¾"

¾" ROUND BAR

16½"

2·11"

1¼" x ¾"

1·6"

1¼" x 1¼" SQUARE

14½"

A. 3 PIECES OF 3 PLY PROJECTING ½ ON INSIDE TO SUPPORT BOTTOM
B. TONGUE TO FIT IN SLOT 8 REQUIRED
C. SLOT TO RECEIVE END OF RAIL 8 REQUIRED
D. SLOT TO RECEIVE TONGUE AT RAIL END 8 REQUIRED

FIG. 1.

A TRAY-

By F. T. B. Hewitt.

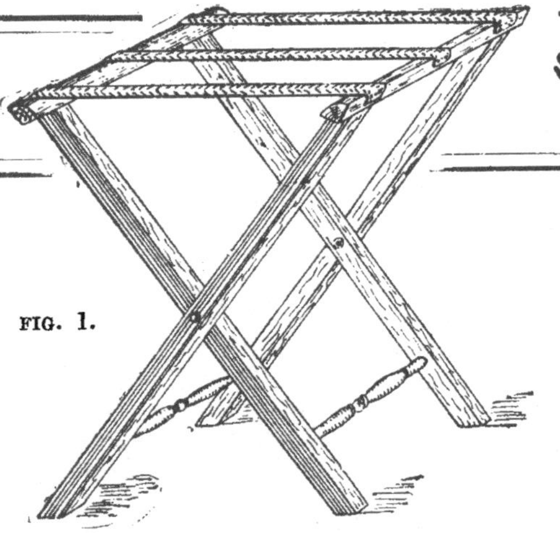

STAND & TRAY.

OAK is just now by far the most popular wood for dining-room furniture, and it is recommended for the construction of the tray-stand and the tray here illustrated and described. Mahogany or American walnut may, of course, be used if preferred, or birch can be adopted and be stained and polished to imitate one of the superior hard woods.

The Stand.

The tray stand, as will be seen from the illustration above, consists of two pairs of legs, one fitting within the other, connected by bolts and nuts, and to enable the stand to open and close easily and yet be rigid when in use, considerable care must be taken in setting out the work and carefully keeping to the figured dimensions throughout the job. Separate drawings of each pair of legs are given in Figs. 2 and 3, the sides and top pieces being in each case $1\frac{1}{2}$ in. by $1\frac{1}{4}$ in. when planed up. Thus four pieces 3 ft. $1\frac{1}{2}$ in. long and two pieces 1 ft. 9 in. long will be required. The two side pieces are in each case mortise and tenoned into the top, the tenons coming right through the top rails where they are wedged and the joint is afterwards wholly or partly covered from view by the webbing.

The top rail is, to each pair of legs, 1 ft. 9 in. finished length, the ends projecting more on one pair than on the other. The sides of the wider legs (Fig. 2) are 1 ft. 6in. apart, out to out, and 1 ft. $3\frac{1}{2}$ in. inside measure. An allowance for clearance of $\frac{1}{8}$ in. on each side makes the outside dimension of the pair of legs (Fig. 3) 1 ft. $3\frac{1}{4}$ in., with inside distance 1 ft. $0\frac{3}{4}$ in. Before framing up, the top rails should be planed up to section as Fig. 4, and the outer side of the side pieces may be finished as Fig. 5, if a hand-reeder is available, or be beaded as Fig. 6. Either treatment improves the appearance, but the sides can, if necessary, be left plain.

The turned rails at the foot of each pair of legs may be turned upon a Hobbies lathe, or may be purchased or ordered from any woodturner. The pattern for turning is given to a larger scale in Fig. 7, and two pieces $1\frac{1}{4}$ in. square and 1 ft. 6 in. long will be necessary. Finish the ends to $\frac{3}{4}$ in. caliper measure, and the shortening and slight tapering to fit the $\frac{5}{8}$ in. holes to be bored to receive them can be done in the fitting and glueing up. The $\frac{5}{8}$ in. holes should be bored 1 in. deep and at 6 in. from foot. When the turned rails have been glued and driven in, to the correct distance, secure each end with a $1\frac{1}{4}$ in. panel pin driven through the side rail.

The holes are next bored through the sides for the fixing bolts; $\frac{1}{4}$ in. bit should be used, and the bolts 3-16th in., the holes being 1 ft. $6\frac{3}{4}$ in. from upper edge of top rails and very carefully measured. The bolts should be $3\frac{1}{4}$ in. long, fixed as shown in Fig. 8. The square part under the head prevents the bolt turning and the nut being loosened when the stand is in use, and each of the two washers prevents the polish of the side pieces being damaged.

The two pairs of legs should now be separated and varnished or French polished with any preliminary staining as necessary, and when this has been done the bolts again fixed, the heads being, of course, to the outside. Cut three pieces of stout English webbing 2 in. wide and 2 ft. 6 in. long. Fold over the ends and fix one end of each piece with three $\frac{5}{8}$ in. tacks as shown in Fig. 9. Then secure the other ends so that the full opening of the stand is 2 ft. 1 in. (See Fig. 9.) If the middle piece of webbing is fixed first it will be easier to get them all the same length than any other way.

The Tray.

The tray shown in Fig. 10 is also made of oak. The outside size may be 2 ft. by 1 ft. 4 ins.; 2 ft. 3 in. by 1 ft. 6 in. or 2 ft. 6 in. by 1 ft. 8 in. Perhaps the middle size will be found most convenient for a variety of purposes. The bottom should be $\frac{3}{8}$ in. thick, finished thickness, and it is probable that a piece of oak will not be readily obtainable of the necessary width. In this case two widths should be chosen with similar style of grain, figured will, of course, look the best, and when partly planed up on both sides fix in the bench screw and carefully shoot the edges with the trying plane. Care must be taken to get both a true line and square edges. When this is done fix one piece in the bench screw after warming the shot edges, glue both edges and place together, slowly rubbing the upper piece backwards and forwards, in true position, finally leaving it in correct position, both as to length and thickness. The pieces so joined should be stood on one side to set, leaving them against another board so that the joint will not tend to come open as it would if leaning against the wall without support.

The next day after joining, carefully clean up both sides with the smoothing plane, mark off to correct size with pencil and square, cut with tenon saw, and plane up the edges. The plane should be sharp and finely set, and a shooting board will be of assistance for the ends. The edges all round should be chamfered as shown in the section Fig. 11. The tray moulding, which is shown in section Fig. 11, is obtainable ready prepared in oak, mahogany, walnut or whitewood. A 9 ft. or 10 ft. length will be sufficient for any of the sizes of tray mentioned. The corners are carefully mitred and glued as for a picture frame, being further secured by needle points or panel pins (a couple to each) if desired. The moulding is fixed to the bottom by a sufficient number of 1 in. fine brass screws with countersunk heads driven from beneath, as shown in the section; five screws to each side and four to each end should be sufficient. The outer side of the moulding should come just to the start of the chamfer as shown in Fig. 11. A pair of brass tray handles should now be fixed, and they may be had in a variety of forms. Fig. 12 shows one of a pair prepared for under fixing and the lugs should be let in flush to the under

side of the bottom of tray. The handles are 3 in. and fixed with brass countersunk screws.

The handles should now be removed, and the moulding separated from the tray bottom, and after French polishing the screws again fixed. The moulding should not be glued to the tray bottom, as the fixing by screws is quite sufficient.

To return to the tray stand for one moment, the legs should be cut off on the splay. To do this, a good method is to set up the stand, and if not perfectly level pack up one or two of the feet as necessary with newspaper; then lay on the floor at one side a piece of 1 in. board, and mark alongside the upper edge with a bradawl; similarly mark the legs on the other side and saw off to the scratches with the tenon saw. A touch of black enamel upon the bolt head and nuts will complete the tray stand.

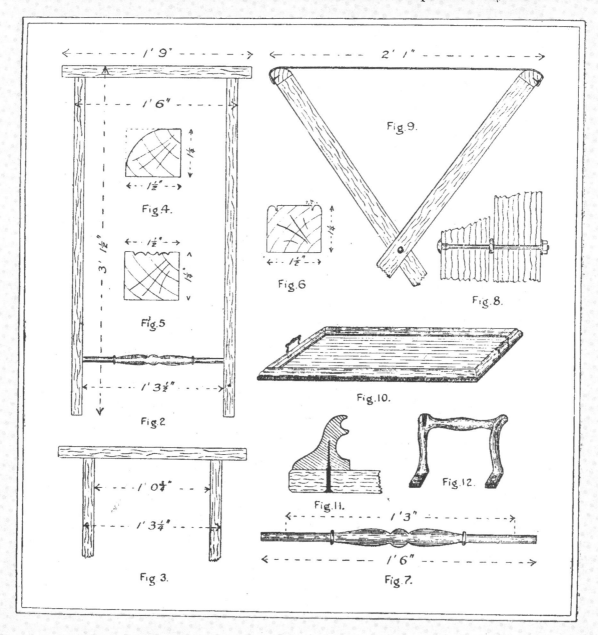

Fig. 4. Fig. 5. Fig. 2. Fig. 3. Fig. 9. Fig. 6. Fig. 8. Fig. 10. Fig. 11. Fig. 12. Fig. 7.

HOW TO MAKE A LEDGE AND BRACE DOOR

THE construction of a panelled door is often beyond the abilities of most amateur joiners, but a door of this kind is easily put together. It is composed of vertical matchboarding held together at the back by horizontal ledges, and prevented from sagging by oblique braces let into the ledges. The boards may be ¾in. or ⅞in. thick ; the ledges and braces should be of 1in. stuff, 6 or 7ins. wide.

Assuming the door to be 3ft wide and 6ft. 6ins. high, the boards should be 6ft. 7ins. or 6ft. 8ins. long. As many boards will be needed as will give a width of 3ft. when the groove of one outside board, and the tongue of the other have been removed.

Assemble the boards and square across them the positions of the ledges. The ledges look smarter and throw off water better if their edges are bevelled all round as shown in the drawing. The braces are bevelled on the edges only.

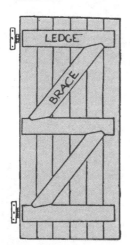

Each ledge is screwed at one end to one outside board. The boards are then cramped tightly together, and the ledges screwed at the other end. The door can then be turned over for the intermediate boards to be nailed to the ledges. The ends of the nails should be clenched flush along the grain of the wood.

Now comes the making and fitting of the braces. To be effective, the braces must run in the correct direction, that is upwards, and away from the hinge edge of the door, so that they shall be in compression. Each end of a brace is square-ended part way across and then sloped off to the edge of the ledge.

To mark a brace, lay the board out of which it will be cut across two ledges, with its edges not less than 2ins. from their ends. Pencil marks are made on the brace over the edge of the ledges ; and it then has the ends shaped and is cut out. The ledges are marked off from the brace, and notches cut in them. Care must be taken that these are not too deep, as the braces must be a tight fit.

Any slack will allow the door to settle and get out of square. When the braces have been placed and nailed on through the front, the ends of the door are squared across, and sawn to their final length.

Hinging and Painting

The hinges to be used are "cross garnets" which should be at least 15ins. long.

A door which is to be painted and will be exposed to the weather, should have all surfaces painted before assembling that will be inaccessible to the paint-brush afterwards ; these include tongues and grooves, and insides of ledges and braces. White-lead paint is the best to use for the joints. If these are well sealed, water will not be able to find its way in.

Low doors of this kind, such as may be used for cupboards, need a ledge at the top and bottom only.

Full instructions for making —

THIS useful cabinet is just large enough to take the usual hair cream, shaving stick, razor and blades that are often left lying around the bathroom. Size has purposely been kept down to a minimum, so as to save space.

The front elevation and side view in Fig. 1 show the general construction and the main measurements. These may be modified if desired, but will be suitable for most requirements.

rail. The top and bottom are 7ins. by 5ins. and 7ins. by 4½ins. respectively. They can be screwed direct to the sides or can be housed in to a depth of about ⅛in. If they are housed they must, of course, be longer according to the depth of the housing.

Glue the towel rail in position at the same time as you fix the sides and then screw the back in place as shown in Fig. 2.

It will be noticed from Fig. 3 that the

A SMALL SHAVING CABINET

JUST BIG ENOUGH FOR ESSENTIALS

With the exception of the small pieces holding the mirror in place, all parts are cut from ½in. wood. Obechi is easy to work and will paint up well if filled in the usual way.

The cupboard portion is made up of two sides, a top and bottom. The sides are shaped to measurement and holes ⅜in. diameter bored to take the towel

door is fixed by means of two hinges which are let in to fit flush. Hinges should be about 1in. long and fixed with countersunk screws. The door measures 7ins. by 8½ins., and may be cut from wood or plywood.

To prevent the door going back a stop made from an odd piece of wood may be glued in place and an ordinary handle

CONSTRUCTION OF THE SMALL SHAVING CABINET

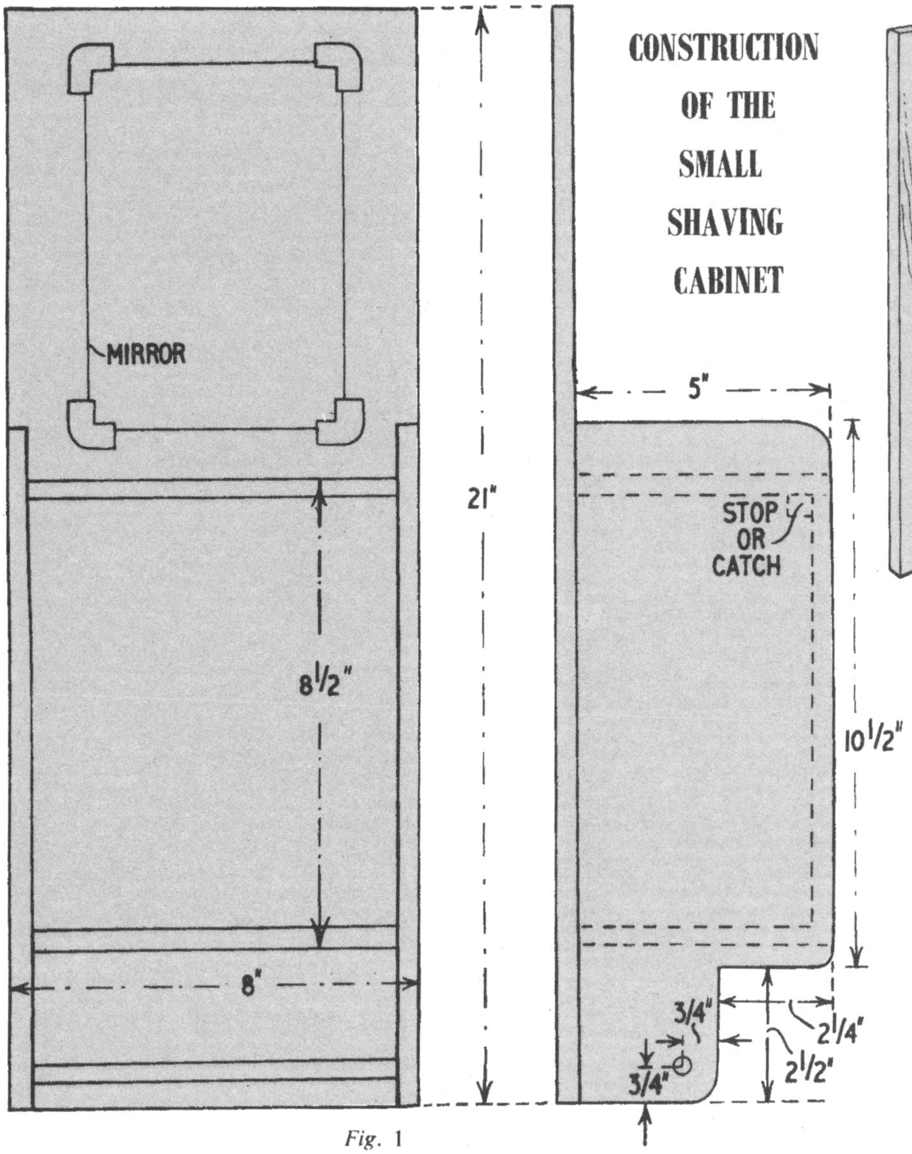

Fig. 1

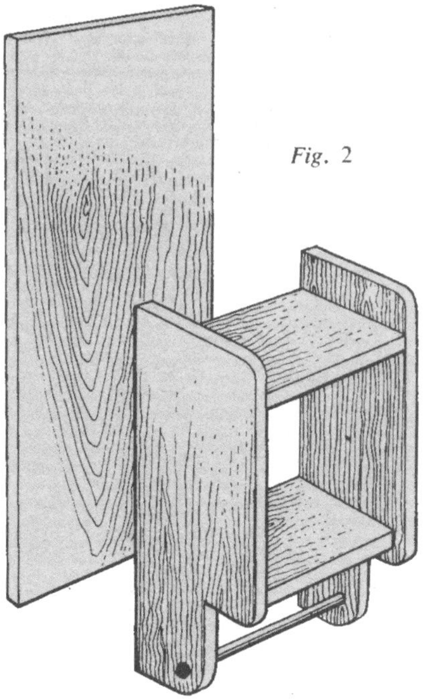

Fig. 2

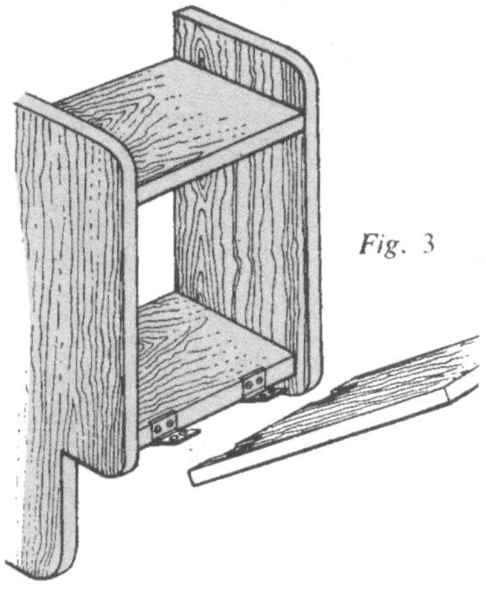

Fig. 3

and catch fitted. Alternatively a special spring catch — Hobbies No. 6224 can be fitted as shown in Fig. 4. The spring is attached under the top and the stop portion to the door. The catch may be obtained from Hobbies Ltd., Dereham, Norfolk, price 3d. A knob of some kind must be fitted to the door to allow it to be pulled out. A piece of chain is fixed in position by means of small screw eyes to prevent the door falling down too far.

The mirror should measure about 7ins. by 5ins., and is held in place by four clips made from wood as shown in Fig. 5. The pieces (A) and (B) are shown full size and are glued together as indicated in the inset diagram. The thickness of piece (A) depends upon the mirror, but ⅛in. thick should be enough. Piece (B) is also cut from ⅛in. wood. The

Fig. 4

clips are glued to the back and strengthened by a fretpin in each.

The cabinet is finished off by painting both inside and out, using high gloss enamel. White is generally suitable for the bathroom, but of course a pastel shade would look equally attractive.

(M.h.)

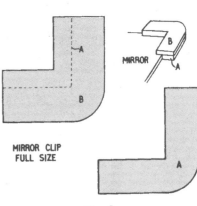

MIRROR CLIP
FULL SIZE

Fig. 5

MECHANICAL DUSTBIN OPENER

Reader's Effort

Labour SAVING

HOME-MADE CHIP POTATO MAKER

A Simple Home-made
TROUSER PRESS

THE SHILLINGSWORTH

COMPACT STOOL TO CARRY ON A CYCLE.

THERE are several kinds of portable stool, but none of them are so suitable for attaching to a cycle as the one shown at Fig. 1. It will be found strong enough for ordinary use, and when

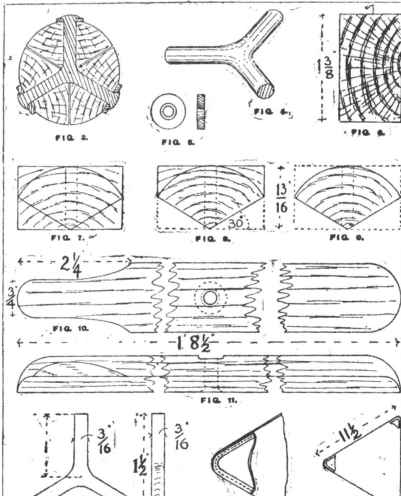

FIG. 2.

folded up as shown at Fig. 2, it may be attached to the frame with steel spring or rubber pump clips. The legs are made of beech, and the seat of leather, a sound piece of basil being very suitable.

A section through the joint is shown at Fig. 3, and it will be seen that the three triangular pieces forming the legs are joined together by a metal "fitting," shown at Fig. 4, which is riveted at the ends over washers; the washer being shown in plan and elevation at Fig. 5. Each leg is 1ft. 8½ in. long when finished, and is cut from a piece of sound beech of the section shown at Fig. 6, 1⅜in. wide and 1 3-16in. thick when finished. Care should be taken that the grain of the wood is somewhere near the position

shown, and then they may be marked as shown at Fig. 7. The sloping sides are at an angle of 30 degrees to the face, and the segment drawn to a radius of 1 3-16in. Before proceeding further with the shaping, the holes shown by the dotted lines, should be bored with a 3-16in. bit, exactly in the middle of each length. The sloping sides

FIG. 1.

FIG. 3. FIG. 4. FIG. 5. FIG. 6.

FIG. 7. FIG. 8. FIG. 9.

FIG. 10. FIG. 11.

FIG. 12. FIG. 14. FIG. 13.

1. Portable seat for a cycle. 2. The seat, folded up. 3. Section through the centre, shewing the joint. 4. The wrought-iron fitting, forming the "hinge" or joint of the legs. 5. Plan and section of washer for the ends of the "fitting." 6. Section of wood for legs. 7. First stage in making the legs. 8. Second stage. 9. Third stage. 10. Plan of one leg. 11. Elevation of one leg. 12. The plan and elevation of iron fitting. 13. The leather seat. 14. Method of making pocket in each corner of seat.

may now be planed down as shown at Fig. 8, taking care that the whole angle is not more than 120 degrees. The lengths may now be placed in a cradle, and the top planed down to the section shown at Fig. 9. The outside should be glasspapered quite smooth, and the ends of each piece shaped as shown at Figs. 10 and 11. The portion at the right hand side of the drawing forms the bottom of the legs; a portion at the top surrounding the hole should be filed or gouged out to take the rivet, as shown at Fig. 11, just enough wood being removed to bring the top of the washer flush; it must not be overdone or the leg will be weakened.

The metal "fitting" as shown at Fig. 12, is made of wrought iron, or may be cut from a piece of 3-16in. mild steel. Any blacksmith would forge up a piece to the dimensions given for a few pence. When prepared the fitting should be placed in the hole in the legs, and each end riveted over the washer. This should be very carefully and thoroughly done for the whole strength of the seat depends on it.

A piece of basil leather of the size given at Fig. 13 should be cut out, and pockets sewn at each corner as shown at Fig. 14. An awl and some waxed end should be used to make the pocket strong enough to stand the strain, or the services of a bootmaker enlisted to ensure this. The pocket should give sufficient depth to take in about 1½in. of the top of the leg, when they are fully extended. Apart from the iron fitting, there is very little real difficulty in making this stool and its comparative lightness, and its compactness, renders it by far the most useful seat for the cyclist. The outside should be given a coat of shellac varnish; otherwise it will soon get dirty.

The most convenient method of attaching the seat to the frame is by means of a steel or rubber clip, but failing this two small straps may be used, twisted once round the frame, and then fastened round the wood.

A WOOL WINDER.

THE wool winder shown at Fig. 1 will be found very effective and may be easily taken apart when not in use. It will be seen in the side elevation at Fig. 2 that here are two reels supported on a stand. In the end sectional elevation (Fig. 3) the method of fitting on the reels is shown, and at Fig. 4, the plan, it will be noticed that the reels are also adjustable and may be brought nearer together and placed farther apart by fitting them in the holes provided.

The stand is very easily made, a piece of

wood being planed up to 2 ft. long, 2 in. wide and 1 in. thick, the ends being carefully chamfered as shown. Commencing 1½ in. from the end bore a series of ¼ in. holes 1¼ in. apart, six being quite sufficient at each end. These holes should be bored to within ¼ in. of the other side of the wood and should be left quite clean. At a distance of 2 in. from each end cut underneath a 1 in. by ¼ in. groove as shown at Fig. 5.

The cross pieces should now be made, these are 8 in. by 2 in. by 1 in. and should be chamfered on the end in the same way as the long piece. In the middle of each piece cut a 1 in. by ¾ in. groove and then cut out underneath a space of ½ in. leaving 1 in. at each end.

The reels, as shown in detail at Fig. 6, should now be made. We shall require four circular pieces of 5-16th in. planed wood, two 4¼ in. diameter, and two 3½ in. diameter. On each piece draw a circle of 1⅜ in. radius and set out twelve equal spaces, this may be done very easily by first dividing the circle into four equal parts and then marking the radius off on each side of the four points on the circumference. The marks thus obtained form the centre of 3-16 in. holes, which should be bored out so that the point of the centre bit used just comes through on the other side.

We now want twenty-four lengths of 3-16th in. round stuff, and these may be obtained from three 36 in. lengths of 3-16th in. dowel pins. They are made of birch and may be obtained from any good timber yard. Before cutting off the lengths, they should be well glasspapered until quite smooth and may be either varnished or french polished. Each length should be 3⅞ in. In the centre of each circular piece bore a ¼ in. round hole right

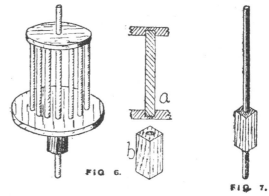

through and then, when cleaned up with glasspaper and either varnished or polished, the round lengths may be glued in ("a" Fig. 6). Seccotine or mendine will be found much cleaner to use than glue and will stick better to the polished surface. We have now to bore a ¼ in. hole through two 2 in. by 1 in. square

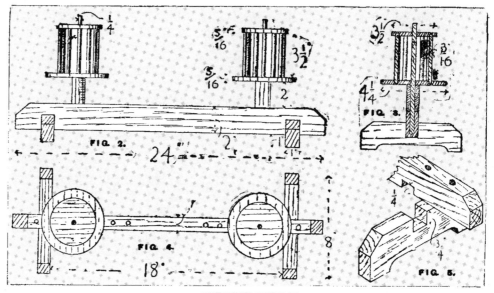

pieces as shown at Fig. 6 "b." These pieces are stuck on a length of ¼ in. round dowel pin so that 1¾ in. projects underneath and 4¾ in. on top. This peg is shown at Fig. 7 and it fits in the holes bored in the long piece of the stand, and on it may be slipped the reel already made. The dowel pins should not cost more than ½d. each, the mending 2d., French polish or varnish 2d.,

circular portions of the reels, this amount being ample.

ILLUSTRATIONS.

1. A wool winder. 2. Front elevation. 3. Sectional end elevation. 4. Plan. 5. Detail of joint for the feet of the stand. 6. Enlarged detail of the reel. 7. Detail of the pin on which the reel fits.

leaving 6d. for the wood for the stand and

Essential for the home 'brewer'

WINE DECANTING STAND

By A. F. Taylor

WHEN home made wine has been bottled and stood by for some time a sediment generally tends to form. On no account should this thick matter be allowed to remix with the wine or its flavour will be seriously impaired.

The amount of sediment varies with different wines and with the method employed in making them, some having quite a thick layer while a few may be practically free from it.

The slightest movement of the bottle will disturb it, and in this condition it is impossible to pour out any wine in the normal way. It is therefore necessary to "decant" the wine and in this operation the clear portion is drawn off without disturbing the muddy bottom layer.

The syphon system

A syphon is used to draw off the wine from one bottle into another and to do this the full bottle must be considerably higher than the one into which it is drawn. To perform this operation successfully a stand is necessary and the one described here will be found most useful for the enthusiastic wine maker.

It has been designed to accommodate an ordinary wine bottle, and any kind of wood can be used to make it. The baseboard should be substantial in order to hold the upright quite rigid — a piece 8½in. long, 5in. wide and ½in. to 1in. thick will do very well.

A piece of wood 25in. long, 4in. wide and ½in. thick is next cut and screwed

firmly to the centre of the baseboard to form the upright. This must be at right angles to the base and very rigid, and to achieve this a support is fixed to the lower half. It can be shaped as shown or

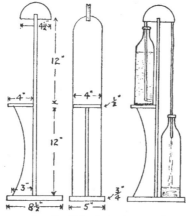

Details of the decanting stand

left as a parallel strip of wood 12in. long, 3in. wide and ½in. thick.

The shelf is 4in. long and 4in. wide and is also held secure by this same support. All these pieces are fixed with countersunk screws. On top of the upright is a half circle of wood about 4½in. across and ½in. wide with a groove

cut in the curved edge. This is to support the rubber tube leading from one bottle to the other and to prevent any sharp bends which might stop the flow of the liquid or prevent the syphon from working.

Starting the action

Starting up the syphon is quite easy. Get a piece of rubber tube 33in. to 36in. long with a diameter of about ¼in. A length of cycle valve rubber will do just as well although it will take longer to empty the bottle. Place one end of the tube into the full bottle to a distance of about ¾ of the way, the bottle being on the top shelf, and then pass it over the top support and down to the empty bottle on the baseboard.

If you put this end in your mouth and draw slightly you extract all the air in the tube, and because one side, measured from the highest point, is much longer than the other the liquid will start to flow in this direction.

Watch the level of the wine in the top bottle so that the tube is always in the liquid and as this is drawn off gently lower the tube, but do not let it get nearer to the sediment than about ¼in. As you get nearer to the bottom it is a good idea to nip the tube a little to slow down the rate of flow and keep the sediment from being drawn up too. Some wines may need decanting several times at intervals of a few weeks but the majority can usually be cleared in one operation.

How to Make

Fig. 2.

Fig. 3.

ONE of the most useful articles of furniture which can be made by any amateur, and at a cost which is hardly worth consideration, is a small Folding Bookshelf. The above sketch indicates the general idea of a simple one, and a few hints and suggestions will enable any lady or gentleman who possesses a hammer, saw, and a little common sense to make it.

Firstly, as to woods, almost any material may be used, and the choice can safely be left to the worker. Of the commoner woods, Pine, Ash, Birch, and Elm will be found the most suitable, and of the better qualities, Oak, Mahogany, and Walnut might be used.

For a small two-space Book Rack as shewn, procure five pieces of wood about 30 inches long, 6 inches wide, and $\frac{5}{8}$ inch thick. It will save the average amateur a considerable amount of trouble if he buys the wood ready planed; but to any one who knows how to handle a plane, it will certainly be found cheaper to purchase the wood in plank form. Two boards for the Sides should be cut as indicated in Fig. 1. The Shelf spaces will be 9 inches and $7\frac{1}{2}$ inches respectively, and the other sizes are marked on the illustration. The shaped pieces at each end may easily be cut with a Keyhole Saw, or with an ordinary Fretsaw if a large blade is used. To those who may not happen to have these tools at hand, and who must therefore try something more simple, any of the methods shewn in Fig. 2 are suggested.

Should it be desired to have the Rack standing on a mantelshelf or on any article of furniture, the lower ends of the sides might be made a few inches longer so that

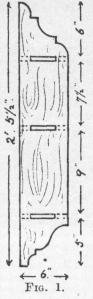

Fig. 1.

extra book space could thus be provided. In this case the end could be finished off square, or it might have a small semi-circular cut as in Fig. 3.

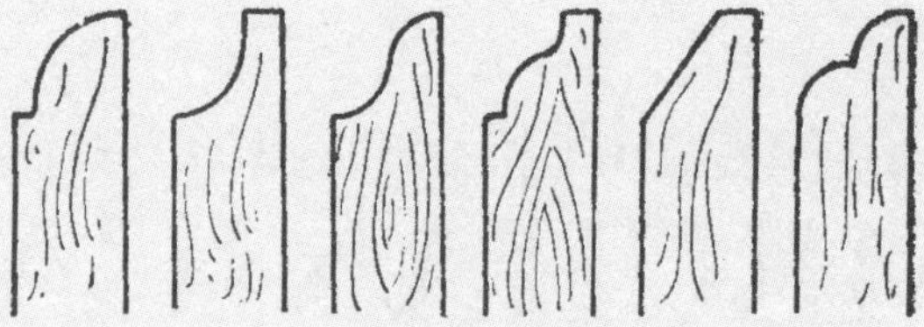

The three Shelves must be carefully cut to an equal size, or the article will not fit closely. If only $\frac{5}{8}$ inch wood is being used the Shelves should not be over 22 or 24 inches in length. Each one should be cut at the ends as shewn in Fig. 4; the projecting portions may be 2 inches long, and about $3\frac{1}{2}$ inches wide. These pass through corresponding holes which

Fig. 4.

must be cut in the uprights, and they are held in position by wedges (Fig. 5) which slip through the small holes in Fig. 4, and thus hold the entire article firmly. All this part of the work must be done with great care, as the more accuracy the greater strength. If the projecting notches of the Shelves fit too easily, the whole Book Rack will shake, and thus prove a very unsatisfactory piece of work.

It will be seen that, by adopting this method of construction, the article may easily be taken to pieces when desired. At the same time, if carefully made, it will be perfectly strong.

Brass Catches (as Fig. 6) should be fixed to the upper and lower Shelves in order to screw the Rack to the wall.

Fig. 5.

Fig. 6.

The question of polishing or staining must be left to the worker's judgment. Ordinary woods may be stained or varnished, but Mahogany and Walnut appear to better advantage when polished.

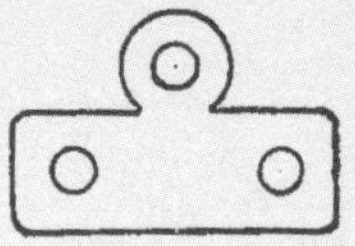

With regard to the spacing of the Shelves, it may be of advantage to state that the common sizes of small bound books are—Foolscap 8vo., $6\frac{3}{4}$ inches; Post 8vo., $7\frac{1}{2}$ inches; Crown 8vo., $8\frac{1}{4}$ inches; and Demy 8vo., 9 inches. In the spaces, $\frac{5}{8}$ inch extra is usually allowed for "finger room."

Such an article as this could be elaborated to any degree. A scroll ornament might be cut on the Sides with a Fretsaw, or small panels might be carved or inlaid. Again, the Book Rack could be of a larger size, and have four or five Shelves instead of three. These variations and additions need not be discussed here; it is only necessary to point out the principle and general method, and the amateur who can lay claim to a little ingenuity will know how to carry out a scheme of improvements.

Something unusual for a handyman to make—
MECHANICAL BELLOWS

HERE is the design for a very novel type of fire bellows, in which the stream of air is obtained by means of a small fan revolved at a fairly high rate by a hand-wheel.

Study the diagrams first to get a general idea of how the apparatus works, and then start construction by first cutting the base (A) from ¼in. wood, the wedge-shaped block (C) and the pieces (a), (b) and (c), also from ¼in. wood ; (a) and (c) are 2¾ by 3¾ins., while (b) is 3ins. by 4½ins., and the dimensions of (C) are given in Fig. 4.

Assembly

Assemble these parts with the side-pieces (e) and (f), which are from two sheets of 1/8th plywood fashioned as (D), and slightly cut at (e) to bend round the angle in the base. Use a series of ½in. sprigs through to the ¼in. material (A) and (b).

The squares (a) and (c) are held by suitable screws up through the base and through from (b), with several small screws going through from the sides to (a) and (c). When together, all these parts form the very sturdy box-like shape clearly shown in Fig. 6.

The moving parts, the fan, handwheel and belt are partly of wood and tin, and partly from items which can be obtained from any model-maker's shop.

First the fan. This is shaped from a 4in. diameter circle of fairly thick tin, marked along the 45 degree lines and cut to nearly the centre as Fig. 7, the sectors so formed being given a 30 degree twist at the top to make the blades.

Fitting the Fan

The spindle is 3/16in. rodding, and the fan is held to it by screw collars at either side, with a touch of solder if the tin seems inclined to slip. The screw collars are only a few pence each and five will be required in completing the bellows.

Holes for the fan-spindle bearings are pierced at the centre of the square section of the body, the blades being made to revolve as near the base as possible without touching. The bearings themselves are two rectangles of tin (M) held over the holes by four small screws each, each having a hole in which the spindle revolves comfortably.

Accurate placing of the bearings is obtained by carefully adjusting these tins before finally screwing down.

On the end of the fan-spindle a 1½in. or 2in. diameter pulley is fitted, being held by its own screw collar. The assemblage of the whole spindle is clearly shown in Fig. 8, but note that the fan is set at the far end of the rod behind the block (C).

Improving the Draught

When the fan position is established, corner blocks (P) are fitted as shown as close to the blades as possible, these being to improve the draught by reducing the amount of spilt air. They are secured by suitable screws through the base, piece (b) and far side.

Opposite the fan, and with the spindle as centre, a 2¾in. circle is scribed and divided into eight parts (given by the intersection of the 45 degree lines). At each intersection, 1in. diameter holes are drilled as Fig. 5, as air inlet vents.

The large hand-wheel is 6ins. diameter, and is

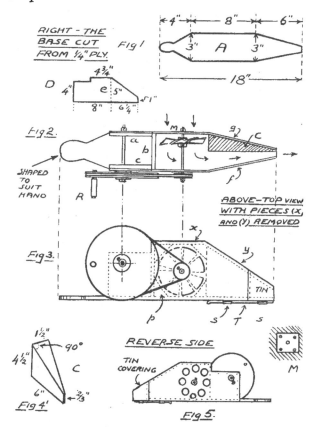

RIGHT — THE BASE CUT FROM ¼" PLY. *Fig 1*

Fig 2.

SHAPED TO SUIT HAND

ABOVE — TOP VIEW WITH PIECES (X, AND (Y) REMOVED

Fig 3.

Fig 4.

REVERSE SIDE

TIN COVERING

Fig 5.

built up of three circular pieces of wood, the centre one being slightly less than this diameter.

The wheel could with advantage be turned from one piece on a lathe and in any case a final turning on a lathe would be good. Its spindle (a further piece of the fan rodding) is secured through two holes in (a) and (b) and as the wheel rotates in

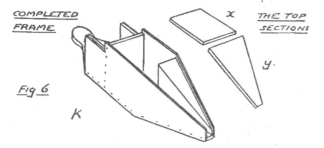

COMPLETED FRAME

Fig 6

K

x THE TOP SECTIONS

y.

this case *on* the spindle, the rod may be jammed into the holes which are 3ins. from the base and ½in. in diameter.

Assembly of Wheel

The whole axle and wheel is assembled as shown in Fig. 2 and Fig. 9, with a thin washer between the wheel and outside screw collar, and a washer (or washers) on the inside, between the wheel and bellows side. A further screw collar at the other end makes everything secure. Before finally fixing, tin bearings as for the fan spindle are put into position to prevent the holes in (a) and (b) from enlarging.

Handle and Belt

The handle (R) is best bought ready made, but can be assembled with a short bolt run through the wheel near its circumference. A nut is placed on the inside, and a loose cover fitted on this with two small nuts on the far end—one to act as a lock.

The belt is a length of spring coil wire sold for small machine belts by model makers, and will cost

only a few pence. The main thing in fitting the belt is to get a nice tension without causing the fan pulley to press too hard on its bearings. You may be able to get a rubber band of suitable length.

Top sections (x) and (y) can now be shaped and put in position, (x) is 3ins. by 4¾ins. and (y) is a truncated piece 3ins. wide at the one end, narrowing down to only ½in. at the other. It is a trifle under 7ins. long and by a little bevelling must be made to fit tightly against (x). Both are held by a

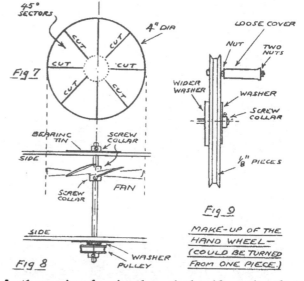

Fig 7

Fig 8

Fig 9

MAKE-UP OF THE HAND WHEEL— (COULD BE TURNED FROM ONE PIECE.)

further series of sprigs through the side, seeing that (y) presses hard on the block (c).

All is now complete except for the short length of metal (T) which is held by two straps of tin (S) and is to push out to rest on a bar of the grate while blowing, and the covering of a short length of the nose with thin tin, this being simply tapped round and secured in position with a few short pins.

The whole apparatus should be finished with a heat-resisting enamel.

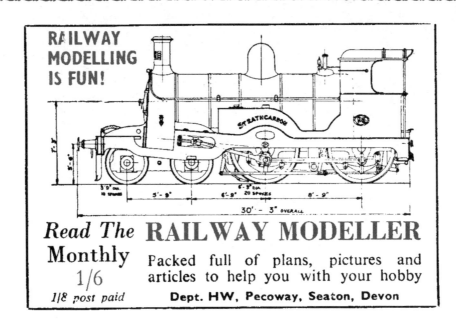

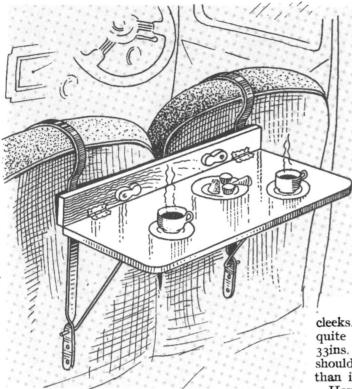

A CAR SEAT TABLE

tend to mark the upholstering, but if desired, you could prevent any likelihood of this happening by inserting rubber tubing over the prongs—or again, by adhering strips of inner tubing around the underside of them with rubber solution.

Shaping the Cleeks

The most difficult part about this novel table is, perhaps, the making of the cleeks. Once started, however, you will find it quite straightforward, for the bars only measure 33ins. by ¾in. by ⅛in. thick, and mild steel, it should be remembered, is softer and more pliable than iron.

Having procured the bars from a local ironmonger or hardware store, bend them to the dimensions provided at Fig. 1 with (1) two iron sash cramps or (2) one sash cramp and an iron vice or (3) a vice and a wrench.

Commence operations by inserting 2ins. of the bar into the jaws of the cramp or vice, and use the rest of the bar as a leverage to obtain the slight curve necessary. Insert the bar 3ins. in the jaws of the implement used, bend as before, then insert a further inch and so on until the curve is completed.

The curve, naturally, will not have a smooth roundness, but this cannot be helped, though the "planes" would be reduced considerably by resorting to ½in. insertions. If you use a sash cramp for the bending, it is to be assumed that you will have it clamped firmly in a bench vice, i.e., the ordinary wooden kind.

When the crook has been shaped satisfactorily, insert 3½ins. of the other end of the bar into the cramp or vice. Another cramp (or large monkey wrench) should be tightened about 1in. above it and the bar twisted as shown.

The three holes at this end are 1in. apart and should be drilled with a 3/16in. twist bit. The

CAR picnics are ripping—sometimes! It's awful starting out on a bright, early morn with fleecy clouds and clear blue skies overhead—skies that lure us out into the open, as it were, and then sprinkle those "pennies from heaven" just when we're miles from anywhere. Br-r-r-r! We can't very well have that much-needed snack sitting—or standing up like cows—in a damp field, and to sit huddled in the car eating foodstuffs from the seats is enough to make us "fed up" before we've even had a mouthful!

Really Useful

The idea you see sketched on this page is thus really indispensable on these occasions. These trays grip on the side of cars much in the way illustrated, but as they are used principally for holding coffee and hamburgers, they are very small.

The article shown measures 23ins. long by 9ins. wide, is light, collapsible, easily erected and suitable for seats up to 3½ins. thick. The cleeks or grips, though bent from mild steel bar, do not

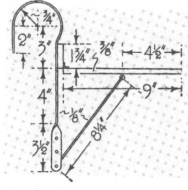

Fig. 1—Side view with dimensions

Fig. 2—Attaching the cleek

Fig. 3—The wire supports

Fig. 4—A detail of one of the stops

holes required at the top end of the bar (see Fig. 2) are drilled and countersunk to suit ½in. by 6 flathead iron screws.

The Table Board

At this juncture, obtain a piece of plywood (preferably birch) measuring 24ins. long by 12ins. wide by ⅜in. thick. This size, besides fitting in with the exemplar per square foot plan favoured by all woodwork supply stores, allows—if desired —an extra inch in the length and width of the table. The measurement suggested, you see, is a usual one suitable for most car seats.

Having planed all edges of the plywood straight, cut off a strip 1¾ins. wide. The ragged edges of both pieces are trimmed up to make a neat join, after which two ornamental brass hinges (No. 5379) are screwed over same about 2ins. from the ends. The foremost corners of the table should be rounded, a penny making a template.

Attach the strip to the bars as seen at Fig. 3. The wire supports are bent to shape, there being two methods. One is to just hook a support to a screw-eye (see inset at Fig. 3) and the other is hooking it to two screw-eyes, this having the advantage of keeping the supports steady.

If you prefer the latter method, the screw-eyes must be inserted to the table before slipping in the shaped rod and turning up the end as shown. The material used in making the supports should be ⅛in. solid mild steel rod. It is advisable to slightly round the free ends with a file. It wouldn't be a bad idea to file the edges of the cleeks if they are square and sharp.

Perhaps you are wondering at *three* holes being made in the cleeks ? Extra holes have been provided owing to the tilt of some car seats and enable necessary adjustment.

To prevent the table rattling against the cleeks, two plywood stops (see Fig. 4) are screwed to the cross strip. As a finish, the cleeks and supports should be enamelled black, using a good stove or bicycle enamel. The woodwork looks well if french polished a dark mahogany or walnut colour.

MATERIALS REQUIRED

1 piece birch plywood, 24ins. by 12ins. by ⅛in. thick.
2 pieces mild bar, 33ins. by ¾in. by ⅛in. thick.
2 wire rods, 12ins. by ⅛in. diameter.
2 ornamental hinges (No. 5379).
Several brass screw-eyes, (Mild steel bar and rod obtainable locally).

REPLIES OF INTEREST

Brass Book Ends

SOME time ago, in one of your issues, I saw an article on how to make decorative brass plates for book ends. I am unable, however, to find this article among my copies. Could you send me the date ?—(E.H.)

THE article on making bookends which I think you have in mind, appeared in our issue, dated August 31st, 1935.

Plant Frame Heating

COULD you suggest a small heating apparatus for a plant frame size 3ft. square ?—(D.P.)

RAISE the frame on a brick foundation, leaving space for the lamp. Make the frame of wood but line bottom with zinc. A grooved wooden bar is in the centre to allow of sliding panes of glass being fixed. Have wooden knobs at front to keep glass from slipping and raise the back of frame a few inches so that moisture will run off. Have frame facing the sun. When frame is completed, fill bottom of it to the depth of 9ins., with cocoa-nut fibre, and keep this moist. Into this plunge the pots or boxes with seedlings, so they may have a genial moist heat. If the pots, pans or boxes are plunged in the fibre up to their rims, little watering will be necessary.

Gunpowder

I WOULD like to know what " F " Gunpowder means. I would also like to know the best kind of glue to use when making fireworks.—(W.R.F.)

THE name " F " gunpowder is given to a particular grade, namely that of a medium grain. Any kind of glue at 2d. or 3d., is suitable for sticking the cases, etc. when making fireworks. Say ordinary fish glue.

A Spot Light

COULD you tell me how to make a spotlight from a car head lamp ?—(G.M.)

THE headlamp referred to can be converted to a spot light for mains operation (if A.C.) by means of a small mains transformer, the primary being wound for the supply voltage (probably 230 to 250 volts). The secondary should be either 6 or 12 volts according to choice of lamp bulb. If the head lamp is of American make, the bulb is probably 6 volt, but 12 volt bulbs can be had from most motor agents and garages. You will find by trial that the current supplied to one filament gives a bright light and a straight beam. This is the contact to use (the return is via the metal part of the lamp). The second filament throws the light sideways and is generally not so bright. You could use a change-over switch and leave a straight beam for spot lighting, and a spread beam for soft floodlighting if desired. The transformer must be able to deliver sufficient amperes at the required voltage—usually 6 amps. at 6 volts or 3 amps. at 12 volts. Secondhand transformers as used in wireless mains units for charging purposes might do, if of the requisite power output, or you could get a Ferranti or a Heybeard model railway transformer, which gives an output of about 12 volts at 2½ to 3 amps. In any case, a regulating resistance capable of continuously carrying the required current should be used in the circuit to ensure a correct voltage, otherwise the lamps will quickly burn out. A valve of 0 to 12 ohms with a 6 amp. carrying capacity will be about right.

Hobbies WEEKLY

January 31st, 1945   Price Twopence   Vol. 99. No. 2572

A Simple Home-made

TROUSER PRESS

A TROUSER press is invaluable in these times of clothes rationing. One has to take better care of one's best pair of pants, which is where the press helps greatly, as it keeps the material stretched and the creases from going "baggy" at the knees.

Another thing, too, there are many men who cannot crease their trousers properly with a damp cloth and smoothing iron. The trouser press saves this frequent ironing and prevents the possibility of "burning" the cloth or putting a delightful "shine" on it in some conspicuous quarter. A press saves all this trouble, and as press fittings are now unobtainable, we have designed a special home-made type which anyone can construct.

The Materials Used

The press is built from common deal flooring boards measuring 4½ins. wide by ½in. or ⅝in. thick. The usual fittings are replaced by ordinary coach bolts and batwing nuts. Such materials, fortunately, are still obtainable, and their use results in a close resemblance to the more conventional type of press made from ¼in. birch plywood and special chromium-plated fittings.

The size of the press, it must be added, will take gents' and boys' trousers. A larger size, measuring 28ins. long by 16ins. wide, is more suitable for the trousers of corpulent men. The dimensions just mentioned cover the size of the press top only. The overall length, which includes the end stretcher, remains 32½ins. as shown in the top plan at Fig. 2.

The Baseboard

To make the baseboard, you need three lengths of flooring 28ins. long. These boards could be merely rub-jointed together, but as strength is wanted, it is advisable to dowel them together. Assuming that the thickness of the wood is ⅝in., use 5/16in. dowelling, as indicated at Fig. 1.

Having glued and cramped the boards together and allowed the glue to set, clean both sides of the baseboard with a smoothing plane, then trim the ends and side edges. Note that the corners at one end are

rounded (to the diameter of a penny which serves as a template).

Six battens of wood are then prepared to length and width. Five measure 18ins. by 2ins. by ⅝in. The other is made the width of the baseboard (13½ins. long). It is screwed to the centre of the underside of the baseboard. The end battens are attached about 2½ins. from the ends, as shown. Use 1in. *flathead* iron screws, by the way, two screws to each board.

Top Press Boards

The top press boards are connected together similar as the baseboard, excepting that only two battens are used. Flathead or roundhead iron screws may be used. Note how the

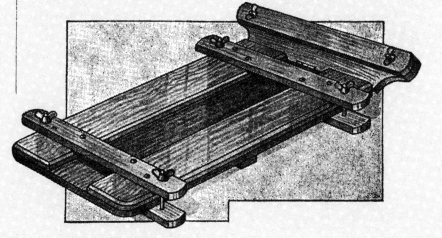

screws are "staggered" so as to avoid weakening the centre of the battens; this also applies to the baseboard battens.

It will be seen that the corners are rounded at one end. There is a reason for having these corners rounded. They ensure that the top press always fits down on the baseboard the right way about, as fitted.

You will also see that the top edges are bevelled. Plane a 5/16in. bevel on the side, top edges first, then proceed with the bevelling of the ends. Use a finely-set, sharp, smoothing plane or block plane.

At this point the stretcher pieces can be prepared. The shape and

entailed in stretching out the trousers prior to finally clamping down the top press.

Fitting the Bolts

The sixth batten goes on top of the stretcher (see Fig. 2) to be flush at the end. In this case, you need two 1½in. long by 5/16in. thick carriage bolts. plus a couple of iron washers and suitable batwing nuts.

Now, there is a certain manner in which the bolts are fitted. The sectional view at Fig. 1 explains a lot. It will be seen that the bolt head is sunk flush into the underside of the batten, with the washer let into the topmost batten.

Therefore, in order to sink the heads neatly, find the diameter and

be in an accurate position. Keep the holes about ½in. from the edges of the boards.

Having forced the bolt heads and washers into the battens and stretcher, the latter can, be screwed to the baseboard at the end shown. It is imperative, of course, that the bolt washers should be a tight fit. otherwise when inserting the top press over the bolt ends, the latter might push the washers out.

Should the washers be loose, a good idea is to drive ⅜in. by 6in. round-head screws close beside them so the screw heads screw partly on the edge of the washers. Two screws for each washer, one opposite the other, would suffice.

Complete the press by staining the wood and polishing it walnut, mahogany, etc. A very high gloss

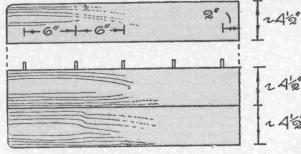

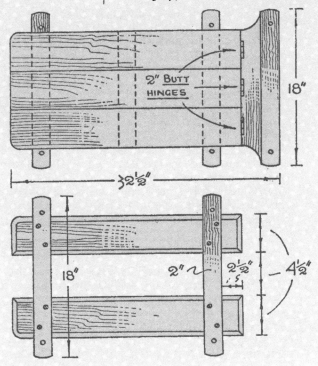

Fig. 1—Details of stretcher piece, bolt and joint with dowelled baseboard

Fig. 2—Plan of baseboard, and upper press parts, with cross brace pieces in place

sizes of the main piece are detailed at Fig. 1. Cut it from flooring board. The 2in. notches are for 2in. long butt hinges.

Screw the hinges to their notches so the "knuckles" sit slightly above the surface sides of the wood. Use 1in. by 4ins. flathead iron screws. Smaller screws would be too weak owing to the amount of strain

understand, the bolt holes must all bore suitable holes halfway in the stretcher, including the underside of the baseboard battens. Having that done, bore ⅜in. holes right through.

The topmost battens are prepared by finding the diameter of the washers, boring suitable recesses, then boring ⅜in. holes right through. As you will

is not wanted. After applying the stain (a spirit stain is the best, as it does not cause the grain to rise so much as a water stain) brush on a coat of thin polish.

Allow to dry, then apply a second coat and, when dry, rub it down with fine glasspaper. The final coat of polish is best rubbed on, or else just mopped on carefully.

through the front. This treadle actuates a rope passing round two pulleys. The other end of the rope is fixed to the arm on an eccentric lever which automatically raises and lowers the lid as required.

The Lower Stand

Let us first examine the stand itself. Four posts 2ins. square and 14ins. long are required, and around the front and two sides are fitted rails of ¾in. material 3½ins. wide. The front rail is 14ins. long, the two side rails are 13¼ins. long, being halved into the leg as can be seen in the picture at Fig. 1. The back rail is 5½ins. wide and 14ins. long.

All these four rails are screwed securely to the upright corner posts so the top edge is 12ins. from the ground. The stand made up allows for the use of a 16in. diameter bin, and in order to get it to stand comfortably between the corners, a triangular section must be taken off to form corner stops as seen at Fig. 1.

The pedal part is ¾in. material 4½ins. wide and 21ins. long. The front end has its corners just cut off to make it more shapely, and a little strip of stuff is added beneath to make the stop when it is pressed down. The back end is fixed

ASK any housewife or maid who has to deal with the dustbin, and they will tell you they are the most awkward things to deal with when attempting to use them. The labour-saving instinct of modern days has not been carried into this particular appliance because whenever anything is taken to the dustbin it has to be stood down, the lid taken off, the contents of the receptacle emptied, and the receptacle stood down in order to replace the lid before picking up the receptacle again to take away.

How much of this can be saved by the ingenious piece of woodwork here shown, is obvious. The idea is utilised in a good many instances in doctors' and dentists' surgeries where appliances are controlled by the foot, leaving the hands free.

Simple Pedal Action

So far, however, we do not know of this having been put to such everyday and practical use as that in the illustration, where the foot controls the lid of the dustbin, lifts it according to requirements, and allows the contents of any receptacle to be emptied without having to stand them down.

Upon releasing the treadle, the lid automatically falls into place without any trouble. The article concerned is really a simple piece of woodwork which any amateur carpenter or handyman can undertake, and the picture of it with the dustbin taken away, but with the lid fixed on, clearly shows the style and proportion.

The wood used can be ⅜in. and ¾in. deal, with four 2in. by 2in. posts to form the corners of the stand.

The general principle of the article is seen by the detail. The stand is built to lift the dustbin about 12ins. above the floor, and at the same time to allow for a hinged treadle action projecting

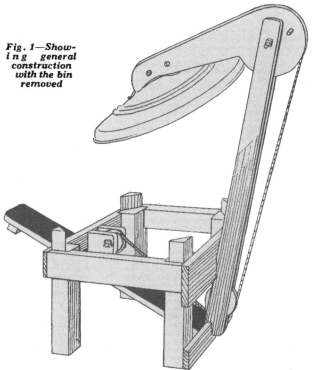

Fig. 1—Showing general construction with the bin removed

centrally to the inside of the lower support to the frame, being held by a strong 2in. hinge. 6ins. back from the front of this pedal piece a hole is bored to take the rope.

Inside the front framework, the projecting piece must be fixed to hold the pulley. The size of this largely depends on the actual pulley used, but we would recommend readers to get these as large as possible. The measurements given are

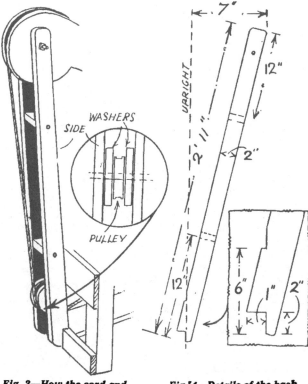

Fig. 2—How the cord and pulleys work

Fig. 4—Details of the back support

assuming that one is using a pulley 3ins. in diameter with a ⅜in. groove.

Pulley Supports

The two supports for this pulley are ⅜ins. thick and 3½ins. square. They must be glued with just sufficient space between to allow play for the pulley and long screws should be driven through from the front to make them quite secure.

If you are able to form a metal bracket to carry the pulley, so much the better, but the wooden brackets mentioned, form a satisfactory joint. The fixing of this pulley piece and the pedal piece is shown in Fig. 1.

To the back of the stand is fitted a lower rail 1¾ins. wide 14ins. long and ¾in. thick. This is fixed flush with the bottom of the legs, and from there rise the two sloping back arms at an angle. This back arm can clearly be seen in the back view at Fig. 2 and a detail of the arm itself is given at Fig. 3 with the necessary dimensions. Notice that the top is 7ins. out of upright when fixing.

Cut both these parts from ⅜in. wood and hold them apart by two blocking pieces 1½ins. wide,

2ins. long, to fit between the arms themselves at a point 12ins. from each end.

At the lower end a shaped pulley is fixed between these arms. One such as is used in the Hobbies Anchor machine is suitable, but you will probably be able to obtain one locally from a cycle or ironmongers shop. The pulley should have a flat groove of ⅜in. wide to take the cord.

This pulley is fixed on a bolt, and side play is prevented by adding two wooden washers which can project well beyond the pulley itself to prevent the rope sliding off. The enlarged view at Fig. 2 shows a suitable method of fixing.

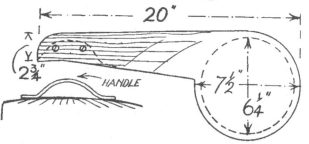

Fig. 3—Dimensions and shape of movable arm

At the upper end of this back support comes the movable arm, and a detail of this is given at Fig. 4, with the necessary dimensions for cutting to the shape shown. Two are required in ⅜in. wood and a hole is cut at the point shown to take a spindle bolt driven through the support, and held with nuts.

The Movable Arm

Between the two arms comes a further wooden piece to take the cord running from the treadle. A little piece of dowelling stuck through the back of the arm is merely to act as a stop when the lid is lifted.

The lid itself is fitted by the handle between the two arm pieces, and can be fixed in place with wire or screws and bolts. All this is a matter of trial with the bin and lid in place.

Test

Having completed the stand and fitted it together, put the bin in position. Thread a piece of strong sashcord through the hole in the pedal and tie a knot underneath to prevent it pulling through. Carry the sashcord behind the front rail, up over the pulley, then down again to go beneath the other pulley at the bottom of the back arm. Carry the cord upwards to the groove formed by the part between the two arms at the back, and test out the length for lifting the lid. Tack the sashcord temporarily in place for this.

Fix the lid to the arm, then depress the pedal to see whether it lifts the lid far enough. It should raise it well up as shown in the photograph. When this is satisfactory, carry the sashcord round the large wooden space piece in the top arm, and nail it on the underside securely.

The whole thing should be now given a couple of coats of creosote, then when dry it is ready for use.

Every reader should join The Hobbies League

HOME-MADE CHIP POTATO MAKER

HERE'S a handy labour-saving device that any house-wife would appreciate—and you can make it! It chips "spuds"—especially the small kind—with no great effort and little waste, or to be more correct, there is no waste at all!

You simply peel the potatoes, wash them under a tap, then place one under the cutter arm as in the illustration and—champ!—the spud is no more. It has literally fallen to pieces, all neat, square and ready for the pan. What would take fifteen minutes or more to do can be done in five minutes—and done much better, too!

It Will Not Rust

Labour saver? You bet, because it is—unlike the bought article—easily cleaned after use. Just a wipe over with a dry cloth and you can hang it up without fear of rust impregnating the cutters, spoiling them, and also tainting the next lot of chips. Wood will not rust, nor will galvanized wire, which incidentally, does all the cutting and explains everything.

You would hardly think wire would be suitable. It has been experimented with, however, and found proficient in every way. Naturally, it is of fine gauge and requires a little extra pressure, but that's all.

The chips are made as though with an elaborate set of knives, and although the finished device may look a trifle crude, none can deny its utility, simplicity, and cost, which, if you have the necessary wood at hand, is only about 3d.

The Base

As many workers will realize, a device of this nature must be made fairly strong. Being constructed throughout from wood, we have resorted to the limit of thickness and selected oak or birch as the most suitable material. That is

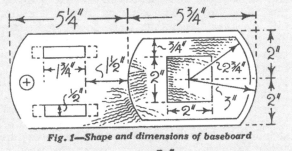

Fig. 1—Shape and dimensions of baseboard

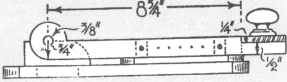

Fig. 2—Side elevation and details

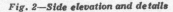

why it appears somewhat primitive, for to use lighter and milder timber would "put pay" to the idea immediately.

With this in mind, cut out the ½in. thick base board as detailed at Fig. 1. It should be stated that this diagram also gives the shape of the ¼in. thick dias piece having a 2in. square cut-out. This 2in. square aperture, therefore, must *not* be made in the base board itself. The dias piece should be cut from ¼in. plywood, then glued and nailed in position.

The Arm Supports

At Fig. 4 we show the arm support, two being required. They are cut from ½in. wood with the grain running in the direction indicated. Before doing so, however, we would advise drilling the ⅜in. dowel pivot holes in same first, as this makes for convenience and eliminates the aptitude of the wood splitting asunder if attempted later.

Be sure to drill the holes as accurately as possible. To save guesswork, ask a friend to watch your drill and brace chuck from two viewpoints, i.e., side and endwise.

Tell him to let you know when you lean the least fraction out of true perpendicular. This will ensure true drilling better than anything else, such as the frequent testing with a set-square, for instance.

Teeth Blocks

Having glued the supports to the base mortises, make 16 tooth blocks as seen at Fig. 4. These are shaped from pieces of stripwood measuring 1in. by ½in. by ½in.

Pare the ⅜in. deep taper point with a chisel, then cut to length. An alternative is to make the complete set of teeth from a solid block of wood 2ins. square by 1in. thick. It is accomplished easily with a tenon saw, the block being held firmly in a *bench* vice or screwed to a thin lath of wood which, in turn, is nailed to the bench.

It only necessitates holding the saw at an angle and cutting across the ¼in. equally divided tops to ⅜in. deep. Cut the V-channels *across* the grain first, then channel the others. Beforehand, too, the side tapers should be made with a block plane.

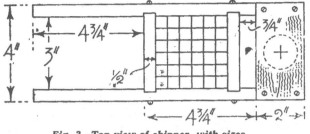

Fig. 3—Top view of chipper, with sizes

Whatever method you have decided upon, when made, glue the teeth in position, after testing them in the dias aperture, of course. If you have preferred the stripwood method, test all in place, then glue one row of teeth, another, and so on until complete. If uneven at the top, a rub of coarse glasspaper will remedy matters.

The Chipper Arm

The chipper arm (Fig. 3) is composed of five pieces of wood. The arms are clearly seen in the elevation at Fig. 2. They are shaped from pieces of wood 11½ins. by 1½ins. by ½in. thick.

Drill the dowel pivot holes first, then cut out and check the *inner* sides (½in. wide by ⅛in. deep) at the distances shown, same being for the short cross pieces measuring 3¼ins. by ¾in. by ½in. thick.

These cross pieces, as like the sides of the arms, should be neatly divided and suitable holes drilled ¼in. apart for stringing the wire network (see elevation). An ordinary fretwork drill suffices,

---

MATERIAL REQUIRED

1 *base board, 11ins. by 4ins. by ½in. thick.*
1 *dias piece, 6ins. by 4ins. by ½in. thick.*
2 *arms, 11½ins. by 1½ins. by ½in. thick.*
1 *handle block, 4ins. by 2ins. by ½in. thick.*
2 *cross pieces, 3¼ins. by ¾in. by ½in. thick.*
2 *supports, 6ins. by 6ins. by ½in. thick.*
1 *dowel pivot, 4ins. by ⅜in. diam.*
1 *wooden knob, 1½ins. in diam.*

---

as the wire used is only about 3/64in. thick, or slightly less than the gauge of paper clip wire. The thinner the wire, obviously, the easier it cuts ; but, strength is a more important factor, so don't incorporate extremely thin stuff.

Attach the arms to the cross pieces with glue and single 1in. by 6 roundhead brass screws. The handle block at the top end is cut from a piece of wood 4ins. by 2ins. by ½in. thick. Rebate the ends, then screw to the arm checks. A wooden knob (1½in. diam.) is obtainable from the 6d. stores at 1½d.

The Network

As previously explained, the wire used must be galvanized. It is procurable from any wire merchant or tin smith, a 1d. coil being more than sufficient.

For convenience in affixing, unscrew the handle block from the arm. Drive a small roundhead screw into one of the arms near the cross piece. Now thread a 3ft. length of wire through one end hole and affix with the screw. Push the wire end through the opposite hole, then into the next, and draw tight. Continue in this manner until all the wires are running lengthwise, then attach the end with another small screw.

In carrying out this procedure with the

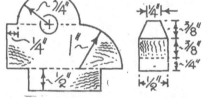

Fig. 4—Arm support with teeth shape

crosswires, entwine them through darning fashion, then affix the ends to the cross piece screws. The sketch of the complete article should make this clearer. An alternative in fixing the ends is to drill slightly bigger end holes and thread the wire around once or twice.

Screw the handle in place again and pivot the whole to the supports with a 4in. length of ⅜in. dowelling. By the way, this must turn in the supports and *not* in the arms. As a finish, this is optional. If you use varnish, nevertheless refrain from coating the teeth and particularly the wire network.

A Reader's Effort in Ships

THIS just shows you what even a young reader can do. The ships are, of course, cut from the Hobbies Designs being H.M.S. Nelson, the Elizabeth Jonas and the Queen Mary. Quite an interesting comparison of the sea, isn't it ? The models were made by G. T. Corin, who resides in Wynberg, Cape Province, South Africa, and is only 14 years of age. Congratulations on such excellent and realistic pieces of work. They appear to be beautifully done, and finished in a painstaking and attractive manner. Notice what a difference a display base makes, particularly with the card bearing the name and details.

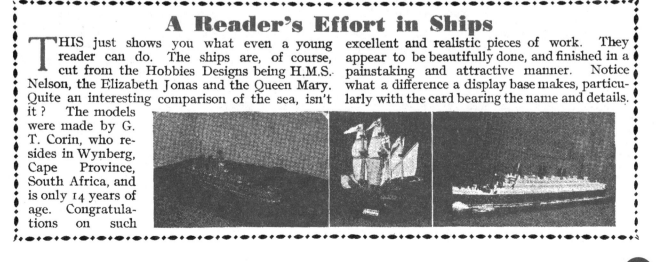

Sweet or Plain?

NOVEL BISCUIT SERVER

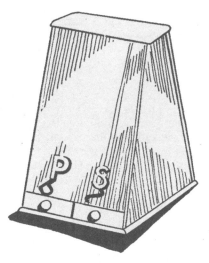

THIS very useful biscuit server works similar to a slot machine, and delivers a biscuit when one of the drawers at the bottom is pulled out. Having two separate compartments, one can be used for plain biscuits while the other may hold the sweet ones.

It has been designed to hold the average size square biscuits about 2½ins. across or round ones of the same diameter. If the server is required to house other sizes this can be done quite easily by making slight alterations to the measurements given.

The kind of wood to use is an important point to consider, and as the server will, no doubt, be placed in a prominent position, it should be something that is attractive. A wood that will harmonize with the sideboard or other furniture in the room and preferably a hardwood such as oak, walnut or

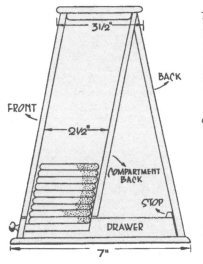

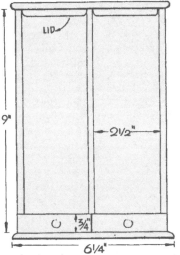

mahogany would be very suitable. If you can obtain wood with a good figure it would add considerably to the attractiveness of the finished article, especially if nicely french polished or varnished.

With the exception of the two drawers all the wood used is ¼in. thick, and even these can be made by gluing three pieces together to produce the required thickness. By cutting the base first and then building the other parts on to this the job of assembling will be simplified somewhat.

Make the baseboard 6¼ins. long and 7ins. wide and round off the top edge all round as shown in the drawing. Now cut the two sides and the middle partition which are all the same size, and fix them to the base. These are 9ins. long and 5¾ins. wide at the bottom, while the

top end tapers off to 2½ins. Glue all three pieces firmly to the base, adding a few fine panel pins driven in from underneath for extra security. The distance between each of these pieces which will form the two compartments for the biscuits will be exactly 2½ins.

The backs to the two compartments are fixed next, as it might be a little difficult to get them in the exact position after the front is fitted. Cut two pieces of wood 8½ins. long and 2½ins. wide and glue them in position as shown in the side view. There must be a gap of ¾in. at the bottom for the drawers to pass in and out, and the bottom edges of these compartment backs must be very slightly bevelled, also the fronts.

Small corner blocks can be glued to the compartment backs to hold them secure if desired and they will not be in the way, as the triangular space behind

is only to make room for the drawer to shut tight.

Cut a piece of wood 8½ins. long and 5¾ins. wide for the front and glue this firmly in position, leaving a gap of ¾in. at the bottom as before. When the glue is set we next fit the drawers and there are two ways of making them.

They can be cut in one piece or made to the necessary thickness by gluing three ¼in. pieces of wood together for each one. The latter method is probably the easiest, as the gap in the front for the biscuits to fit into can be kept to one board thick, while the back portion consists of two more glued on top: two drawers each 5¾ins. long and 2½ins. wide are needed.

The drawer fronts 2⅞ins. long and ¾in. wide, are glued on afterwards and don't forget to bevel the front slightly to

enable them to fit snugly. Make the drawers to slide in and out easily. A ¼in. square strip of wood will serve for the drawer stops and these can be glued in the correct position before the back is fitted on. Two small knobs fitted to the fronts of the drawers will finish these.

The back is 9¼ins. long and 5¾ins. wide and can now be glued in position after the top edge has been bevelled to fit.

For the top a piece of wood 6¼ins. long and 3½ins. wide is needed, and this has all four edges rounded as shown in the drawings. In order to keep the container air tight, it is necessary to make this lid fit closely, and this is done by making two inner caps 2½ins. square and gluing inside the lid. Owing to the slight tilting of the biscuit compartments two edges of these inner caps will need slight bevelling in order to fit correctly.

It will be seen that the sink in the front drawers has been made ½in. deep. This is much deeper than most biscuits and is to allow for varying thicknesses. A square of wood should be cut and dropped into the space, so that when a biscuit is placed on top it is just level with the top of the drawer.

The letters (P) and (S) fixed over the two drawers are cut from thin wood and stand for the plain and sweet biscuits which the server contains. If you always have the same kind of biscuits, you could fit small panels with the names carved on them.

Glasspaper the entire cabinet and finish with a coat of varnish or french polish. The compartments should also be well smoothed and it is advisable to give these a rub over with french polish or a coat of varnish. (A.F.T.)

Rustic Knick-Knacks and Geegaws

USE YOUR FRET-SAW

A BISCUIT BARREL

BEDROOM TUMBLER BRACKET

ARTISTIC WOODEN NECKLACE HOLDER

The artistic craftsman can make many kinds of
RUSTIC KNICK-KNACKS

A S ornaments tend to become more and more "plastic" the charm of genuine "rustic" articles increases. At the present moment there is the added advantage that they can be made from comparatively "green" wood.

The articles described here were made from holly destined for burning. But any other wood with a smooth bark and close texture will serve. Hazel, sycamore or beech should be excellent.

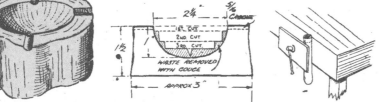

Fig. 1—An ashtray   *Fig. 2—How to cut*   *Fig. 3—Holding work*

Cut the branch from a growing tree and store for a time in a dry place. Do not put it in a warm cupboard or it will split. Nor should it be left out in the weather or the bark will peel off and the heart start to rot. A well-aired outhouse is the best place. A few months seasoning is quite enough.

If you like to use wood that has been lying outside for a time then peel off the bark until the brown inner skin is exposed, glasspaper carefully and polish with clear varnish. Quite beautiful results can be obtained this way. Generally it is safer not to use branches more than 3ins. to 3½ins. in diameter as they are very liable to split in a warm room.

An Ashtray

The ashtray in Fig. 1 could be turned out on a lathe, but the writer's experience is that quicker and better results are obtained by the use of an expanding bit and gouges. If an expanding bit is not available the outside edge could be marked with dividers and a deep incision made with a sharp-pointed knife or large-radius scribing gouge. As large a hole as possible could then be drilled in the centre and several other holes to a lesser depth all round. After that the job could be completed with gouges.

By using the expanding bit in several stages very little gouging is necessary (see Fig. 2). Use a ½in. gouge (outside ground and preferably bent) to do the preliminary clearing out, and work round the cavity rather than straight down. Finish with a flat bent gouge, or a 'spoon',

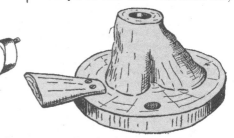

Fig. 4—Napkin rings

gouge, or a 1in. O.G. gouge. Leave the tool marks, as they add rather than detract from the appearance. Now fair the top off with a broad chisel making sure it is really keen. Work round and slightly in toward the centre otherwise the bark will be liable to break off. (For this reason a plane is hopeless). Cut the cigarette rests with 5/16in. scribing gouge and the top (except for polishing) is complete.

All this part of the job has been done with the log of wood clamped in the vice, as shown in Fig. 3. It is practically impossible to work on an irregularly-shaped piece of wood otherwise. Now cut off to the required depth.

Where the wood has been cut, a good finish is imperative. Like a piece of granite that has been polished on one face the beauty results in the contrast between what Nature did and what man can do to improve on it. Fix a piece of fine glasspaper on a flat surface and rub the top and bottom surfaces on it until they are perfectly flat and begin to take a dull polish.

Rub the end of a candle on to the glasspaper and give a final polish with that or, if you like, apply shellac with a small piece of cotton wool wrapped in a cloth.

Napkin Rings and Candlesticks

Having done that you will probably want to make a few more! The napkin rings shown in Fig. 4 follow the same principles. Start by drilling as large a hole as possible, as straight as possible, for as far as possible down through a short branch of wood about 2ins. in diameter. Saw off pieces about 1in. wide and gouge them to about ¼in. thick. Smooth the tops and bottom as with the ash-tray and polish with wax. The stand was,

Fig. 5—A novel candlestick

in this case, a piece of cherry twig stuck in an odd scrap of holly—any shape will do.

A simple circular candlestick is shown at Fig. 5. Another, without handle, is illustrated in use at Fig. 6. This one can be made by sawing a piece about 3ins. long off at the stump of a branch.

Bore a 13/16in. or ⅞in. hole for a candle and a ½in. hole in any convenient position for used matches. Make all the surfaces smooth as before, then polish. The whole can be mounted, if preferred, on a 5½in. diameter base and a handle 3ins. long fitted, using ordinary brass screws for fixing.

There is little danger from the candle flame, but if you feel doubtful, line the hole for the candle with some form of cement, in which case, of course, you will have to increase

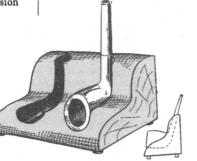

Fig. 6—Another type of holder   *Fig. 7—Twin pipestand*

Fig. 8—A simple but artistic penstand

the original diameter slightly. Alternatively, one can make up a small, cylindrical cup out of brass or copper.

A Pipestand

The shape of a pipestand is given in Fig. 7. In this case a ½in. hole was drilled vertically for the stem and a ⅜in. hole horizontally to meet it, for the bowl. After that, gouges were used to shape the recess and make it suitable for the pipes it had to hold. A hole was drilled in the top for spills or pipe cleaners. Dimensions can be 4½ins. long 3½ins. wide and 3ins. high.

Inkwell Holder

The inkstand (Fig. 8) is made from a slip of sapwood 8ins. by 4½ins. with the bark peeled off and the surfaces highly polished. Sapwood is, of course, liable to warp and split, but in some cases one is lucky, especially if the wood has been carefully seasoned.

If nothing better is available, small meat-paste jars make perfectly good ink wells. You may have to drill the hole right through the wood to accommodate them but if feet are screwed to the stand this will not matter. If you have a lathe you can turn wooden caps as shown. If not, you can use the original metal caps and paint them with bright glossy paint.

For the feet, cut discs of cherry or hazel twigs, leaving the bark on.

Drill a hole through the centre for the screw, drive into the base of the stand and slightly countersink. A simple arrangement like this enables you to fit new feet if the wood should warp later.

A Pen Tray

For the pen tray, first mark the size wanted with a straight edge and a steel marker. Incise all round the mark with a sharp knife or chop with a chisel and proceed to gouge out with an outside-ground gouge.

These are only a few simple things that can be made. An ingenious person will think of many more as he handles the odd scraps of wood that are left over from the saw.

The thrill of "Build it yourself"

Mobile Crane made with Meccano Outfit No. 3

How much better it is to make your own toys! Make them as you want them, and make them work. Make them with Meccano. When you've made and played with one model, you can take it to pieces and build another with the same parts. Meccano grows in interest as you keep adding to your stock of gears, wheels, girders and strips — it is *"the Toy that grows with the Boy"*.

MADE IN ENGLAND BY MECCANO LTD., BINNS ROAD, LIVERPOOL 13.

THE ✤ LATHE ✤ AND ✤ ITS ✤ WORK.

PART IV.—By S. A. Sears, B.Sc.

A BISCUIT BARREL.

THIS week we will take a biscuit barrel as our example in wood turning and metal spinning.

A sketch of the finished article is shewn in Fig. 1. The best wood to use is oak which is polished when finished. To set off this to the best advantage, silver should be used for bands, handle and lid. As this would make the article expensive, brass will be used instead of silver, the metal work afterwards being silver plated by a home method which is very inexpensive.

The barrel is constructed of 12 pieces of wood cut to the right shape (Fig. 2.). To set this out correctly, a gauge must be made (Fig. 3.). The angle is 30°, and is set out by striking an arc of a circle from any centre and measuring a distance *a b*, with the compasses without altering the radius, that is *a b* is equal to *a d*, then with the compass on *a* make an arc at *c*, and also with compass on *b* make another arc to cut the first at *c*. Join *c d* and the angle between the lines *a d* and *c d* is the correct angle 30°. It is well to set off this angle on a piece of wood, and make a gauge as in Fig. 3, the size shewn 1⅝ in. at the top is correct for a barrel of 6 in. outside diam.

The pieces of oak should be 7 in. long and when correctly shaped to the gauge are glued together and held tight in position by being firmly tied round two or three times with a stout string or wire.

The Turning.

When the glue is thoroughly set, the rough barrel is screwed to the face plate (Fig. 4), the outer end being tied tightly round with two or three turns of stout iron wire. The inside may now be bored out, if necessary. A recess must be bored as shown and the bottom glued in, this is a piece of ¼ in. or ⅜ in. oak previously turned or cut circular. The inside dimensions are determined by the size of the jar which it is proposed to insert. A useful jar is a 2lb. marmalade jar of white ware; for a jar 4 to 4¼ in. diam., the wood is made 1in. thick, which gives 4¼ in. inside diam. It would be well to start with the jar and set out the size on paper to save boring the barrel.

After the end is glued in, a small hole is made in the centre of the bottom, and the tailstock is adjusted to that to steady the work while turning the outside, which must be stained and polished before parting from the face plate (Fig. 4, lower half).

The Metal Work.

We must now make the metal work; for this two pieces of hard wood 7in. diam. by 1¼in. thick, turned to the shape shown in Figs. 5 and 6. Fig. 5 is the shape for the central bands, and the lid, which is rounded. A sheet of metal is cut to 7in. diam., and screwed firmly on to the chuck as shown; it is then pressed into the hollow space by working the tool first from, and then toward the centre. No. 22 or 24 gauge brass should be used for this, being annealed before spinning, and perhaps during the process. The Portion *x y* is used for the bands, and must be made about 1-16in. larger than the barrel at the point where the bands are put on, also of the correct taper. The metal is cut at *x y* for the bands, and, nearer the centre for the lid, which should be 4⅛in. diam. Before cutting, the lid is bored 3-16in. diam. in the centre for the knob. Cut the smaller circles first, the bands being ⅝in. wide.

Fig. 6 is the shape for top and bottom bands. The metal used is 6¼in. diam., screwed to the chuck as shown and then pressed to shape. The bottom band is ½in. deep, being trimmed at *z* and *w*. The top band has also to support the lid, and is, therefore, trimmed at *z* and *v*. These bands are fastened by round headed brads, about three to each band.

The handle (Fig. 7) is made out of a piece of 3-16in. brass rod 17in. long turned at the ends to ⅛in. diam., 1½in. long, the metal being gradually tapered between the two sizes. A ball (Fig. 8) is turned from a piece of ⅝in. brass, and when polished is drilled with a 3-16in. hole, this is done before the ball is parted from the rod, the drill separating the two when it is right through. The ball is then threaded on to the centre of the brass rod, which has previously been tinned, the two are then heated to melt the solder, thus joining the ball firmly to the rod, which is afterwards bent to the form of a semi-circle (Fig. 9), the two ends being also bent as shown. Two fastenings for the handle are made of sheet brass as shown in Fig. 10, the ends of the handle being threaded into the holes before finally clinching them together.

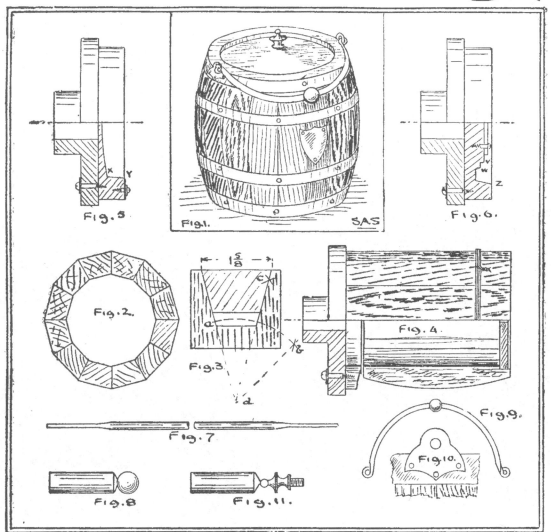

Fig. 5.   Fig. 1.   SAS   Fig. 6.

Fig. 2.   Fig. 3.   Fig. 4.

Fig. 7   Fig. 9.

Fig. 8   Fig. 11.   Fig. 10.

A brass knob (Fig. 11) is turned for the lid; the shank being turned first 3-16in. diam., and screwed to fit a brass nut, the knob is then turned and polished, afterwards being parted off

A shield may be cut out 1½in. wide by 1¾in. deep and fastened as shown in Fig. 1.

To silver plate the metal it must be polished with fine emery knife powder or crocus powder and afterwards rubbed with a paste made by dissolving ¼oz. nitrate of silver in ⅛th pint of water, and adding ¼lb. cream of tartar with ¾lb. common table salt, ground fine, adding water until the consistency of thick paste. When sufficiently silvered after a minute or so rubbing with the paste, wash well in cold water and polish with whiting; when polished, coat with pale glaze. The silver will then retain its lustre for years. In silvering the handle, scrape away any solder round the ball, as that would blacken the silver if not removed.

NEW WAY TO MAKE A SOLDERED JOINT.

THE method herein described and the accompanying cut show how to make a soldered joint on brass, copper and lead pipe.

The pipe is cleaned and tinned, then placed in a mould made of two pieces of wood. One piece or one-half of the mould is shown in Fig. 1. The two parts of the mould are placed around the pipe joint to be soldered and held in position with clamps, as shown in Fig. 2, while the melted solder is poured through the apperture provided for the purpose at the top of each half section. Figure 3 shows the completed joint with one-half of the mould removed.

Instead of the two clamps shown we advise the use of the Hobbies square-shaped clamps.

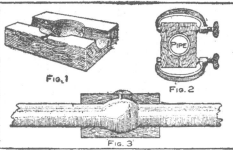

Fig. 1   Fig. 2   PIPE   Fig. 3

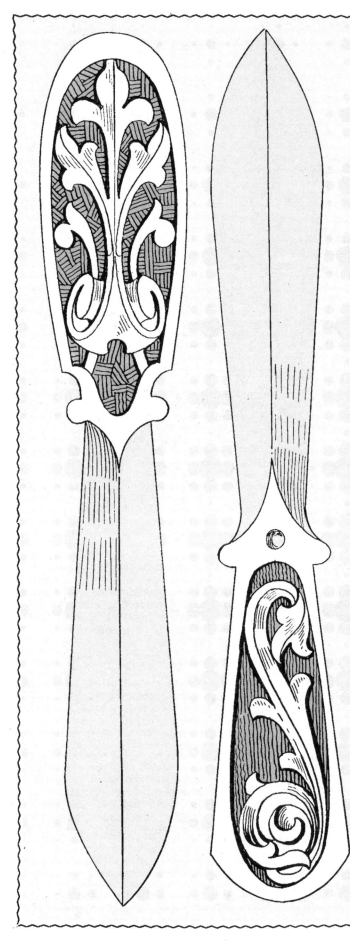

Suggestions for
TWO CARVED PAPER KNIVES

IN these days when most of our time is busily occupied, it is nice occasionally to have something which we feel we can execute and complete in about half an hour or so. Here is a practical suggestion in the making of a paper knife.

They are handy little things for slitting open letters, and are usually much appreciated as a gift to a friend for almost any occasion, even apart from using one yourself. Nicely made, they are ornamental enough to occupy a position on the sideboard or hall table, and we are sure readers will be able to complete them satisfactorily.

Use Fancy Wood

Two complete designs are shown and they are each cut out from ¼in. or ⅜in. wood. It is best to use a close-grained fancy variety such as satin walnut or beech rather than oak which is perhaps apt to slit and be awkward to carve.

Trace off whichever pattern you are going to make, on to the wood, and paste down the actual paper design shown here. Cut out the outline with a fretsaw then commence to shape up the article.

The blade should have a ridge down the centre of each side and from there taper gradually to a more or less sharp edge in each direction. This can be done with a penknife, finishing up with a fairly smooth wood file and finally glasspaper.

A good plan is to mark a line down the edge of the wood half way across its thickness. This will indicate the point to which you have to taper the wood of the blade.

Do not, however, get it so sharp that it is apt to become knotched or broken in use, but rather leave a very slightly rounded edge which is, however, still sharp enough to slit open paper envelopes.

With Carved Handle

The handle, as will be seen, contains a panel of carved work, and this is so simple that even the beginner can undertake it. You should, of course, have the proper carving tools, but no doubt even with a penknife or small chisels and gouges many will be able to execute it very satisfactorily.

The carving can be carried out on one side only in order to allow you to get depth into the work without fear of splitting it. Mark out the design carefully, getting the edges of the work straight down to the ground.

This is shown shaded in the design, then the various curves can be marked in with a knife, and the various layers of wood cut away to form the scroll and leaf work shown. The ground should, of course, be perfectly flat but it can afterwards be roughed up with a matting tool.

The whole knife can be oiled over to get a semi-gloss or stained and waxed. If you want a polished effect you can apply Hobbies Polish.

ARTISTIC WOODEN NECKLACE HOLDER

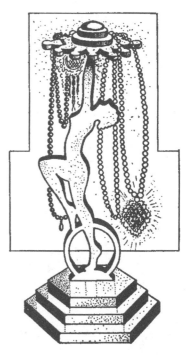

ALTHOUGH intended for use in the home, this novel necklace holder would make an excellent display stand for jewellers (!) and those catering in pendants, rings, etc. The holder is very fashionable, and of course, looks much better in reality than as depicted in the sketch.

It is made easily and cheaply from plywood and enamels of bright colours. A disc of lead is secreted in the base as a precaution against top-heaviness.

The only way you can profit from such articles would be to make them by the dozens, and before actually doing so, it would be wise to make one only, take it round all likely buyers and thus learn the number required, after which you can consider whether the idea would be worth while or not.

The Weighted Base

The weighted base could be attended to first. It consists of three layers of ¼in. plywood, the central one having a circular aperture for the lead disc. Now, in marking out the hexagon shapes, there is, apart from the details given at Fig. 2, a simpler method whereby you can obtain true shapes any size desired.

All you need is a pencil compass. Set it to the diameter radius required which, in the case of the top (mortised) base piece, is 1/16in. to give a 2⅛in. circle. Scribe the circle, then without altering the compasses in any way, set the point on the radii (circumference) line and mark two ticks. Set the point on the ticks and mark four new ticks.

By ruling straight lines from tick to tick, you will complete a true hexagon. To mark out the others, simply increase the radius by ¼in. and proceed as described.

Having glued the central piece to the largest base piece, cut an 1½in. circle in a scrap piece of ¼in. stuff and nail a suitable piece to the bottom. Soot it, then melt some old lead piping in a tin and pour it gently into the mould.

Prior to removing, level the lead flush with the mould, using a flat file for the purpose. Fit the lead disc in the base aperture and glue the mortised piece on top (see section at Fig. 4).

Having marked and cut out the figure outlined in ½in. squares at Fig. 1 glue it to its base. The figure, as like the plain discs (Fig. 2) and holder (Fig. 3) is cut from ⅛in. material.

....
MATERIAL REQUIRED
1 piece birch plywood 6ins. by 6ins. by ⅛in. thick.
1 piece birch plywood 6ins. by 6ins. by ¼in. thick.
1 wooden toe (No. 19) ½in. across.
1 piece green baize 3¼ins. by 3¼ins.
....

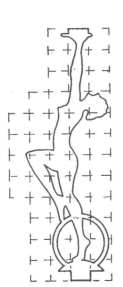

Fig. 1—The Statuette shape in ½in. squares

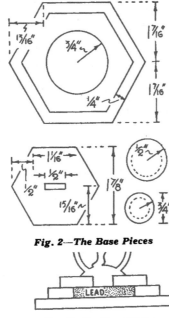

Fig. 2—The Base Pieces

Fig. 4—Section of base, showing lead

BEDROOM TUMBLER BRACKET

The ⇒⟶ indicates direction of grain of wood.

Brackets B
Cut one of each ¼ in. thick.

B

B

For this design we can suppl_
a panel of ¼-in Mahogany (A
15" × 10½".

Price 1/-, postage 6d. extra.

D

Cut one
¼ in. thick.

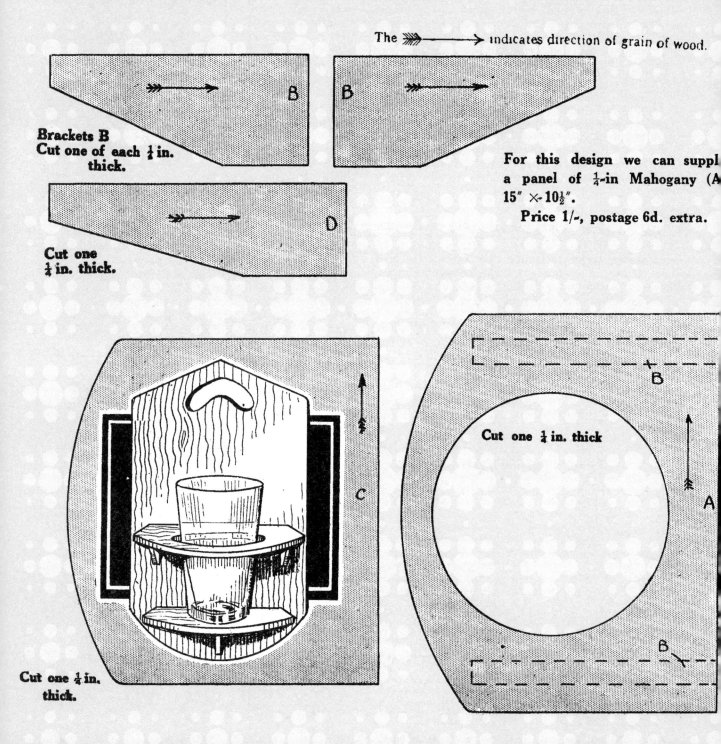

C

Cut one ¼ in. thick

B

A

B

Cut one ¼ in. thick.

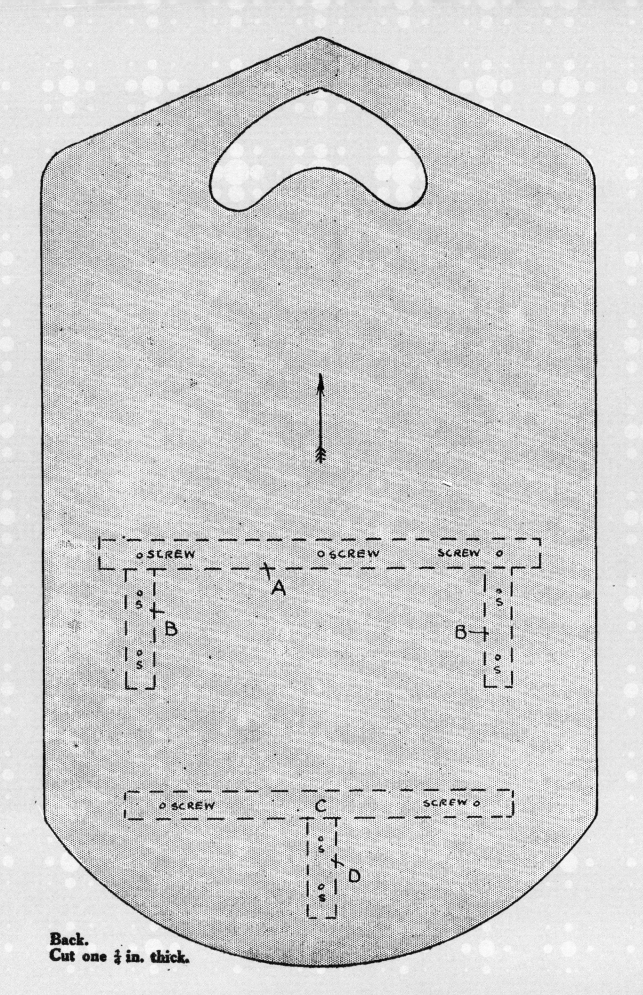

Back.
Cut one ¾ in. thick.

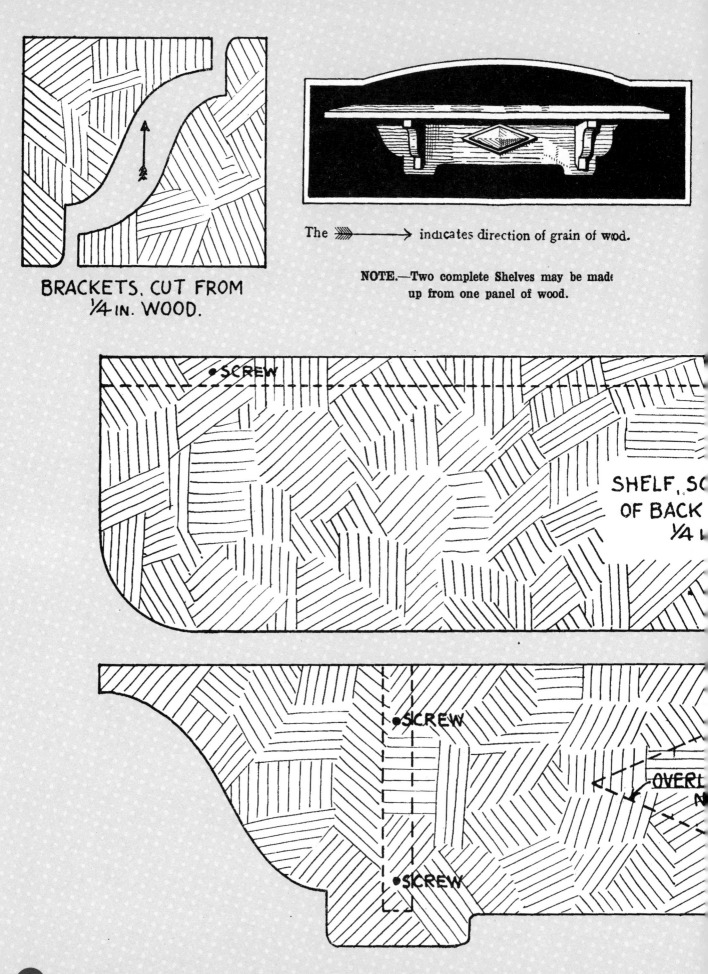

BRACKETS. CUT FROM ¼ IN. WOOD.

The ⫸⟶ indicates direction of grain of wood.

NOTE.—Two complete Shelves may be made up from one panel of wood.

• SCREW

SHELF, SO OF BACK ¼ I

• SCREW

OVERL N

• SCREW

CHINA SHELF.

ELEMENTARY SERIES.

For this design we can supply a panel of wood, "A," $15'' \times 10\frac{1}{2}''$, Price 1/-, and a Diamond Oak Overlay, No. 208, Price $1\frac{1}{2}$d.   Price complete $1/1\frac{1}{2}$. Postage 6d. extra.

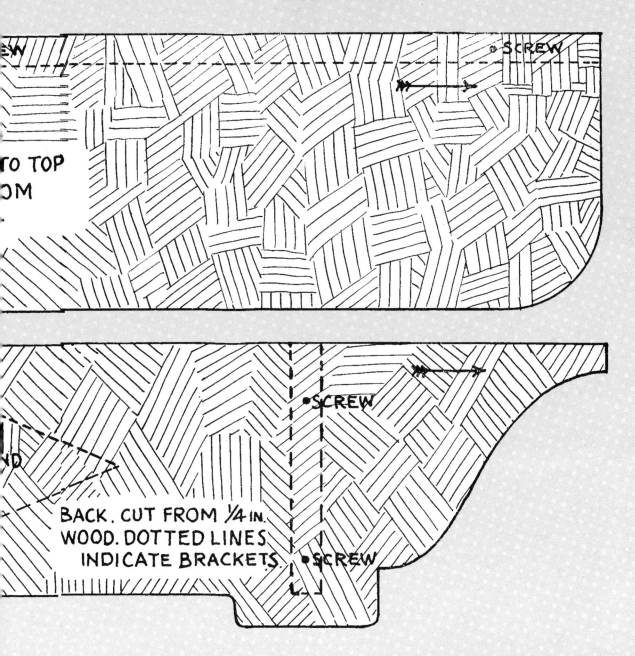

Simple woodwork project

AN ATTRACTIVE LETTER-RACK

THE original of this little letter-rack was made in sycamore, but any hardwood of pleasant appearance would be equally suitable.

Four pieces of wood are prepared to the sizes shown in Fig. 1. All wood is ⅜in. thick. It must be noted that the grain of the base (which is prepared to 4½ins. wide) runs from front to rear, and not from left to right.

Do not attempt any shaping at this stage, or it will be impossible to mark out the joints with any accuracy.

By K. Blackburn

First, the back must be dovetailed into the base as shown. Square lines round on both pieces ⅜in. from the ends, and mark out the dovetails on the back part. When these have been sawn and the waste removed, draw round the tails onto the end of the base with a very sharp pencil. Square the lines down the base to the shoulder line, and remove some of the waste with a coping saw, finishing off with a chisel.

The distance between back and middle section is 1¾ins. Square the two lines right round the base after checking the distance between them by placing the centre section in position. Square a line round also ⅜in. from the bottom of the centre section before marking out the joints with a marking gauge.

Note that the centre part of the upright is cut down only to within ⅛in. of

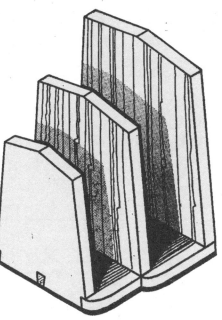

the shoulder line: this raised middle portion will fit into the groove between the mortises in the base. The side pieces, of course, are cut right down to the shoulder line.

The positions of the mortises in the base are marked by placing the centre section flat upon it as shown in Fig. 2. The gauge is then set to each of these four marks in turn, and the joints marked on top of, and underneath, the base.

Use a ⅛in. chisel for chopping out the mortises, reversing the wood when the mortise is half-way through. Then the ⅛in. deep groove is cut between the two mortises with the same chisel.

The front is dovetailed into the base in the same way as the back. Next mark out the shaping on the three upright sections, and plane down to these lines with a finely-set plane, using it in the direction of the arrows in Fig. 2.

These three sections are now fitted into the base, when the shaping on it can be marked with no danger of error. Use a marking gauge for the straight part which has to be cut away, and draw in the curves freehand. The shaping is done with a tenon-saw and a wide chisel, used vertically downwards while the base rests flat upon a piece of wastewood.

The inner surfaces are then cleaned up with fine glasspaper. Do not glasspaper inside the joints, or their fitting will be spoiled.

Polishing tips

You will find it easier to do the polishing of the inner surfaces before assembly. Give a few brush-coats of French polish, using flour grade glasspaper to rub down between each coat. A few more coats of the same polish applied with a rubber will give a delightful finish. The rubber consists of a piece of cotton-wool (which holds the polish) wrapped in a piece of cloth.

When polishing, be very careful not to allow any polish on the joints, as this would prevent the glue from penetrating properly.

After gluing up, wait until the glue is like a stiff jelly, and you will find that it will peel off the polished surfaces quite easily.

The joints are then cleaned up on the outside, and the outside surfaces polished in the same way as described earlier.

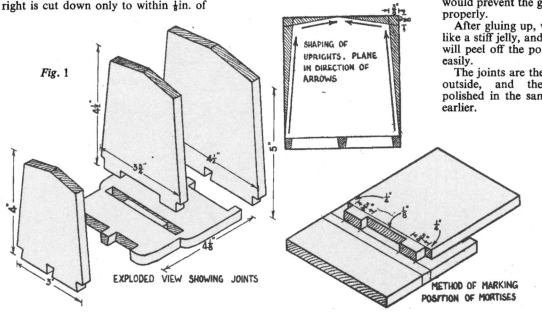

Fig. 1

Fig. 2

SHAPING OF UPRIGHTS. PLANE IN DIRECTION OF ARROWS

EXPLODED VIEW SHOWING JOINTS

METHOD OF MARKING POSITION OF MORTISES

A MUSICAL SAW

STEAM LORRY

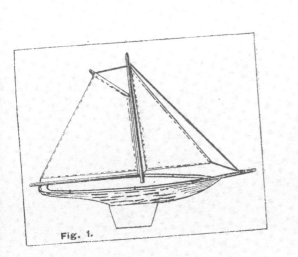

Fig. 1.

Wet Weekends

SUPERMARINE SPITFIRE

A WORKING MODEL CRANE

Full-size patterns provided for this excellent little
WORKING MODEL CRANE

WITHOUT doubt our model makers will be pleased with the fine working crane. It is made in wood, and it has been designed as a working toy with proper winding drum, gears, etc., and the whole thing is made to rotate with its load and deposit it at any desired spot.

A practical addition to the mechanism is the ratchet wheel and pawl which so acts that when the load has been raised to the desired level it is held there ready for the jib to be swung round to any angle.

Then, when it is required to lower the load, by lifting a handle at the side the ratchet wheel is released and the drum allowed to unwind.

Useful Designs

Our illustration gives a good idea of the crane, the full size diagrams of most of the parts of which we have been able to include in the centre pages of this issue. This means that all the worker has to do is to stick down the patterns of the various parts to the wood and cut them out direct with the fretsaw.

In commencing to build, first make the base, which in turn holds the main supporting spindle of the crane and the gear wheel for traversing.

This base is just a plain square flat box and is constructed as Fig. 1 shows from six pieces of 3/16in. wood. Two sides measure 6ins. long by 1½ins., and two 5⅝ins. by 1½ins.

The top and floor are each 6ins. square and centrally in the top there must be a hole cut 3/16in. for the passage of the upright spindle.

The Base and Spindle

A corner of the base in Fig. 1 has been shown broken away to give a view of the interior where a small washer is glued to hold the lower end of the spindle.

The spindle consists of a 5½in. length of 3/16in. dowelling or rod and it is seen in position in Fig. 1 ready for the crane and jib to be put over it to rest on the gear wheel underneath.

At this stage it will be advisable to turn to the centre pages of this issue and see there the portions of the crane which are to be mounted on the wood for cutting cut with the fretsaw.

Gear Wheels

The four gear wheels on the left half of the sheet should first be dealt with and cut carefully with a fine grade fretsaw using wood 3/16in. thick. One of the larger wheels will be put over the spindle as mentioned and glued as a fixture to the base.

It is round this wheel that one of the smaller gear wheels will act in traversing the crane. A detail of the traversing gear, consisting of spindle with hand-wheel at the top and gear wheel below is given in Fig. 2.

Floor and Sides

The next part to make up is the floor and sides of the crane. All three parts are given full size on the sheet and ready for cutting out. Cut the bearing holes carefully. The most accurate way of doing these would be to bore them with a twist drill.

Cut out also the two cross braces—shown at the top of the sheet, and fit and glue them into A and

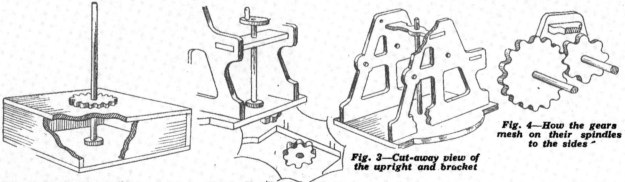

Fig. 1—Base and spindle construction   Fig. 2—Handle to turn crane

Fig. 3—Cut-away view of the upright and bracket

Fig. 4—How the gears mesh on their spindles to the sides

B in the sides. Then glue the latter to the floor, to the dotted lines there shown. Two countersunk screws should be driven in to make the "frame" strong.

The detail Fig. 3 shows the "frame" with portions of the near side cut away to show the spindle and its bearing in the top cross brace.

Winding Drum

The winding drum consists of a cotton spool fastened to a piece of 3/16in. rod, and this passes through the holes marked C in the sides.

To this spindle will also be attached the second of the larger cog wheels which in turn engage a smaller cog wheel on the handle spindle. The little detail at Fig. 4 shows these two wheels on their respective spindles.

The crank arm, shown on the sheet, will be cut out and glued to the outer end of the handle spindle and a short piece of dowelling glued in the arm to form the handle, just as seen in Fig. 5.

When threading on the wheels, and the winding drum on to the spindles, the spacing washers must also be put on and glued to prevent too much lateral movement. They thus hold the spindles properly in place.

Fig. 5—The crank handle   Fig. 6—The ratchet gear

The ratchet wheel, pawl and handle are next cut out with the former glued to the extremity of the handle spindle. The pawl will be loosely pivoted with a round-head screw at point D on the frame and should engage, if properly cut and fixed with the ratchet wheel as in the detail, Fig. 6.

The Jib Portion

The jib of the crane is made up in three pieces. There is a main centre section, with fret-cuts to represent iron lattice framing, and the two outer side sections.

On the centre detailed sheet these sections are given full size so the worker can stick these patterns down to the wood direct and cut them out with the fretsaw. The two outer side pieces of the jib can, of course, be cut together to save work and for accuracy of shape and fit.

Glue the pieces together and then cut off a length of dowel rod to act as bearing for the lower end of the jib. Cut off also a piece of rod to short length for the bearing of the pulley wheel at the top end of the arm.

For this pulley see the detail on the sheet. Here are shown two discs of 3/16in. wood which must each be chamfered on one edge so when glued together they form a deep-grooved pulley as shown in the detail.

Let this pulley revolve freely about the spindle and let the cord which passes over it pass also round a second pulley which must be made similarly to the one above.

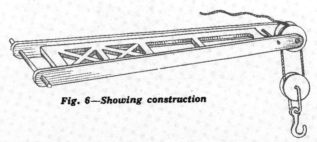

Fig. 6—Showing construction

In this second pulley a wire loop must be fitted to hold a hook as at Fig. 7. A hook may be made from wire.

The "rope" for the crane will be fastened to the drum and brought up over the fixed pulley on the jib and round the loose hanging pulley. It is finally fastened to a cross bar of wire, also at the head of the jib just to the rear of the fixed pulley.

A Suitable Finish

This completes the model, with the exception of its finish of paint or varnish either of which finishes would be suitable to represent steel or similar metal, with black dots for rivets.

Two strips of lead or iron could well be used to weight the base of the crane, these strips being screwed or pinned to the sides or floor sections. The teeth of the gear wheels should be rubbed with a lead pencil now and again to make for ease of working.

A MUSICAL SAW

YOU may have seen and heard at a concert or theatre the fellow who plays music brilliantly with a bow across a handsaw. Some of these saws, of course, are specially made, but if you have a

good quality ordinary one which is quite bendable, you can try it out for yourself.

To play the saw you must hold the handle of it firmly between your knees with the back edge of it away from you. Now grip the upper and free end of it with your left hand and bend it slightly in two opposing directions so that it curves like an elongated letter S.

This done, take a well resined violin bow, and move it forth and back on the edge of the saw, when it will give out appealing sounds something like a wailing human voice.

The reason you can learn to play it easily is because you have only to bend the saw to a greater or lesser degree in order to get the note you want.

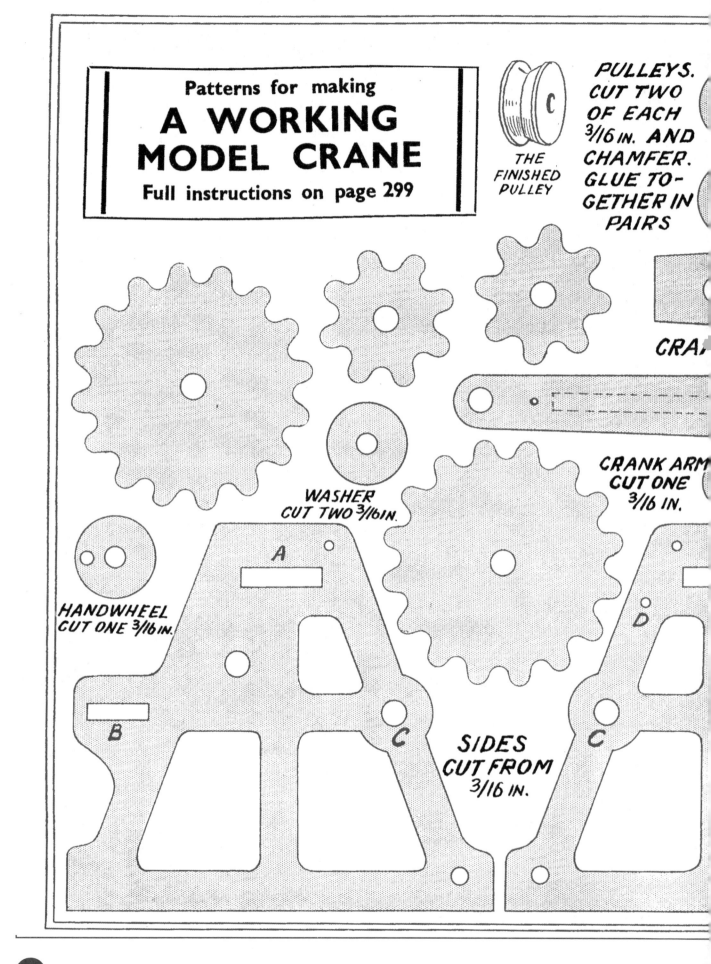

Patterns for making
A WORKING MODEL CRANE
Full instructions on page 299

THE FINISHED PULLEY

PULLEYS. CUT TWO OF EACH 3/16 IN. AND CHAMFER. GLUE TOGETHER IN PAIRS

CRA

CRANK ARM CUT ONE 3/16 IN.

WASHER CUT TWO 3/16 IN.

HANDWHEEL CUT ONE 3/16 IN.

A

B

C

D

C

SIDES CUT FROM 3/16 IN.

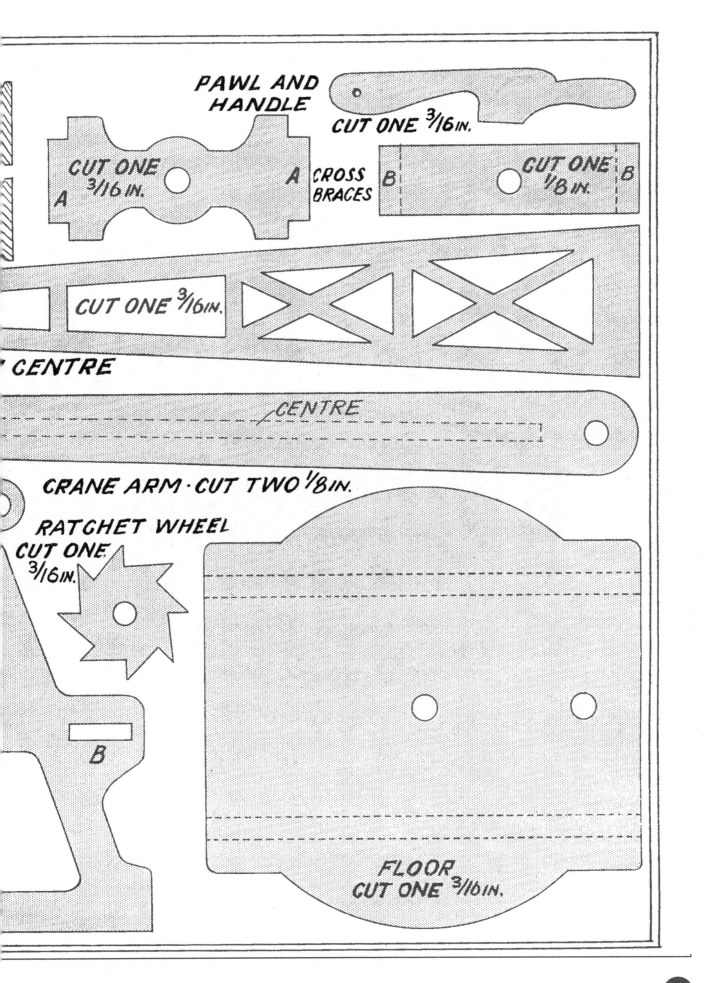

PAWL AND HANDLE

CUT ONE ³⁄₁₆ IN.

CUT ONE ³⁄₁₆ IN.

A   A

CROSS BRACES

B   B

CUT ONE ⅛ IN.

CUT ONE ³⁄₁₆ IN.

CENTRE

CENTRE

CRANE ARM · CUT TWO ⅛ IN.

RATCHET WHEEL
CUT ONE
³⁄₁₆ IN.

B

FLOOR
CUT ONE ³⁄₁₆ IN.

OUR MONTHLY MODEL

STEAM LORRY.

WE publish this week full details for making the interesting little model shown in our perspective sketch on this page. The model is as true to type as it is possible to make it in wood, and is not at all difficult to make up as it is itself pretty large and therefore each particular piece of wood is easily cut and handled.

The length of the lorry is 14¼ins. overall, its width 5ins. and its height 8ins. From these dimensions it will be gathered that this is a model which can be used as a real toy, with doors and all at the rear to open, and real Dunlop tyres on the wheels. Any good class wood would be suitable to use for this, ¼-in.

cutting this to shape also. Now set down two lines on the main chassis ¾-in. from the edge as shown at Fig. 4. To these lines glue and screw the bearers which must before this is accomplished, however, be holed as shown for the axles of the wheels and for the gear axle. The positions of the holes are given in Fig. 4 and they should be bored with a ¼-in. twist bit and brace. The bearers are now braced or strengthened by the two pieces B and C, B measures 2¼ins. long by 1¼ins. wide, and C measures 2¼ins. by 2¼ins. wide. These are cut and squared up accurately and then glued and screwed in between the bearers as shown in the detail.

FIG. 1.

pine or mahogany being first class and easily worked. Briefly described the model may be made up in three distinct portions—the chassis, with wheel brackets and wheels, the engine and hood, and the body or box portion. We will commence work upon the chassis, and for this ¼-in. wood is used throughout. The top of the chassis consists of one piece 14ins. long by 4½ins. wide, and to this must be glued and screwed the wheel bearers or brackets, shown at A in Figs. 1 and 2, and in detail in Fig. 4. Choose a straight piece of wood, 2¼ins. wide and 14ins. in length and mark off the dimensions given in Fig. 2. Cut this piece to shape with the fretsaw, and then lay it on a similar piece, similar in length and width, and draw round the shape in pencil afterwards

The Wheels.

We now turn our attention to the wheels and their axles. At Fig. 5 is shown the type of wheel, and Fig. 6 and 7 the two methods of making them. Now, as real rubber Dunlop tyres are used—they may be purchased from Hobbies at 1/4 per set of four—some provision must be made for grooving the wheels themselves so that the tyre may be sprung on as real tyres are. Each wheel may be cut circular from a single piece of ⅜-in. wood and the groove made by placing it in a vice and filing round with a circular or half-round file, or they may be made up in two distinct layers and glued together as seen in Fig. 7. Here, each piece will be filed or chamfered round before they are fixed together. If this latter method is adopted

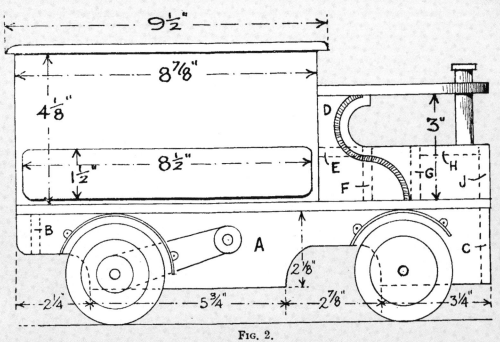

FIG. 2.

engaging with the rear wheel on this side. Thus the gearing and drive of an actual lorry is more or less truly represented. To fix the wheels, first glue one on to each axle, then insert this through the holes in the bearing and finally glue on the two remaining wheels, care being taken to allow of a slight clearance so that the wheels and axles move freely. If mudguards are to be represented, these should be cut from thin wood and bent round and held in place by small wooden bracket pieces fixed to the bearer sides, or again they may consist of metal, cut to shape from a tin box. This latter would perhaps be the simpler method as the bending is easily done, and the fixing can be carried out by leaving small lugs on one side of the strip through which may pass the pin or screw for fixing. The metal guards are shown in detail in Fig. 8.

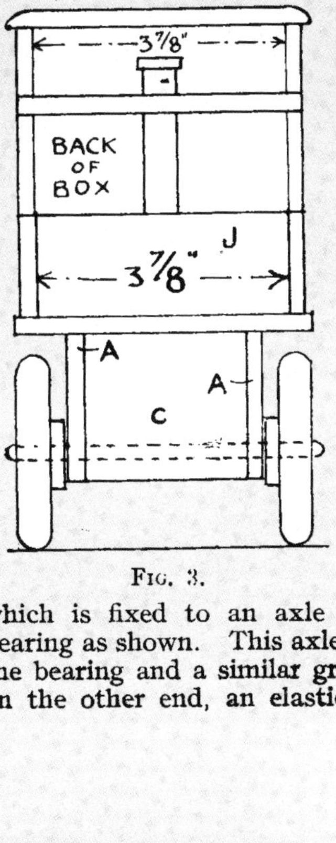

we should recommend that the spokes, as seen in Fig. 5, be drawn and cut in one piece only of each wheel so as to give strength to the whole when glued up. The centres of the wheels will be bored with a ¼-in. twist bit ready for the axles which consist of ¼-in. diameter rod glued into the wheels. On each of the four wheels will be glued washers 1in. in diameter, these will be glued on the back of the wheel and will act as washers between wheels and bearings. The two washers on the back wheels should be grooved with a round file, so as to permit of an elastic band running round and connecting up to a similar grooved wheel,

The Engine and Cab.

We now lay the completed chassis aside and proceed with the fore part of the model, that is, the engine and cab. From Fig. 1 we

FIG. 3.

FIG. 4

which is fixed to an axle further along the bearing as shown. This axle is carried through the bearing and a similar grooved wheel glued on the other end, an elastic band here again

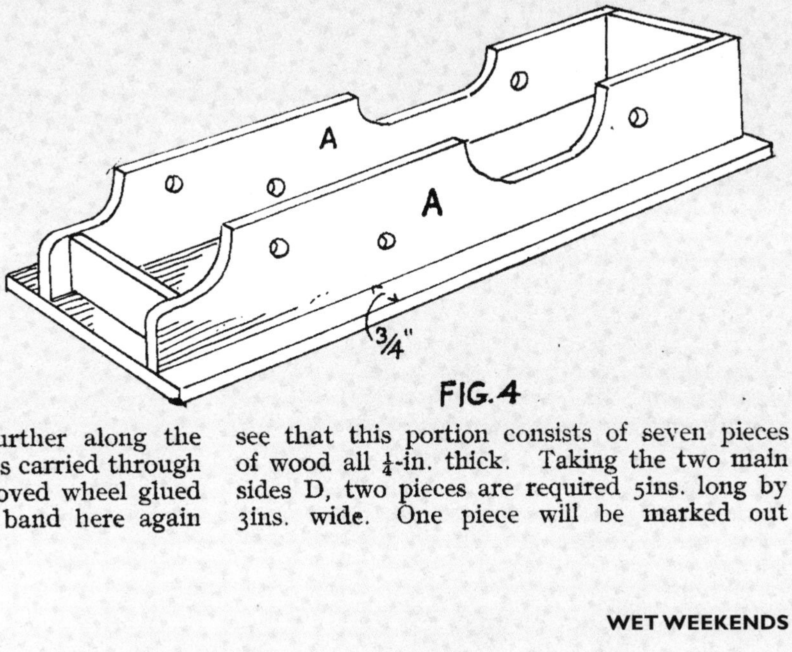

see that this portion consists of seven pieces of wood all ¼-in. thick. Taking the two main sides D, two pieces are required 5ins. long by 3ins. wide. One piece will be marked out

according to the dimensions given in Fig. 9 the corresponding other side being got by drawing round this after it has been cut out with fretsaw. Now cut two rectangular pieces measuring 3⅞in. by 1⅛ins., these being for positions marked G and J, in the diagrams. A top piece H will be cut to size, 3⅞ins. long by 1⅝ins., and will be glued in between the former pieces to form the engine. Now cut another piece of stuff, same size exactly as G, for front of seat F, and glue to this the top piece E, which should measure 3⅝ins. long by 1¼ins. wide. Glue up all these pieces and finally glue them to the chassis, the front edge of the engine section being flush with the edge of the chassis. The next step will be the cutting and fixing of the hood over the boiler and cab. Looking at Fig.

FIG. 5

11 we see this piece on plan fully dimensioned and giving the point from which to strike the curve at the front. Note the ½-in. diameter hole for the chimney, cut this carefully to a good fit for the round rod which forms same. Cut off a length of rod as mentioned 2½ins. long and pass it through the hole in the hood so that it reaches the top of the boiler, at the same time allowing the rear part of the hood to rest upon the

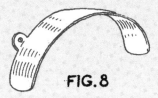

FIG. 6   FIG. 7

sides D. Glue and screw all together and, finally, cut a disc of 3/16-in. wood to a ¾-in. circle and glue to the top of the chimney to form a capping. The box portion will now be made and this consists of two sides each measuring 8⅞ins. long by 4⅛ins. wide, a back measuring 4⅛ins. by 3⅞ins., a roof, length 9½ins. by 4½ins. All these pieces may be cut and properly squared up and glued and pinned together as shown in the front and rear views of the lorry, Figs. 2 and 3. The roof section will have all its four edges carefully rounded off and sandpapered, and, as will be seen from the diagrams, this piece overhangs the sides and back to a slight degree. Small gluing blocks may be glued along the inside angle between roof and sides, or triangular fillet would answer better, to give rigidity to the box before it is fixed to the chassis.

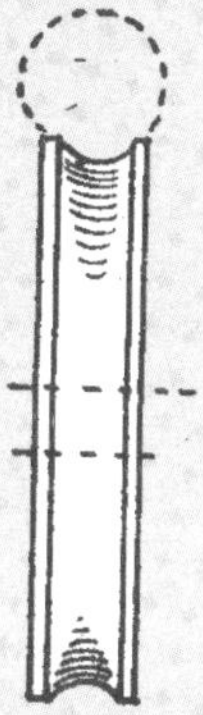

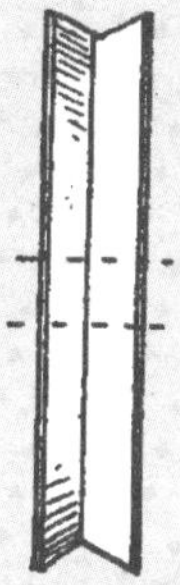

The Doors.

Here will be encountered the part of the work which needs careful marking and fitting, if sound and nicely fitting doors are to be desired. Mark out and cut two pieces of wood, ¼-in. thick, to the sizes 4½in. by 2⅛in. Test them when cut for fit at the open end of box and trim away any wood necessary to make an easy fitting. Cut in shallow recesses for the tiny hinges, as shown in Fig. 12, which gives a rear view of the lorry. Screw the ½-in. hinges to the doors so that they rest flush when laid flat in the recesses. Now open each flap of the hinges and hold them against the sides of the box and, finally, after pricking the holes for the screws insert these and run them in. The plan, Fig. 11, shows how the doors will open, and from the rear view will be gathered the method of keeping the doors closed. This is done by a small brass strip filed to the simple shape shown and drilled and screwed to the left-hand door. On the other door a pin or shaped

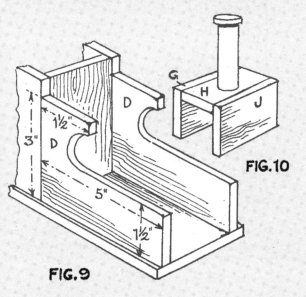

FIG. 8

piece will be fitted for the catch to drop into.

As an added feature to the sides of the box portion two thin overlay pieces may be cut to the shape and size shown in Fig. 2, and glued and pinned each with four pins at the corners. The whole model may now be painted approved

FIG. 9

FIG. 10

FIG. 11.

colours and certain portions picked out and lined up, and to make the model even more realistic a business name may be painted on the sides somewhat after the manner shown in our sketch. Several little gadgets may be added to the model, such as the necessary hose pipe for water filling—this pipe being hung just in front of

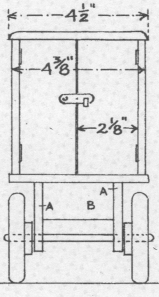

FIG. 12.

the side gearing, and a number plate, too, may be made and pinned on. We will, however, leave these "trimmings" to our workers to choose and make for themselves, and we trust at completion the little model may be found of interest and will give enjoyment to the lucky person for whom it is made.

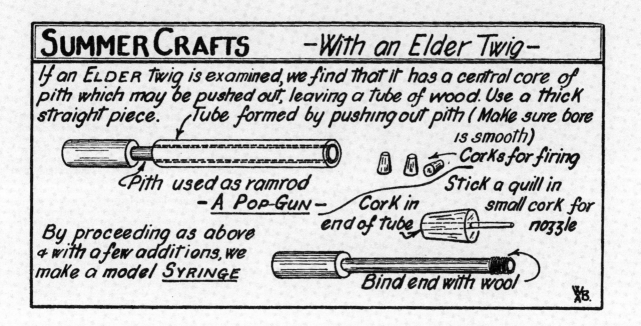

SUMMER CRAFTS —With an Elder Twig—

If an ELDER twig is examined, we find that it has a central core of pith which may be pushed out, leaving a tube of wood. Use a thick straight piece.

Tube formed by pushing out pith (Make sure bore is smooth)

Pith used as ramrod —A POP-GUN—

Corks for firing

Cork in end of tube

Stick a quill in small cork for nozzle

By proceeding as above & with a few additions, we make a model SYRINGE

Bind end with wool

Famous Fighter Aircraft

SUPERMARINE SPITFIRE I

WHEN it was first adopted by the Royal Air Force for issue to its fighter squadrons, the Supermarine Spitfire was claimed to be the fastest military aeroplane in the world. It owed much of its remarkable performance to the experience gained by its makers in the design and construction of high-speed seaplanes for the Schneider Trophy contests. The aircraft was made entirely of metal, had a retractable undercarriage and the pilot was enclosed by a glass cockpit cover.

The Spitfire was powered with a Rolls-Royce Merlin engine developing 1,025 h.p. at 16,250ft., which gave it a

3ins. by 1½ins. for the tail units; two 1in. pins or about 2ins. of 20-gauge wire, brass or galvanised, for the undercarriage legs and thin sheet metal for the undercarriage fairings. Wheels, both undercarriage and tail, may be purchased or may be made from linen buttons. Similarly the three bladed airscrew with spinner may be purchased or the blades can be made from thin sheet metal and the spinner from wood turned on a lathe, or carved by hand. The plastic cockpit cover can be obtained from any model shop.

The method of constructing the Spitfire is very similar to that of the Hurri-

There are two separate parts to be made which fit on the underside of the wings. (See Fig. 3 for shape and 3-view drawing for position). These two parts are (a) The Glycol radiator (Glycol was the liquid used for cooling the Rolls-Royce engine) and (b) air intake to carburetter.

When the wing has been glued into position, it should be faired to the fuselage (Fig. 4). For this plastic wood can be used.

Painting

The Spitfire I was camouflaged dark earth and dark green on the upper

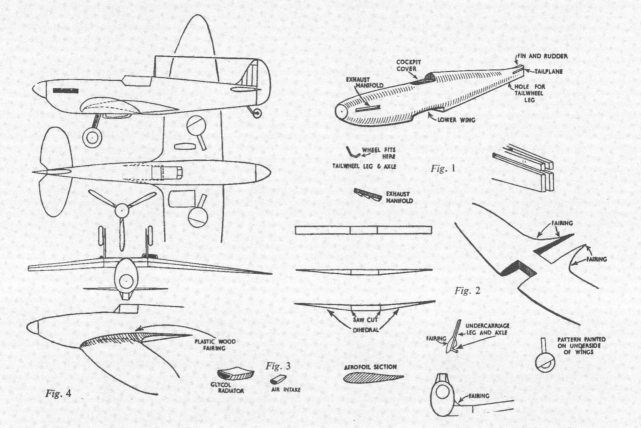

Fig. 1

Fig. 2

Fig. 3

Fig. 4

maximum speed of 375 m.p.h. at 18,000ft. Later versions had a speed well in excess of 400 m.p.h. It was a day-and-night fighter and was armed with eight Browning machine-guns, fixed in the wings, four on either side.

With the Hurricane, the Spitfire achieved its greatest fame in the destruction of the German Luftwaffe in the Battle of Britain.

HOW TO CONSTRUCT THE SCALE MODEL

The drawings are to a scale of 12ft. to 1in. Tracings to a scale of $\frac{1}{12}$nd can be obtained from the Editor.

Materials required are a block of balsa 4¾ins. by 1in. by ⅝in. for the fuselage; a sheet of balsa 7ins. by 2ins. by ¼in. for the wings; a sheet of balsa

cane. Prepare the fuselage (see Fig. 1). For the short exhausts cut two narrow channels in the fuselage $\frac{9}{16}$in. by $\frac{1}{16}$in. by $\frac{1}{16}$in. Next cut two pieces of balsa, $\frac{9}{16}$in. by ⅛in. by $\frac{1}{16}$in., shape half their width to the design in Fig. 1, and glue into the slots.

Next prepare the wing and give it its correct dihedral (Fig. 2). Bore two holes at the correct angle in the underside of the wing for the undercarriage legs. For the wireless mast a pin with its head removed will serve admirably.

By D. G. Norton

surfaces. On the under surfaces it was sometimes very pale blue, or light grey. Sometimes the undersurfaces . the wings were light grey on one side and dark grey on the other and the underside of the fuselage would be divided in exactly the same way. The wheel hubs, undercarriage legs and tail wheel leg were light grey. The fairings of the undercarriage legs were the same colour as the undersurface of the wing. The spinner and propeller blades were black, each blade having an orange tip.

Red, white and blue rings were carried on the sides of the fuselage and on the undersurfaces of the wings. But on the top surface of the wings the rings were red and blue only. Red, white and blue vertical stripes were carried on the fin, red being at the front.

THIS WEEK'S TOY

SMALL MODEL SAILING BOATS.

THE smaller varieties of sailing yachts are always in demand in the summer months, especially at sea-side places, and the best time of commencing a stock is during the winter months. The proportions of the ordinary small model sailing yacht differ very much, but as many of the shapes on sale do not float satisfactorily, it is as well to consider a really good form. The yacht shown in perspective at Fig 1, and in side, end and sectional plans at Fig. 2, will be found quite satisfactory, and can be depended upon to float in a vertical position. The dimensions are those suitable for a medium small size and providing the main proportions are adherred to, alterations may be made in length and beam. It is not advisable to utilise the proportions for a longer yacht than 18in., as other considerations will enter into the construction and will materially effect the design.

The Construction.

The first step in construction is to prepare the hull, and as several operations are necessary, the various stages are shown at Fig. 3. In the first place the block of wood should be roughed out from some soft even-grained wood, such as American whitewood, poplar, pine or any similar timber, to 9½in. by 2½in. by 1½in. If a quantity of 2½in. by 1½in. short ends can be obtained it will be a great advantage, as the cost of the material will be slight compared to long lengths of prepared timber. The wood should he shaped with a hand and bow-saw to the shape shown at "b," and then sawn along the base with a circular saw, as indicated at "c." It will be seen that the saw cut is not carried right along, but is stopped 2⅔in. from the bows, as indicated in the section at Fig. 4. Further, rough shaping should now be done, as indicated at "d," Fig. 3, and again at "e." The main shape of the hull is now seen, and the rest of the work requires the use of plane and chisel to work out the correct shape shown at "f." The wood should be finished with glasspaper, if necessary using a rasp and file to prepare the surface to a sufficient degree of finish.

We may now prepare other portions of the

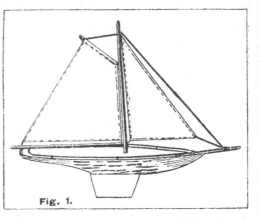

Fig. 1.

work, the first being the spars. Ordinary dowelling, 3-16in. diameter, is very useful if it can be obtained in soft wood, otherwise it will have to be prepared from 3-16in. wood with a beading plane or on a machine. In using a beading plane, one side is worked first, as shown at Fig. 5A, and then the wood is turned over, as shown at "b," and the edge again planed, as shown as "c." The work is very quickly done and the spars do not cost much to produce. To each boat 22in. of spar will be needed. For the mast 8in. the boom 6in., the gaff 3¼in., and the bowsprit 4in. The ends of the first three spars should be trimmed off, as indicated at Fig. 6, and the bowsprit should be shaved off as shown at Fig. 7. Various wire fittings are necessary to hold the spars together, and thin coppered iron wire is most suitable for this purpose. The bowsprit has to be attached to the deck with two brads, the mast is fitted in a hole ½in. deep, bored in the deck at a distance of 3⅝in. from the bow and has a rake of ¾in., that is the top when fitted in place is ¾in. behind the base. At 1¼in. up from the bottom of the mast, a length of wire is fitted through the wood and the ends turned over to form loops as indicated at Fig. 8. The same thing is done 4in. higher up, as indicated, and 1in. from the top a hole should be bored right through in the same direction as the others, but is not fitted with a pin. The end of the boom and also the gaff are fitted with a wire loop, the wire being driven in the end grain and then turned round, as shown at Fig. 9. The best way to do this is to have a strong pair of pliers for pushing the wire in and a small pair of round nose pliers for forming the ring or loop. A hole should be bored in the end of the boom, ¾in. away, and on a line with the loop at the end.

We may now prepare the sails. The main sail measures, when complete, 4¾in. along the foot, the back 5½in., the head 2¾in. and the luff 4in., as shown at Fig. 10. Cheap white sateen forms a good material and as the edges have to be hemmed, it will be as well to cut out a shape in cardboard, thin wood, or sheet metal, so that a number can be cut out the correct size. To allow for the hem, it will be necessary to allow 3-16in. on each side over and above the above dimensions, and as a wide hem must be left at the head, so that the sail can be slipped over the gaff, it will be necessary to cut the back and luff lengths ½in. longer. The fore sail should be 3¼in. along the foot, the leach 5½ and the luff 6½in., as shown in the sail plan at Fig. 10. In this case, 3-16in. should be added all round, in cutting out the pattern, to allow for the hem. A hole should be made at the corner, as shown and indicated at tack and a wire loop filled at the other, as indicated.

Having now constructed the spars, fittings and sails, we have to complete the hull and provide white string or thread for the rigging.

The hull now requires a keel, made of thin sheet iron, cut to the shape and dimensions shown at Fig. 11. Scrap metal will do quite well for this, but ordinary tinned sheet unless very stout is useless. The correct balancing of the boat deepnds in the weight of the keel and many boats are rendered quite useless, owing to disregard of this essential. The metal should fit tightly into the saw cut and it is as well to provide the metal before the saw cut is made so that it will fit in properly.

A first coat of paint should be given to the hull, placing it deck downwards and brushing the paint well into the keel slot. The keel should also be painted and then driven in place, the pointed end at "a" being driven into the bow end of the hull. The effect of driving the metal into the wood and the fact that the work has been painted will hold the keel quite firm. A darker coat of the same colour should be painted round the top of the hull to give a finish and if desired a line or couple of lines may be made by wiping the darker colour away with a pronged piece of metal or wood. The deck should be painted white and to give a finish a length of coppered iron wire should be fitted all round to attach by means of four wire supports similar to those driven in the ends of the boom and gaff. The wire should be ¼in. inside and ¼in. above the deck. The ends of the wire should be driven in at the stern to touch the sides of the bowsprit. When the above work has been completed, the sails may be fitted in position and the rigging fitted up. A length of the string should be tied round the top of the gaff, carried through the hole in the mast. It should be twisted round the mast

twice and then threaded through the top of the foresail carried to the hole and twisted round once more and finally carried down to the end of the boom. One or two turns should now be given round the bowsprit, and the end taken through the hole, looped through the sail and carried back again and after being carried round about twice more may be tied up and cut off. The mainsail is of course already threaded in the gaff and should be hooked to the mast at the bottom and threaded through and tied to the boom. A length should now be left, threaded through a hole in the stern of the hull and tied to the end of the boom, allowance being made for adjustment. The hole should be large enough for another length of string, so that those children who like to have their boat securely held may attach the end of a length of string.

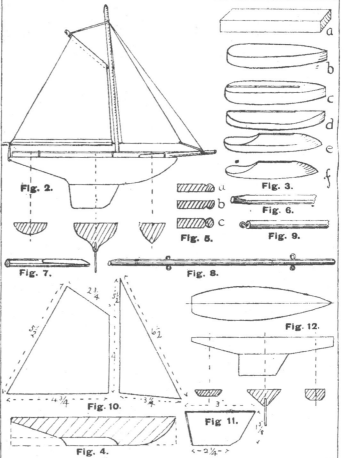

Fig. 2.

Fig. 3.

Fig. 5.

Fig. 6.

Fig. 7.

Fig. 8.

Fig. 9.

Fig. 10.

Fig. 11.

Fig. 12.

Fig. 4.

The Selling Price.

The yacht should now be ready to sail and for sale. The actual selling price of this boat in normal times would be 1s., but owing to scarcity of material and the high cost of labour, it is impossible to produce them for sale at the wholesale rate of 6s. 9d. dozen. The lowest price at which a quantity of these boats could be made now is 10s. 6d. per dozen.

ALARUMS

A HOME-MADE UKULELE

Making a Sycamore Whistle

CORNCRAKE RATTLE

An effective mechanical wind

AEROPLANE BIRD SCARER

IT is the movement of this model aeroplane—not the noise, for it is silent in working—that scares the birds away from your garden or allotment. It is a rather unorthodox sort of "plane," for it has to be given a large tail fin and a giant of a propeller in order that both will undoubtedly catch the wind and work according to plan.

It looks small in the illustration, but actually the model has a length of over 18ins., with a wingspan of 16ins., the propeller being 12ins. long by 2ins. at the widest part of the blades.

Of course, the model has to be this size so it will catch the eyes of the birds better and frighten them off.

The writer has seen many " noiseless " types of aeroplane scarers fixed up on posts in rented plots of land. In comparison, they were rather rough and crude models, but obviously effective, although they swung stiffly and were badly balanced. The model to be dealt with is correctly balanced and swings on a special pivot ; the hub of the propeller, too, is fitted with face plates that ensure continual easy working.

Fuselage and Wings

Some idea of the size and shape of the fuselage of the 'plane can be gathered from the side elevation at Fig. 1. It is cut from ⅞in. deal and checked ½in. deep for the thickness of the wing and tail-piece as shown.

The wing shape is detailed at Fig. 2, with an alternative beneath. The tail and fin is included at Fig. 1, all being cut from ½in. thick wood. Note that the tail is checked to accept the tenon of the fin, the tenon fitting tightly.

Before going further, however, the base of the fuselage has to be drilled for the pivot. First of all, bore a ⅛in. hole 1in. deep, then continue right through with an ⅛in. or 5/32in. drill. It would be advisable to square up the hole position on both edges of the fuselage and bore from both edges to have the hole perfectly true perpendicularly and horizontally.

Pivot and Plate

Having attached the wing and tail parts to the fuselage, make a plate for the pivot pin (see details at Fig. 3). The plate is cut from 1/16in. sheet brass, copper, etc., and drilled for the pivot and screws, the holes of the latter being countersunk if flathead screws are used.

An ⅛in. thick nail or piece of brass wire serves for the pivot pin, the length of which is about 5ins. The pin is filed to a blunt point as shown and then " eared " with nippers about 2¼ins. from the point.

Lubrication

It is then set into the fuselage hole and covered with the plate. It will be found that the plate prevents the pin coming out due to the ears which act as a collaring. Incidentally, the ⅛in. hole space inside the fuselage could be filled with grease that would always lubricate the pivot. Vaseline is ideal.

The pivot pin should be fitted into a wooden holder shaped from ⅞in. wood as shown in the elevation. The shoulder arm is drilled and countersunk for two screws (see illustration). This enables the plane to be attached to a shed, clothes-line pole, etc.

Making the Propeller

The propeller can now be made. Obtain a piece of deal 12ins. by 2ins. by ⅞in. and mark out the frontal shape (Fig. 1). Be quite certain to get the exact centre of the hub.

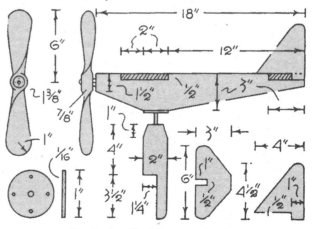

Fig. 1—Details of the various parts

When cut and pared as shown, drill a hole through the hub (from both sides) to take a 1¾in. by 8 roundhead brass screw or black-japanned iron screw freely. For instance, if the screw shank is 3/16in. thick, the hub hole should be slightly larger by a 1/16in.

Fix Hub Plates

This also applies to the two hub plates required, same measuring 1in. diameter by 1/16in. thick, using sheet brass. Four other holes are drilled for small roundhead or flathead screws. One could use nails, but this means hammering and unsightly heads; they are liable to work out in time, moreover.

The screws are best and should be, at least, ⅜in. long by 3. When the plates have been carefully attached, insert the pivot screw and test for freedom.

If satisfactory, the propeller can then be screwed to the nose of the fuselage, with a small metal washer or nut between (see Figs. 1 and 3). The

threads of the nut are likely to work around the threads of the screw and jam the propeller—that is, if the nut is rather on the wee side.

Anyway, when you have painted the model, it is

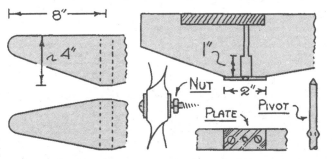

Fig. 2—The Wings Fig. 3—Fuselage and Propeller details

complete. A little oil applied to the propeller will keep it lubricated for a long time. Weather conditions should not have any effect on working parts if you have followed the instructions faithfully.

Have a home-made band with these
MUSICAL PIPES

EVERY reader of Hobbies Weekly will be sure to get hours and hours of enjoyment out of this simple home-made pipe. The materials required are a piece of bamboo and a cork—nothing more. As regards tools, a pocket knife, a saw and a few files are all that are really necessary, though other tools may come in handy if you have them.

You will soon find that you can play hundreds of tunes with this little pipe. A few simple ones to begin with are " Drink to Me Only," " Old Folks at Home," " Barbara Allen," " The First Noel,' " Three Blind Mice," " The Vicar of Bray," " Camptown Races," etc.

Complete Pipe Bands

You can have some good fun playing together if your friends make pipes exactly in tune with yours, and it may interest readers to know that hundreds of boys and girls in various schools have learned to make and play pipes like this.

They not only play simple little melodies which everybody knows, but also play tunes by the great composers such as Bach, Handel, Haydn, Mozart, etc., thus proving that this humble little pipe can be a real musical instrument in the hands of a good player.

The Bamboo Tube

First select a piece of bamboo about 11ins. in length and not more than 1in. in diameter. Choose a piece which is as straight and as round as possible, free from cracks, and with only one joint, or node.

Begin by filing out the layer of fibre inside the

bamboo at the " node," i.e., make the bamboo so that you can see right through it if you cannot already do so.

Now saw out a mouthpiece at one end of the pipe, as shown in the diagram (see Figs. 1, 2, 3, 6). Begin by sawing half way through the bamboo ¾in. from the top. Then cut away the lower half and slope the sides upwards, as shown, and file or glasspaper the rough edges.

The Wind Opening

Now mark the centre of the " window " 1¼in. from the top of the pipe (Fig. 2). Bore a small hole and enlarge it to an oblong ¼in. wide and 3/16in. deep. Make a neat job of this if you want to get the best out of your pipe.

Now cut out (with knife or chisel, and file) a shallow " passage " about 1/20 in. deep from the window to the top of the pipe on the inside (see Fig. 3). Make the bottom of this passage perfectly

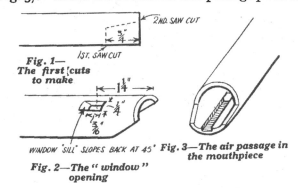

Fig. 1—The first cuts to make

WINDOW 'SILL' SLOPES BACK AT 45°

Fig. 2—The " window " opening

Fig. 3—The air passage in the mouthpiece

flat, and the sides quite square. Beware of making it too deep, especially towards the window end, and make it the exact width of the window.

Now return to the window and cut or file back the lower edge of the oblong opening at an angle of 45° (i.e. half a right angle), to form a sharp edge or "sill" for the air to strike. (Fig. 2). Take care not to enlarge the size of the window opening when doing this as a deep window spoils the tone of the pipe.

Cork Fitting

The next thing we require is a cork which will fit tightly into the top of the pipe and reach just to the top edge of the window opening. If the cork is too long, cut off a piece. It is usually best to cut this piece from the narrow end, but it may be cut from the wide end if the cork fits very tightly.

When the cork is exactly the right length, cut or file a piece off the top as shown in Figs. 4 and 5. Beginning near the narrow (or window) end, start cutting off a very thin strip, and cut with a gradual slope downwards towards the mouthpiece end.

It is important to note that whilst scarcely any cork should be cut from the window end, there should be quite a large "air" space at the mouthpiece end (See Figs. 4 and 6).

Push the cork in, and the pipe should now play a note. Breathe very gently and listen to the low note, not the high one which is produced by blowing slightly harder. Gentle breathing is essential. When the note is satisfactory, trim off the cork to make a nice mouthpiece (see Fig. 6).

To make the other notes of the scale, finger holes must be carved in the pipe. If you do not want the pipe to play in any particular key, begin right away and make the first or lowest hole. Measure the distance from the centre of the window to the bottom of the pipe. Divide this by four, and mark (with pencil) the position of the first hole, this distance from the bottom of the pipe. (Fig. 7). Do not pierce the hole yet.

Now mark the top hole 2½in. from the centre of the window. There will be six holes in all covered by the three longest fingers of each hand.

Forming the Notes

Place these fingers on the pipe (right hand below left, unless you are left-handed), and mark out the remaining four holes between Nos. 1 and 6, either equally spaced, or in two groups of three, where the fingers naturally fall. You are now ready to pierce the first hole.

Bore a small hole, and gradually enlarge it with any tool you find convenient until the pipe plays the second note of the scale (i.e. "ray"). Keep blowing the pipe to test the note, and beware of making the hole too large. As soon as "ray" is exactly in tune, begin to make the next hole ("me") in the same manner.

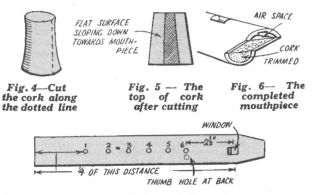

Fig. 4—Cut the cork along the dotted line

Fig. 5 — The top of cork after cutting

Fig. 6 — The completed mouthpiece

Fig. 7—The finger hole spacing

Remaining Holes

The third hole (" fah ") will be a small one because the distance from " me " to fah " is only a semitone. Holes 4, 5 and 6 will give " soh," " lah " and " te," and to give top " doh " we make a small thumb hole (i.e. to be covered by the thumb of the left hand) immediately behind hole 6, at the back of the pipe. This will be a small hole for the same reason as hole 3.

Take care not to force the tools when making holes, as the bamboo splits very easily, and then all your work is spoiled, as a cracked pipe will not play. You might, of course, seal up any cracks which you happen to make by filling them with liquid glue or plastic wood, but it is better to avoid them altogether by taking care.

If you cover the bottom three holes only (or perhaps the bottom two only) and blow harder, you can play top " ray," and you may, by experimenting a little, find out how to play top " me " as well.

The fingering for these extra notes varies on different pipes, but is soon discovered if a little patience is exercised.

With the Piano

If you want to play the pipe with someone accompanying you on the piano, or with other pipes, it should be tuned to the piano. When the pipe plays its first note (i.e., before any holes are made), saw small rings off the bottom until it plays D exactly.

When deciding how much to saw off, allow ⅛in. to raise the pitch a semitone, and beware of sawing off too much. When the pitch has risen to D exactly, mark out the holes according to instructions, and tune each hole in turn to the next note of the scale of D major.

If you like, there is no reason why you should not make a C pipe (i.e., one which will play the scale of C major), though a pipe of this kind is usually pitched in D.

For celebration or bird scaring you can't beat a
CORNCRAKE RATTLE

A CORNCRAKE is, of course, the name aptly applied to a bird frequenting cornfields and having a peculiar, raucous, crake-ing cry, or call. The novelty illustrated is a gadget giving a fair imitation of the cry of a corncrake—hence its name. Perhaps the word "rattle" would be a better name for it for it was made to create noise! Not just mere noise, but an awful din serving to show the delight and exuberance of spirit of the user.

When our victorious Allied armies are returning, bringing peace and happiness, we shall want to cheer them as they march along, which is where the corncrake will help to swell the applause. There is no need, however, to make and keep the corncrake until then. Make a couple, and give one to a youngster to play with.

A single-tongue type is described. It is possible to make a double-tongue model, which naturally creates double noise. The latter is made in exactly the same way as the former, excepting you need an extra cog-wheel, or agitator, with side piece and filling block.

The Side Shapes

To make the single-tongue type, cut out two side shapes from $\frac{1}{8}$in.

wood to the size shown at Fig. 1. The tongue is cut from similar wood, preferably ash, oak or birch, as some springiness is wanted. Deal, being soft, is liable to break or splinter at the tip. The latter, as you can see, is neatly rounded.

The most important part, the cog-wheel, consists of three shapes, one $\frac{1}{4}$in. thick and the others $\frac{1}{8}$in. thick, cut to the size shown. To ensure strength, the shapes are assembled together, with glue, like a piece of 3-ply wood.

The grain directions cross, as indicated by the arrows. The thinner pieces run in the same direction, whereas the thicker, central piece runs crosswise between them. If this is not done, the four short-grained teeth on the agitator, being weaker, are easily knocked off. By crossing the grain, all teeth are strengthened.

The Handle

The handle is made from a 6in. length of $\frac{1}{2}$in. dowelling. A pivot, $1\frac{1}{4}$ins. long by $\frac{1}{4}$in. square, is cut at one end, as you can see. If a double tongued corncrake is being made, the pivot needs to be made longer by about $\frac{3}{8}$in.

At this point, you need two filling blocks 2ins. long by $\frac{3}{8}$in. wide by $\frac{3}{8}$in. thick. Glue these to the tongue, as indicated at Fig. 2. The blocks are

then glued between the side shapes, flush at the end. A few panel nails should be added to hold the parts firmly together.

The squareness of the ends of the filling blocks are rounded to the shape of the side pieces. Pare off the waste wood with a sharp chisel, then rasp, file and glasspaper the end neatly.

Assembling the Parts

Having made the agitator wheel and two $\frac{1}{8}$in. thick by $\frac{7}{8}$in. diam. washers, glue the latter centrally on each side of the agitator. Test the handle pivot through them. If it goes through satisfactorily, set the agitator between the "jaws" of the sides and push the handle pivot through. A smaller $\frac{1}{8}$in. washer, $\frac{1}{2}$in. diameter and having a $\frac{1}{4}$in. square hole cut in its centre, is glued over the projection (see sketch) to complete the construction.

To finish the novelty, it should be brushed with a thin coat of light brown polish. If desired, a spirit stain could be applied only. The teeth of the agitator should be lubricated by rubbing in a smearing of candle tallow.

To use the corncrake, of course, one merely swings it around by the handle with a circular motion of the hand. This particular corncrake can be swung in a clockwise or anti-clockwise direction, as desired.

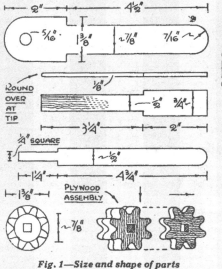

Fig. 1—Size and shape of parts

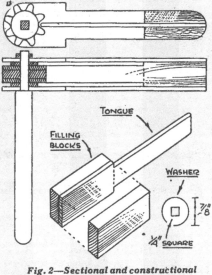

Fig. 2—Sectional and constructional views

Making a Sycamore Whistle

IN these days of synthetic pleasures a lot has been lost of the simple enjoyments we had as children. When some of us were young, money was hard to come by and we had to provide most of our own amusements and construct many makeshift toys. We learnt to make four-wheeled carts from odd planks and sugar boxes and soon became adept at doing odd jobs.

A Prize

To those of us who lived in the country our first pocket-knife was a prize indeed, as it opened the door to

BARK MOISTENED, TAPPED WITH BACK OF KNIFE HANDLE & SLIPPED OFF.   CUT AROUND WITH KNIFE EDGE.

FIRST STAGE   REMOVAL OF BARK

MOUTH PIECE SHAPED THUS   AIR HOLE CUT THUS

SECOND STAGE   BARK REPLACED & MOUTHPIECE & AIR HOLE SHAPED

FLAT CUT ON TOP FOR AIR PASSAGE   HOLLOW UNDER AIR HOLE EXTENDED & PITH DUG OUT

THIRD STAGE   BARK REMOVED & WHISTLE HOLLOWED

unlimited possibilities. With it we could produce bows and arrows, walking-sticks, stilts and a variety of fascinating objects.

It would be a good thing if we who can remember our childhood prowess with the pocket-knife would hand on to our children the secrets we discovered. They would appreciate the gesture and be proud of being able to produce toys which hitherto they have understood to be obtainable only from a shop and in exchange for money.

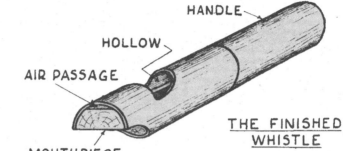

HANDLE

HOLLOW

AIR PASSAGE

MOUTHPIECE

THE FINISHED WHISTLE

In spring, when sap was in the sycamore shoots we made whistles—and what could be better than a whistle made with our own hands. And if we broke our whistle or became tired of its note we could make another.

Making the Whistle

To make a sycamore whistle a young branch or shoot of up to ¾in. in diameter should be selected. The smaller the shoot, the easier it will be to slip off the skin. Having cut a length to suit, a ring cut should be made from two to three inches from the end, making sure the blade penetrates to the full thickness of the skin. The section of skin beyond this cut must now be removed without splitting or damaging it. The skin is moistened—we naturally placed it in our mouths—and then tapped all over with the back of the knife-blade. This wetting and tapping process is repeated several times, and between times the end should be grasped firmly and twisted. After a

few minutes it will part company with the stick and may be slid off. The skin is replaced for the shaping of the mouthpiece and the cutting of the outlet hole. This could have been done before loosening the skin, but it would have been more difficult to avoid splitting.

The skin is again removed for a final finishing of the inside wood. A sliver is cut from the top of the mouthpiece to form an air passage and the hollow beneath the outlet hole is extended and the pith dug out. On replacement of the skin the whistle is finished, to be blown with delight by any small boy.

I recently made a whistle of this type for a young boy and it was not long before nearly every small boy in the neighbourhood was blowing a similar one. With one lesson these youngsters were fashioning their own.

It may be noted that the simple freeing of a portion of the skin as shown in the first illustration forms a whistle which will sound a variable note when blown across the end. A warbling note may be sounded by sliding the skin up and down while blowing.

The note of the more orthodox whistle is determined by the diameter of the wood and the amount of hollowing. The various stages of making the whistle are shown in the illustrations.   (L.J.B.)

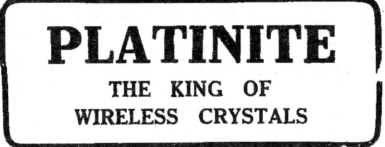

A HOME-MADE UKULELE

A UKULELE, of course, is just an instrument for vamping or harmonizing in accompaniment with (chiefly) a vocalist or yourself, whether humming or singing. The construction presents little difficulty, more consideration being given to the tonal qualities of the wood selected for use.

Ordinary thin birch plywood could be used throughout. This, however, is not so sonorous and resonant as plain thin fretwood such as white chestnut, silver spruce or deal. Birch fretwood, and other hardwoods like beech, sycamore and padouk produce quite a good tone.

Any of these can be also used for the neck handle, although whitewood is often employed. An excellent combination would be a birch handle, with a padouk body surface and birch back. The bent sides could be 1/32in. thick birch plywood cut short-grained to alleviate the bending, with the interior flanges cut from ⅛in. stuff, the blocks, of course, being ⅞in. deal.

Construction of the Body

Commence work by striking out the body shape as seen at Fig. 1, this being mostly compass work. Be sure to find the correct radius centres, otherwise the radii lines will not meet properly. The sound hole, naturally, is only required in the face piece which, as mentioned, could be cut from padouk to give a nice contrast to the rest of the work.

Having cut it out and trimmed neatly with glasspaper, use it as a template for marking out the back piece. The shaped flange pieces are cut in separate portions, i.e., they stretch from top to bottom only; the cross bars are affixed separately later. One cut-out flange will mark for the other three required.

The body can now be assembled. To do so, glue the flange parts around the edges, allowing

All parts supplied in Parcel No. T.M.355 for 5/-, or sent post free for 5/9.

1½in. space at top and bottom (in the centre) for the blocks which measure 1½ins. long by 1⅞ins. wide by ⅞in. thick. The face of the bottom block is rounded to conform with the curvature of the body. Incidentally, the blocks and flanging must show an even 1/16in. wide margin all round as in Fig. 1.

The Plywood Sides

When the cross bars are fitted and glued in position, glue and panel pin the shaped face and back portions to the blocks—or, if possible, just use glue, a powerful tube glue such as Certofix. The sides are formed with two separate strips of thin plywood meeting at the corners of the violin shape, the topmost strip measuring about 15ins. by 1⅞ins. by 1/32in. thick, with the bottom strip about 12ins. long by the same width and thickness.

Glue the bottom strip around first, the ends being mitred neatly at the corners. If there is much resistance in bending, the strip should be steamed into the desired shape. It is held firmly in place with strands of cord or tape tied around same and the framing until the glue dries. The topmost strip is also centred, then nailed to its block and bent around to "test" for the correct mitre length.

Owing to the "inside" curvature, you will—after having tied string around—need to force wedges of wood in at this point, or better still,

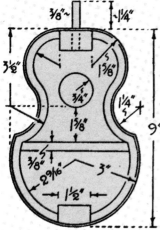

Fig. 1—Back view of body front showing dimensions and general parts

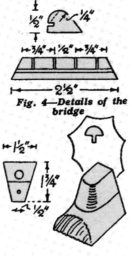

Fig. 4—Details of the bridge

Fig. 3—Shaping of neck at shoulder with sectional front view

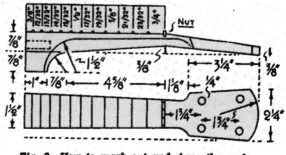

Fig. 2—How to mark out and shape the neck

use similarly shaped pieces of wood and wedge the whole between two upright lengths of ¾in. diam. dowelling in a scrap piece of thick wood, the projecting tops of the dowels being pulled into alignment with cord.

The Neck

The neck is cut and shaped as detailed at Fig. 2 from a piece of wood measuring 11ins. long by 2¼ins. wide by ⅞in. thick. Before doing so, however, set out the fret positions with pencil and square and score or cut across them to a depth of not more than 1/16in.

A small block of the same wood (2ins. long by 2¼ins. wide) is glued to the shoulder end, whereupon the top and side shaping can be carried out with a panel saw and keyhole saw, the rest of the neck being cleaned up with the spokeshave, rasp and glasspaper. The shoulder end must be dead square. It is bevelled as seen at Fig. 3, then drilled for a ⅜in. dowel 1⅜ins. deep and for an 1½in. by 6 flathead iron screw, this necessitating countersinking. The peg holes are drilled with a ¼in. bit.

A dowel hole to correspond with that of the handle is made in the body so that the finger board is flush with the surface. The bodywork is glasspapered prior to gluing and screwing the neck in place; fill the screw hole in with plastic wood.

MATERIALS REQUIRED

1 handle (birch) 13½ins. by 2¼ins. by ⅞in. thick.
1 body back (birch) 9ins. by 6ins. by 1/16in. thick.
1 body front (padouk) 9ins. by 6ins. by 1/16in. thick.
2 pieces plywood (flanges) 9ins. by 5ins. by ⅛in. thick.
2 end blocks (deal) 1½ins. by 1⅞ins. by ⅞in. thick.
1 plywood side (birch) 15ins. by 1⅞ins. by 1/32in.
1 piece plywood side (birch) 12ins. by 1⅞ins. by 1/32in.
1 bridge (birch) 2½ins. by ¾in. by ½in. thick.
4 wooden pegs.
4 (set) gut strings. Opposite obtainable locally.
1 felt plectrum.

The Bridge and Frets

The bridge, being made from wood and the sole anchorage for the strings, is made and glued in position at this juncture. Shape it from a piece of hardwood 2½ins. long by ¾in. wide by ½in. thick as shown at Fig. 4. First cut a kerf along one side (see section above) then round the top and bevel in the manner shown, the string cuts being made with a tenon saw as indicated by the dotted lines.

The inset at Fig. 3 shows a sectional view of fret wire. You will need a 24in. length or two 12in. lengths, there being enough allowance in case of accident. This wire is obtainable at most local musical instrument shops. It is cut into suitable lengths and then tapped into the sawcuts.

Check the handle ⅛in. by ⅛in. for the nut which can be either a piece of hardwood or bone 1¼ins. by ¼in. by ⅛in. (see Fig. 2). Glue the nut in place and divide its rounded top into four as shown.

Suitable Finish

As a finish, the whole woodwork should be given a coat of clear varnish stain or polished. When dry, insert the pegs and affix the gut strings, the end knots fitting in behind the bridge kerf. Reading from left to right, the instrument is tuned to G.C.E.A. or according to the key in which melodies are played. A felt plectrum is used; but most players are content with strumming with the thumb.

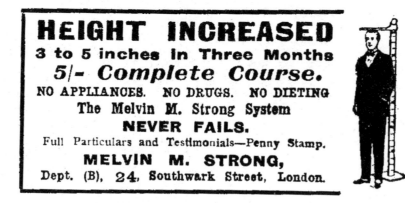

EXCURSIONS

A WOODEN GAS MASK BOX

CAMP WIND-BREAKS

A TOBOGGAN FOR GRASS SLOPES.

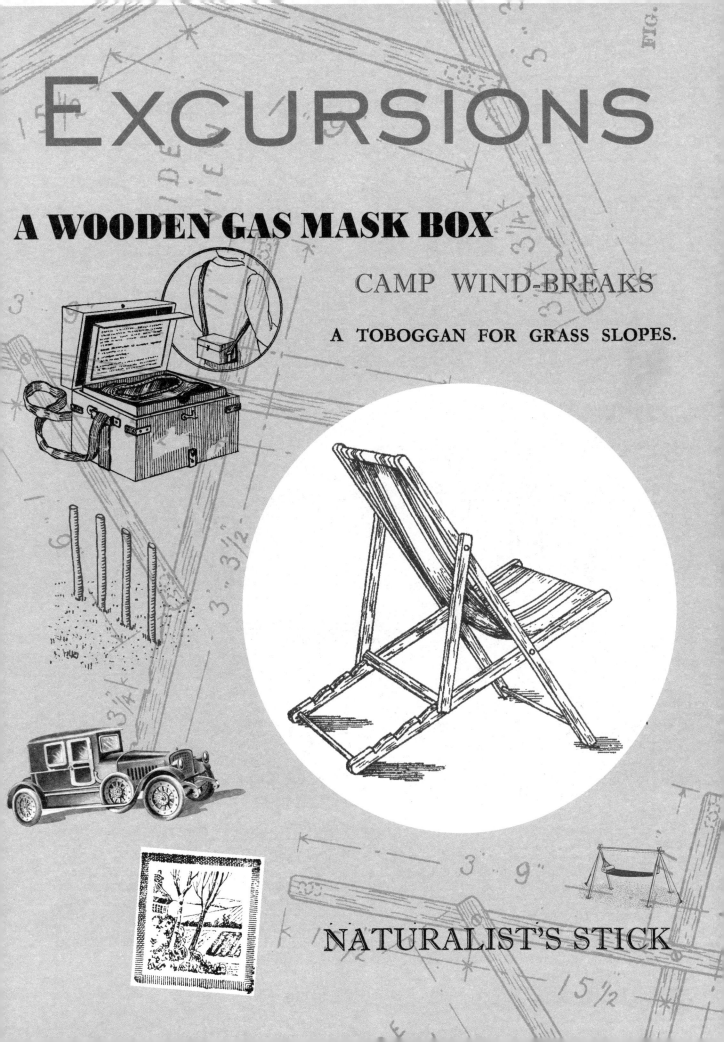

NATURALIST'S STICK

A Garden Hammock Support.

THE amateur carpenter can turn his hand to many things, and in the summer days naturally turns his thoughts to something suitable for outside use. His is the opportunity to make many useful things at considerably less than half the cost of the same things bought in a shop. For that reason the hammock holder illustrated here is sure to appeal, not only because of its usefulness, but also for the ease with which it can be made. As can be seen it consists of two uprights at each end held together by two cross pieces.

This simple framework is made the more inexpensive because all the parts are of a standard size, so that any timber merchant will cut the boards out to the dimensions required. A good hard wood should be asked for, and the wood can be bought in its rough stage straight off the

or 1½in. boards, and all ends are rounded off except the four resting on the ground. These should be left square for the time being. Run the plane down the edges to take off the sharpness of each corner.

The boards are all held together by bolts, which pass through, and are held by double nuts in order to lock them securely. Five bolts are required altogether—three of these to be fairly long. All of them must be stout and threaded well down. The two end supports are held at the top end with one of the bolts, a hole being drilled through them about six inches from the end. The two other boards are fitted one on each side, and are there bolted quite tight. A little recess should be made where the uprights come against these supports in order to make them the more steady. An end view of

saw. This will, of course, necessitate planing, but no great work will be involved in this because the wood has not to be finished as carefully as in ordinary work. Moreover, it will be given a coat of paint or creosote when completed.

All four parts are eight feet long, and can be either 3ins. or 4ins. wide. They are cut from 1in.

the uprights and cross pieces is given to show the detail. As can there be seen, the bolt must pass right through, and be fixed quite tight. In this way the uprights are held firmly, and the cross pieces are prevented from slipping. The uprights thus take the whole of the weight.

In addition to the bolt at each end another should be put through the centre as can be

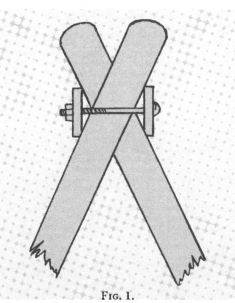

Fig. 1.

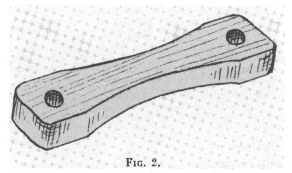

Fig. 2.

the supports, and is tightened up round the tent peg by means of a wooden sliding block. This can also be cut from a piece of waste wood to the shape shown at Fig. 2.

The bottom of the uprights are now put their proper distance apart, and the bottom end cut level with the ground as can be seen in the picture. The whole frame is now ready for use, and the hammock is slung between from each end. There is plenty of room for an ordinary six-feet swing, and the height is ruled by the slinging ropes at the ends.

seen in the picture. A thick block of wood is placed between the two boards, and a hole drilled right through all three parts. Then put the bolt in place, and fix the nut on the opposite side quite tight.

To prevent the frame having any side play a rope is fixed and drawn out to a tent peg driven into the ground at an angle away from the supports. The rope is tied round the top of

As previously mentioned the whole of the woodwork should be treated with paint or creosote. If paint is used a nice shade of green should be used, and two coats put on to make it entirely waterproof.

A TOBOGGAN FOR GRASS SLOPES.

DURING the summer, slopes where the grass is short, often become extremely slippery, so much so that anyone who tries to walk up or down feels almost as if he was on ice. On such a surface it is possible to get just as much enjoyment with a toboggan as one would on a snow covered hill-side. A simple form of to- boggan, which is very easily made, is on the lines shown in the sketch. Ob- tain two staves from an apple barrel ; these tubs are to be found in fruit shops almost everywhere and, as they mostly come from overseas and are not return- able, they are com- monly broken up for firewood. A piece of wood for the seat will also be required and this should be about fifteen inches long and seven inches wide. As well a narrow strip of wood

for a foot rest will be needed. A suitable length for this would be twenty-two inches. Place the barrel staves on the ground and then nail the seat across the inner side about five inches from the end. The foot rest is placed at the other end of the staves a similar distance away and fixed securely. At the ends of the foot rest holes are bored through which a strong piece of cord is knotted to play the part of reins for the toboggan.

It is worth paying a little attention to the under side of the runners of the tobog- gan as the smoother these are the better. First of all rub with coarse, and then finish with fine glass-paper. You can now make a start on a grassy slope and you will find that as the sport proceeds the surface becomes more and more slippery.

Add to your comfort by erecting these
CAMP WIND-BREAKS

GOOD campers never go to camp to be uncomfortable. Indeed, they do all they can to make the alfresco life as easy and cosy as possible, and have absolutely no time for the tenderfoot type who thinks he must of necessity suffer the utmost limits of discomfort when living in a canvas home.

Certain more spartan conditions have to be put up with, of course, but the old pioneer never believes in being cold when a little ingenuity will make him warm, or lying on a hard bed when a softer one can be made.

A beginner has to be a tenderfoot at first, but he should quickly grow out of this stage and bring his inventive faculty to work in the making of helpful items. Fighting nature is half the fun of camping.

Simple Barriers

The comfort-producing gadgets that old-timers can turn out are almost without end and one of the most useful is the 'wind-break'. This can be anything from just a low barrier behind which you sit, to a larger protection, say, for the camp fire. But a 'wind-break' is not a hut and its purpose is just to put something between yourself and a steady wind that may come sweeping across the camping ground for days on end.

Such winds are not necessarily cold, but they can be a nuisance, blowing about any papers you are holding, or in the case of the cookhouse, blowing leaves and bits of grass into the food. So a 'break' is really very handy.

The simplest wind-breaks are made of bracken which is usually plentiful during the camping months. A good amount is required and the collecting should be generous. The fronds are pulled as low down as possible and care must be taken while bringing in to prevent the tops from becoming broken. Crushed limp bracken is useless for the purpose in hand.

For Sitting

Fig. 1 shows a low wind break for sitting behind. Required are four stakes which are placed as shown, driven into the ground. The bracken is then interwoven in strands (two or three pieces together) alternately passing behind and in front of the uprights. The main thing is not to have the uprights too far apart and to be liberal with the bracken. Press each alternate 'strand' well down on to the one below before putting in the next.

By adding supporting pieces as seen in the inset, this wind-break can also become a back rest, the whole gadget becoming a tight and very cosy retreat behind which to read and enjoy the sun without the nuisance of the breeze.

A similar but much taller 'break' can be made for the camp fire (as Fig. 2). Here quite long stakes are required, nearly as big as a person standing, and a cross-bar is lashed on top as (a). It is best, too, to put up guy lines to give full rigidity against the blast.

Quite a lot of bracken is required here and the good camper will not think it beneath his dignity or lowering to his pride if, should there be an odd ground sheet about, he uses this for part of the filling.

It cannot be stressed too much that the old-timer uses whatever he can to attain his purpose, and is not tied down to set rules, but the good pioneer also finds that generally he can get all he wants in nature's storehouse if he looks far enough, and that he has seldom to solicit the aid of commercial items.

A more elaborate 'wind-break' for the cooking fire is shown in Fig. 3. Here we fit a roof also, which is a second framework made quite separately, with a cross bar at the top and bottom, thinner bars going in between. There will not be much strain at the intersections and the lashings can be of quite a simple type. The 'binder' need be no thicker than strong string.

Lash the Roof

Required also are two further stakes (b) slightly taller than those at the back. The roof is placed on top of the break already erected and lashed, the front end thus being held by the two taller uprights. The arrangement is now complete, and if well erected and the stakes sunk a little distance, it will stand quite nicely, but final rigidity is best given by four guy-lines attached as shown and set out at a slight angle.

In making a roofed break like this, do not fall into the common error of making it just too low, which means

continual stooping.

The best of shelters of the kind described is that once the frame is up you can keep improving this with little trouble, even to the day that camp is broken. Then the 'breaks' should be taken carefully apart, the bracken

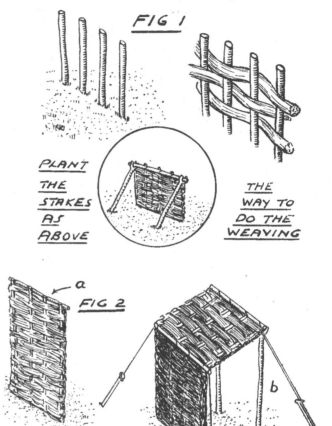

FIG 1

PLANT THE STAKES AS ABOVE

THE WAY TO DO THE WEAVING

FIG 2

FIG 3

either burnt or buried, and the stakes put away out of sight, for nothing looks worse than a camping ground with derelict and broken-down gadgets lying about.

Safe Storage

If you will be using the ground again, the stakes could be stored somewhere and retrieved for further use later on. Should the ground be used by you as a week-end patch, then there is no doubt that the owner would let the wind-breaks stay in position during the intervening days, but see the owner of the ground about this.

Also make sure that the breaks are really solid and that they will not scatter bits all over the place should a really extra strong wind happen along.

Careful selection in the first place will prevent this likelihood.

Carry your impedimenta easily inside this bamboo
NATURALIST'S STICK

THE field naturalist, whatever his particular calling, is often encumbered with a great number of small articles which are very necessary for his work. It is possible to carry many of these in an unusual and useful way, and this article is intended to show how a walking-stick, which in itself is a most valuable asset to the naturalist, can be improvised for the purpose.

The stick itself is of bamboo, about 1½ins. diameter, and this can be purchased from a shop or furniture dealer. It should be about 3 ft. long overall and have only two joints, equally spaced on its length. Burn and hollow out the top to a depth of a few inches, and fashion a small block which will fit tightly or screw into the hole.

This should not be as long as the hole burnt into the stick, as on to the bottom of the new block may be fastened a small trowel or spike which will be most useful for digging up pupae specimens. It can also be stuck into the trunk of a tree to assist in climbing and can be screwed firmly into the base of the stick. Into the head may be fitted a small compass. This should be sunk so its surface is level with the end of the stick, and there is little likelihood of its becoming broken as it is normally shielded by the hand.

Hollow inside of Stick

The complete portion of the bottom joints of the stick is then hollowed out in the same way. This gives a receptacle of 2ft. or so in length. To take the place of the original wood make a small wooden bar of a few inches which fits easily into the hole.

This bar should in turn be hollowed, and the end which will be the end of the stick when it is in position should be shaped so that it will plug into the stick, and also have two small holes drilled into it. A small brass ferrule will strengthen this base of the stick, and prevent it from splitting.

The two small holes are for a loop of wire which may be carried in this hollowed block, together with a fine net which will roll and fit easily into the space as well. This net is useful for catching butterfly specimens and water animalcula. If the ferruled end of the new block fits into the hollowed end of the stick a few extra inches can be added to the stick as a whole if this is ever required.

A small test tube should be carried in the hollow portion of the stick. When netting water specimens this can be fastened to the bottom or centre of the net with an elastic band, and while the water drains from the net the specimens will sink into the tube.

What can be carried

What is carried in the remaining space in the stick is largely a matter of choice.

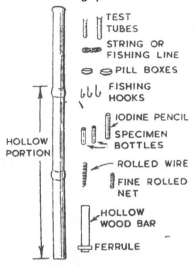

TEST TUBES
STRING OR FISHING LINE
PILL BOXES
FISHING HOOKS
IODINE PENCIL
SPECIMEN BOTTLES
ROLLED WIRE
FINE ROLLED NET
HOLLOW WOOD BAR
FERRULE

HOLLOW PORTION

What the hollow stick can hold

Several small phials may be inserted, as these are always required. A tube of methylated spirits, some cotton wool, string, fishing line and hooks, screws, an iodine pencil, a tape measure, dipping-tube, a small bottle or two. All these can be carried and there should still be some space left. Several small lenses will also take up very little room.

For Measuring

The length of the stick can be marked off with a knife into feet, and will be found a useful measuring-stick. It can then be used to measure heights. If the rough height of a tree is wanted drive the stick into the ground, mark its shadow, and measure it. Then measure the length of the shadow of the tree from which its height can thus be calculated.

An Improvised Telescope

A useful observation glass can be made simply which is easily used in conjunction with the walking-stick. The best lenses for this are a convex 1.50 and a concave 16 or 20. These numbers represent the strength of the glasses. In the lid of an empty blacking tin or a similar one cut a hole about the size of a silver threepenny piece, and place the concave lens in the lid.

To make it fit tightly cut a strip of cardboard and glue it firmly round the inside of the lid to make the lens sit in position. Over the lens glue a piece of black paper with a hole about ⅛in. in the centre. The eye-piece is then complete, and on to it should be soldered a 'screw-eye'. This is screwed into the 'eye' end of the walking-stick when the observation glass is used.

From the bottom half of the tin cut a circle almost the size of the convex lens, and mount the lens inside with a cardboard ring as before. On to the rim of this half of the tin solder the stem of a ferrule which will slide up and down the walking-stick. When in use a strong elastic band will be sufficient to keep this sliding object-lens in a desired position.

It will be realised that when the observation glass is in use one sees all round the object-lens as well as through it, but this is to some extent an advantage as the object to be focused is easily seen before the observation lens is brought upon it. The two lenses are best carried in the pocket when not being used in conjunction with the stick.

An air hole or two may be drilled in the hollow part of the stick, and such specimens as lizards, beetles, and larvae can then be carried inside without them dying.

This simply-made walking-stick will be seen to have a multitude of uses, and is really an invaluable aid to the naturalist.

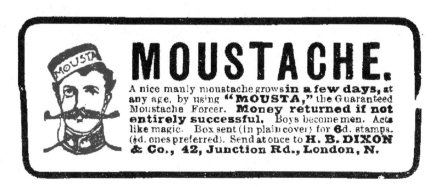

THE CONSTRUCTION OF A DECK CHAIR.

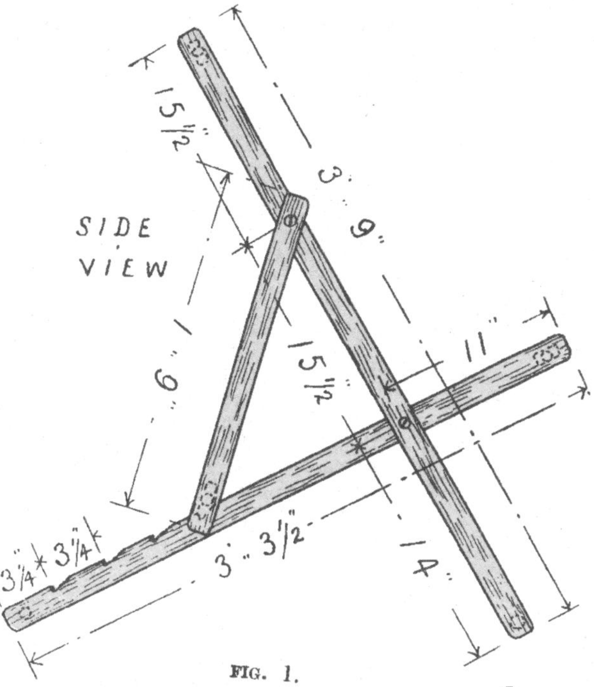

THE chair here illustrated is a folding one, suitable for use on a deck or a lawn. Its seat is of canvas, and the angle of its back is adjustable. The wood may be birch, or almost any kind of hard wood that is available. Ordinary deal could be used, but in that case it would be desirable to slightly increase the sectional measurement of the pieces, in order to give sufficient strength. Dimensions are given on Figs. 1 and 2. Fig. 3 shows how the rigid joints are made, the ends of the pieces fitting between being shouldered down to fit a centre bit hole, about ⅝in. diameter, which does not go completely through the piece it is bored in. A wire nail driven through at right angles secures the joint. An alternative to shouldering down the ends is to cut them to the right length for fitting between and bore then to receive a short length of dowel rod, which projects to form the pin. It will be seen that the two distance pieces nearest the ground are not rectangular in section, like the others, but are simply lengths of dowel rod.

The chair consists of three main parts, each of which must be framed together separately. First there is the seat portion, consisting of two long rails, united at the front by a shorter one of similar section fitting between, and at the back, which rests on the ground, by a length of ⅝in. dowel rod. Next there is the back of the chair, a little longer, but made precisely in the same way, with a rectangular rail at the top and dowel rod at the bottom. The third portion, which supports the back at the angle required, has a distance piece at the lower end only and the edge of this piece is bevelled to fit the notches in the sloping seat rails. There are four of these notches 3¼in. apart by about ¼in. deep.

When these three portions are made they are united by screws, with two washers between the wood at each point of union. Suitable canvas is tacked on as seen in the first illustration.

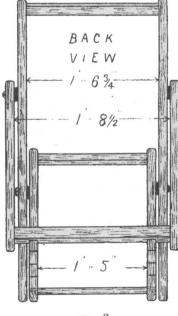

FIG. 1.

SIDE VIEW

15½"
3' 9"
1' 9"
15½"
11"
3¾" 3¾"
3' 3½"
14"

BACK VIEW

1' 6¾"
1' 8½"
1' 5"

FIG. 2.

FIG. 3.

¾"
1¼"
⅝"
1¼"
¾"

For all

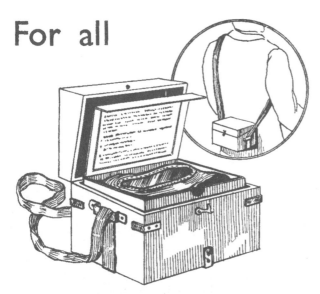

weathers you need
A WOODEN
GAS MASK BOX

•◦•◦•◦•►◄•◦•◦•◦•►◄•◦•◦•◦•◦•◦•◄

When all six parts are fixed thus, the two measurements shown in Fig. 2 one at the front and one at the back of the case should be drawn on and a pencil line made all round the case. Grip the box in a vice and use a small-tooth tenon saw for sawing round the lines.

The case will need to be moved from time to time so the saw does not bind and is prevented from clearing itself during cutting.

Care must be taken when putting the case together in the first place to see there are sufficient screws to hold all parts securely together during cutting and afterwards when the lid portion is severed altogether.

Hinges and Catch

It is now only necessary to add a pair of 1in. brass hinges to hold the parts together. The hinges should have their flaps " let in " so that the two parts of the case fit closely together.

The lid should be strengthened inside by gluing around some strips of ¼in. triangular fillet (Fig. 2).

Two stirrups should be made by angling up some pieces of brass strip about ½in. wide, and drilled for receiving the round-head fixing screws.

The case might be also strengthened by adding four or six angles plates (No. 101, sold by Hobbies at 6d.).

A stout hook and eye completes the case excepting for the paint which should be applied in two coats.

A tough wood such as beech or Spanish chestnut would be best for making up the case.

IN wintry weather it will be obviously necessary to consider the best type of case to make, for carrying your gas mask. We learn that it is detrimental to the mask itself to allow moisture to get at it, and that it should be folded carefully to prevent damage to the rubber.

The cardboard container supplied with the mask is ideal for size, but it affords no protection against rain and snow, and the wet would soon penetrate it and in time the mask would probably be ruined.

Hold the Whole Container

A light wood case seems to be best for protection, and we describe here how to make one up from fretwood, ¼in. thick. It will hold the cardboard container within this wooden case, and the only part to be cut away from it is the side flaps which fold down underneath the top cover.

The instructions on " Packing the Respirator " can therefore be retained, and this inner lid will form a further protection against dust, etc.

The box has a hinged lid, the front of which is made a little deeper than the back to allow quick and easy handling.

The Construction

The construction of the case is shown in Fig. 1. The two sides (A) are nailed or screwed to the ends (B), and over these are fixed the top and floor (C). The holes for the screws—these should be used in preference to nails—must be bored and the tops countersunk so the heads are flush and neat.

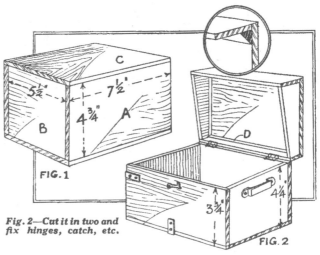

Fig. 2—Cut it in two and fix hinges, catch, etc.

```
CUTTING LIST

A.—Two pieces 7½ins. by 4¾ins. by ¼in.
B.—Two pieces 5¼ins. by 4¾ins. by ¼in.
C.—Two pieces, 7½ins. by 6ins. by ¼in.
D.—Two pieces, ¼in. triangular fillet 7ins. long.
D.—Two pieces ¼in. triangular fillet, 5½ins. long.
```

Look out for details how to make a complete Home Cinema shortly. Don't miss it!

THE BOY SCOUT WOODWORKER.

HOW TO MAKE WOOD JOINTS.

AS every Boy Scout knows, proficiency badges are awarded in connection with a very large number of subjects, and it is the ambition of every true Scout to become honestly entitled to at least a few of them. One of the most coveted badges is that given for proficiency in woodwork, the design of which is shown in the heading above. Every Scout into whose hands this special number of *Hobbies* falls should—if he has not already done so—endeavour to qualify for passing the test in woodwork. It is hoped that the following notes will be of some assistance in helping many fellows to pass it.

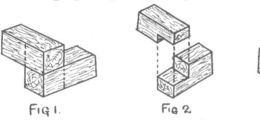

FIG 1.   FIG 2.   FIG 3.

One of the most important branches of woodwork, and one which distinguishes the skilled worker from the " dud," consists in the making of good joints. It is a fairly easy matter to put articles together with nails and screws, but really, no woodworker worthy of his craft will be satisfied until he has mastered the art of making all sorts of joints.

Without attempting to make up any particular article, therefore, it is worth while to practise this branch of the work for its own sake. Get some special wood for the purpose then, you fellows—some nice, soft, even-grained wood, from 1½ins. to 2½ins. square—and just practise making joints ; and don't be content until you have become—in your own estimation at least—really smart at the job.

You will need— among other tools —a square, a carpenter's pencil sharpened to a very fine point, and a tenon or back saw, about 12ins. long. It is, of course, assumed that you have a suitable bench to work at, with other accessories available. So now for a few practical tips.

FIG 5.   FIG 6.   FIG 7.

Half-Lap.

To make a half-lap or corner joint, cut two pieces of wood about 6ins. long, and see that they are nicely trued. Lay one of them down on the bench, and lay the other piece across it at right-angles, so that the corners come together, exactly, as shown in Figure 1. Then with your carpenter's pencil mark the breadth of the top piece on to the lower one. Next, mark on each piece the depth of the cut to be made, so that when the two pieces are fitted together, they will be of the same thickness as a single piece of wood. Lay each— in its turn—flat on the bench, and saw firmly

across the line you have drawn, down to the line that indicates half the thickness of the wood.

FIG 4.

Each piece should then be held upright, preferably in a vice, so that the cheek pieces may be cut away. To do this, hold the saw firmly, and saw downwards, cutting parallel to the edge of the wood.

To fix the joint, smear a little glue upon one piece only, and press firmly together. Figure 2 shows the corner joint ready for fixing, and Figure 3 shows the finished joint.

Bearing Joints.

A bearing joint is used for joining beams required to support fairly heavy loads. Mark off the width of the cut upon each piece, saw through half the thickness of the wood, and with a wide chisel remove the spare parts from each piece. Figure 4 shows a bearing joint ready for glueing, and Figure 5 a completed joint.

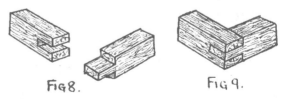

FIG 8.   FIG 9.

Bridle.

A bridle joint is generally used in door frames, and in fact in any frame where a horizontal beam has to rest upon two vertical

posts. To mark out this joint, lay both pieces of wood flat on the bench, and bring their ends together. The thickness of each piece is then divided into three equal parts. Mark round the end of each piece. Stand one piece on its end and cut out a groove, as indicated in Figure 6. Then stand the other piece on end, and cut away the two outside portions, so as to leave a projecting tongue, as shown in Figure 7. Figure 8 shows this form of joint ready for fixing, and Figure 9 shows the job complete.

Dove-tail.

Now try a halved joint (dove-tailed). In this joint a tenon, both sides of which are of wedge form, is cut to fit accurately into a corresponding notch. The arrangement will be clearly seen from Figures 10 and 11, the

FIG 10.

former showing the joint ready for gluing up, and the latter the finished joint.

Other forms of joint which should be practised by the boy scout woodworker include the tongue-and-groove joint, single and compound dovetail joints, blind or hidden dovetail joints, mortise-and-tenon joints, scarfed joints, and dowelling. Scouts will find an instructive article on this subject at page 115 of Hobbies' 1929 Catalogue.

FIG II.

Further, articles on woodworking appear in *Hobbies* from time to time—also many interesting things to make.

There is no knowing how useful a practical knowledge of woodworking may be to you in later life, so now is the time to learn, and—BE PREPARED. .

A CLUB ROOM TABLE AND BENCH.

IN a Scouts' club-room, it is desirable that most of the furniture should be adapted for folding up, so that sufficient floor space may be available for games and sports. The following article will thus appeal strongly to handymen-scouts and woodworkers, since

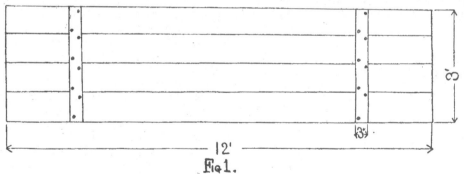

Fig 1.

required. These planks are joined together by stout battens, 3ins. wide, which are fastened to the underside of the boards by screws arranged in staggered formation, as shown in the sketch. The wood should preferably be from ¾-in. to 1in. thick, and should, of course, be well planed.

The table is supported on trestles of the type shown in Figure 4. Trestles to carry the table top above described should be 3ft. wide × 2ft. 6ins. high.

The construction of the hinged members (or frames) of the trestles will be seen by reference to Figure 3. Four of these frames will be needed. They are hinged together in pairs at the top. A hole is bored through each of the lower cross bars, through which a piece of

the table and bench described not only have the above characteristic, but are easy to make, and very effective in use.

The table top may be of any desired size, that illustrated in Figure 1 being 12ft. long × 3ft. wide. It is made by taking a few planks of the desired length, the number of these being sufficient to make up the width of table

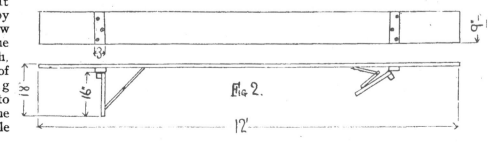

Fig 2.

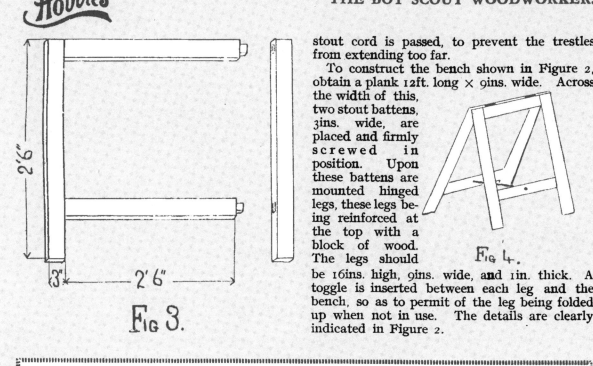

Fig 3.

Fig 4.

stout cord is passed, to prevent the trestles from extending too far.

To construct the bench shown in Figure 2, obtain a plank 12ft. long × 9ins. wide. Across the width of this, two stout battens, 3ins. wide, are placed and firmly screwed in position. Upon these battens are mounted hinged legs, these legs being reinforced at the top with a block of wood. The legs should be 16ins. high, 9ins. wide, and 1in. thick. A toggle is inserted between each leg and the bench, so as to permit of the leg being folded up when not in use. The details are clearly indicated in Figure 2.

A STAVE-RACK.

MOST scouts appreciate the importance of neatness and efficiency, yet they know only too well how very untidy headquarters appear, when staves are left lying about promiscuously in the patrol room. The remedy for this is to construct a stave-rack.

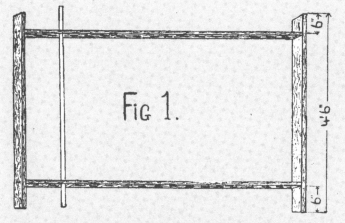

Fig 1.

The rack described below, and illustrated in Figure 1, properly fills the bill. It is not only useful, but quite ornamental, and is extremely easy to make. It comprises two upright supports, 4ft. 6ins. in length, 3ins. wide, and of

½-in. thickness, and two cross members, also 3ins. wide and of ½-in. thickness. The latter are bored throughout their length with a series of holes 2ins. in diameter, as illustrated in Figure 2.

The length of the cross pieces will depend on the number of staves which are to be kept in the rack. The cross pieces are connected to the uprights by passing screws through the uprights from their outer sides.

The rack, after being suitably stained or painted, is placed against a wall, and secured thereto by means of brass eye-plates. A tab containing the name or initials of an individual scout can, if desired, be fixed in front of each hole, so that everyone will know just where to look for his own property.

The rack above described, when it is full of staves, looks remarkably well.

Fig 2.

Don't miss "Hobbies" when on your Holidays.

When are you going to put up those shelves?

SET OF HANGING SHELVES.

THE WINTER LOG BOX

Small Revolving Bookcase

How to Make a Small Revolving Bookcase

THE small revolving book-case illustrated has been designed on very simple lines to hold paper-bound pocket-sized books. It is, accordingly, quite light in construction, but there is no reason why the various dimensions should not be modified to make a much larger case, though the inclusion of an extra shelf will cause slight complications.

If made to the sizes suggested below, the case may well be of softwood finished with brush lacquer or enamel. In fact, such a treatment would be preferable to the use of a stained and polished hardwood, for lacquer will more effectively conceal the butt joints used for the assembly.

Measurements

Wood of ⅜in. or ½in. thickness is used for the upper part of the book-case. The top and bottom are 9ins. square, while the uprights (of which there are four) all measure 9ins. high by 4½ins. wide.

The end-grains of all uprights are glued and they are fitted between the top and bottom, flush with the outside edges. They are held there by oval-headed panel pins, which must be driven well down, and the holes made good with plastic wood. The arrangement of these uprights will be seen in plan view on drawing (A), and it will be seen that each upright occupies the right-hand end of each side when seen from the front. Assuming that wood of ½in. thickness has been used, the dimensions of one side of the completed case will be as given at (B).

This upper case is connected to the base by means of a short threaded bolt of ½in. diameter. The bolt fits down through a hole drilled in the middle of the book-case bottom, and must be a very tight fit; about 1½ins. of bolt should project below the bottom of the book-case.

It is essential that this bolt be so tight

that it cannot revolve inside the bookcase, and there are several ways of ensuring this. If the head of the bolt is sufficiently large one or two fine holes can be drilled through it so that it can actually be riveted to the wooden bottom; alternatively a suitable metal cement can be used to hold the bolt sufficiently tightly.

The head of the bolt is covered with a small block of wood, the size of which will depend on the bolt-head. This block is hollowed out on the underside and is simply glued into place. The block also provides an alternative method of securing the bolt, as the recess in the block can be made to the exact size and shape to make movement of the bolt-head impossible. Drawing (C) gives a view of the centre of the bottom of the book-case showing this block with one side removed to show the hollowing.

This completes the constructional work on the top part of the case, but if desired it can be made neater in appearance by putting an overlay or half-turning on each of the four upright members, or moulding roun bottom.

The Base

The base of the book-case offers plenty of scope for decorative work, but the simplest type is illustrated at drawing (D).

Wood of about 1in. thickness is the most suitable for the base and a piece 4ins. or 4½ins. square is needed. A chamfer measuring ⅛in. each way is worked around the four top edges of the wood.

In the centre of the top of this base a recess is cut in which a nut can be fitted. Again, this nut must be perfectly immovable, which can be arranged either by riveting it down into place, or by ensuring that the recess is a perfect fit for the nut.

A hole of slightly less than ½in. diameter is bored into the centre of the part-thickness of wood remaining below the hole in the centre of the nut. It is then possible to thread the bolt on the book-case down through the nut in the base. This threading will probably be found rather tight at first, but the metal will soon cut suitable channels in the soft wood. The book-case should be screwed down to its full extent, then any thread projecting beyond the bottom of the base can then be cut off.

The assembled book-case is then ready for glasspapering, followed by its lacquer or enamel treatment. A minute quantity of grease can be put on the screw-threads to make the case revolve more easily, and a square of baize glued to the underside of the base to prevent its scratching the table top. (F.H.T.)

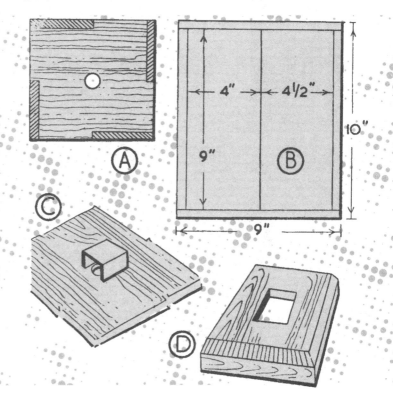

A MODERN WALL BRACKET

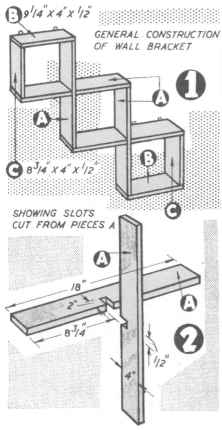

GENERAL CONSTRUCTION OF WALL BRACKET

B 9¼" × 4" × ½"

C 8¾" × 4" × ½"

SHOWING SLOTS CUT FROM PIECES A

18"

2"

8¾"

4"

½"

The following materials may be obtained from Hobbies Ltd, Dereham, Norfolk or from any Hobbies branch or stockist.
Three pieces stripwood 36 in. by 4 in. by ½ in. price 11/-, postage 1/6.
Decorette transfer No. 137B price 2/3, postage 6d.
Wallhangers No. 121 6d. per four, postage 3d.

AS a special wall feature, or as a means of displaying small plants or ornaments, this type of wall bracket illustrated on the front page is ideal.

The diagrams in Figs. 1 and 2 show how to use Hobbies standard stripwood 36 in. long by 4 in. wide and ½ in. thick. Four pieces A are halved together in pairs, and completed by adding the pieces B and C.

The exact size of piece A is indicated in Fig. 2. The halving joint will, of course, be a tight fit, and care should be taken to see that saw cuts are made on the inside of the lines. Naturally, if these pieces are cut from standard lengths of stripwood, the measurements will be scant to allow for the width of saw cuts.

Use glue and nails when assembling the pieces, and wipe off excess glue before it has time to dry. This is particularly important if the wood is to be stained and varnished, because excess glue will seal the wood and prevent the stain from taking.

The appearance of the bracket can be further enhanced by the judicious use of suitable materials for backing the individual 'boxes'. Fig. 3 shows how a coloured print from a magazine can be mounted on a piece of plywood or hardboard, and held in place by ¼ round beading. Other subjects which would be equally suitable are old calendar pictures, jigsaw pictures, and original photographs. For instance it would be a novel idea to enlarge the best of your family snaps, and use it as a backing. Those who are proficient in marquetry might like to design a special panel as a background.

Transfers, too, can be used to good effect. The Decorette No. 137B of zonal pelargoniums looks well if mounted on to plywood and glued to the front of the bracket, as indicated in Fig. 4. Cut roughly round the shape with a fretsaw

COLOUR PRINT, PHOTO OR MARQUETRY PANEL HELD IN PLACE BY ¼ ROUND BEADING AND BROWN PAPER PASTED ON THE BACK.

DECORETTE 137B ON WOOD. GLUE TO FRONT OF UNIT

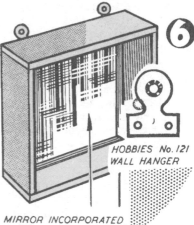

HOBBIES No. 121 WALL HANGER

MIRROR INCORPORATED IN ONE UNIT TO GIVE PLEASING REFLECTIONS

before gluing in position. Some idea of this attractive coloured transfer is shown in the sketch in Fig. 5.

A mirror cut to size and inserted as in Fig. 6, gives a pleasing effect. It will reflect the beauty of ornaments or cacti.

The finish of the wall bracket may be stain and varnish or paint. In any case the wood is rubbed down well with glasspaper. Fill the grain with woodfiller, and lightly rub down again with fine glasspaper. Now stain or give an undercoat of the colour required. Finish off with a top coat of high gloss paint, or with clear varnish.

The bracket may be hung by means of wall hangers as in Fig. 6.   (M.h.)

FIG.1

Wе all know during the dull wintry weather how welcome a brightly burning fire is, and how a good dry log or junk of wood thrown on the fire helps to brighten a dismal room. The unfortunate part is, however, the wood burns away all too quickly and this therefore necessitates keeping a good supply of wood always handy. A convenient box kept in the fireplace recess would at this time of the year then prove a useful and necessary piece of furniture for the dining room or living room.

We illustrate a box of convenient size and of simple construction. The decoration on the front of the box is in the grotesque Maori style, and this being in low relief carving should not be found difficult for our amateur woodworkers to execute. At Fig. 1 we show a general view of the box, and from this it will be seen how the front and back are made to project beyond the ends with bar handles connecting same, and how the lid is hinged, etc.

Taking Fig. 2, which is a sectional plan of the box, we note that the internal dimensions are 1ft. 3ins. long by 10ins. wide inside, by 9¼ins. deep.

The Sides,

These are shaped from pieces of ¾-in. or ⅞-in. stuff and are 1ft. 9¾ins. long by 10ins. wide. The curves are so slight at the ends of these boards that it

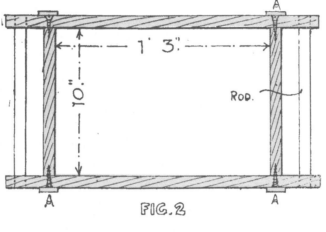

FIG.2

will be a simple matter to mark them out from the detail of the front, Fig. 3. The shaping may be carried out with the fretsaw and all edges smoothed up with sandpaper.

Having done one side, this should be laid on the second piece of wood and drawn round so that both may be identical. Two holes must be made for the handles in each piece 1in. from the end edge and 1in. from the top surface. These holes are made with a ¾-in. brace and bit.

The carving to the front of the box should be carried out, of course, before the various parts are assembled, we therefore at this stage put in hand the drawing out of the design and the chiselling. A series of simple curved and straight lines comprise the outline, which may be drawn in from the front view Fig. 3. The actual work of carving is done with flat gouges and matting tools, the whole being only slightly cut down. A good deal of the work may be carried out

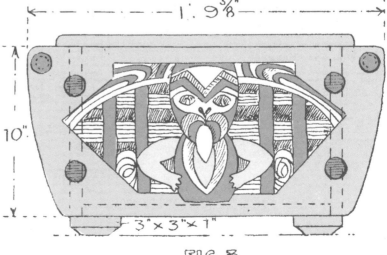

FIG. 3

THE WINTER LOG BOX.

with the veining tools, with the background recessed and finished with a fine matt.

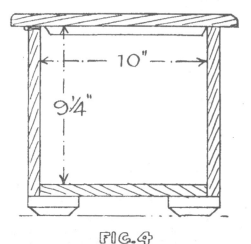

FIG. 4

The Ends.

The ends are plain square pieces measuring 10ins., these are simply screwed to the front and back, the screw-holes being slightly countersunk and afterwards covered by ¼-in. cut discs 1¼ins. in diameter, as shown at A, Fig. 2. The positions of the ends may be marked off on the two large pieces, as shown by the dotted lines on Fig. 3, the holes for the screws being kept central with the ends.

Floor.

This, again, is a plain piece let in between the sides and ends and measures 15ins. by 10ins. Countersunk screws are used for the fixing of this piece, the holes being neatly filled, or stopped, at completion.

Handles.

Two ⅞-in. diam. rods 11½ins. long will be required for these. They will be carefully cleaned up and let into

FIG. 5

the two long sides and glued. The ends where they appear through the sides will be covered with four circular discs cut from ¼-in. wood, 1¼ins. in diameter and glued on.

The Lid.

This should preferably be made up from two pieces planed up and jointed together. If one piece of stuff is used the full width shown, it is liable, unless a thoroughly seasoned piece can be obtained, to warp and twist out of shape. If, however, a good glued joint cannot be made, it is recommended to place on the inside of the lid two stiffeners, as shown in Fig. 5. The lid measures 1ft. 6ins. long by 1ft. 1½ins. wide, and the edges should be shaped slightly, as shown in Fig. 3. The two stiffeners each measure

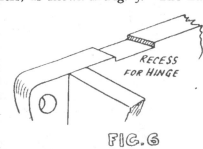

FIG. 6

9½ins. long by 2½ins. wide, and their positions must be carefully set out so that when the box is closed they fit securely inside, as illustrated in the section of the box, Fig. 4.

It now only remains to screw on the hinges and form recesses for the flaps of same in the back of the box, as shown in the detail Fig. 6. To keep the box raised from the floor four simple feet are made and secured to the floor. Four pieces are first of all cut 3ins. square, from 1in. thick stuff and to these are glued four more pieces having a chamfer worked on all edges. Long screws driven into the floor hold the feet securely and form a satisfactory finish.

A SET OF HANGING SHELVES.

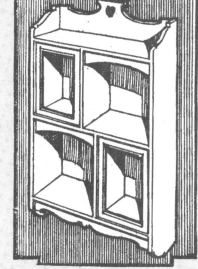

THE handy set of shelves shown completed by the drawing on this page can either be carried out exactly as about to be described (apart of course from possible alterations of the main sizes), or it may be varied in several ways, the chief of which are as follows:—first, the filling in of the back might be omitted entirely, or only put to the two small cupboards, the width of the shelves, etc., being varied accordingly; secondly, the cupboard doors might be omitted entirely, or tenoned together in the orthodox manner: for such a case as the present, however, it will be found quite efficient to simply make them of mitred picture-moulding, or the idea of glazed doors might be abandoned in favour of solid ones as at a in Fig. 1; here three narrow widths of board all slightly v-jointed at their edges are held together by means of two small "ledges" on the inner face where shown by dotted lines: the ornamental hinges indicated (No. 5350), as well as the

various handles, etc., will be met with in Hobbies 1915 Catalogue.

Any of the usual varieties of wood may be employed, and practically a minimum $\frac{1}{2}$in. thickness for the two sides, with $\frac{3}{8}$in. for the residue of the work will suit, especially if oak be adopted. Exclusive of the back (which might be of good three-ply) the wood required will be a 5ft. 6in. length by 7in. by $\frac{1}{2}$in., 10ft. of 7in. by $\frac{3}{8}$in., and 7ft. run of a plain rebated oak picture-frame moulding, unless solid doors are substituted.

Fig. 7 will serve to show the main construction, and the work may be commenced as follows:—The sides b and c 7in. by $\frac{1}{2}$in. and 2ft. 7$\frac{1}{2}$in. long all shaped top and bottom to the curves set out in Fig. 6; next the three horizontal shelves are prepared, 6$\frac{1}{2}$in. by $\frac{3}{8}$in. (7in. by $\frac{3}{8}$in. if the back is omitted) and 19$\frac{3}{8}$in. long, a rectangular piece $\frac{1}{2}$in. by $\frac{3}{16}$in. being cut out of the front corners as at d in Fig. 4, leaving projecting ends which should be housed into

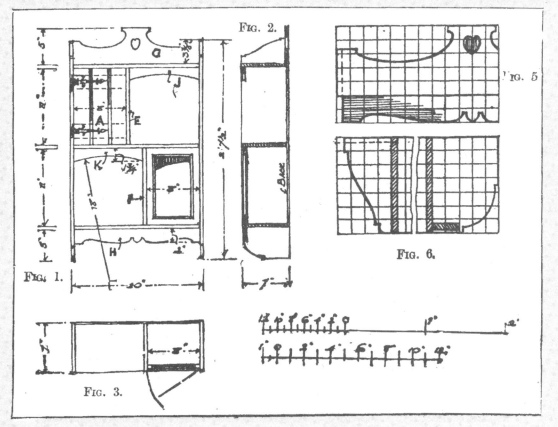

FIG. 1.   FIG. 2.   FIG. 3.   FIG. 5.   FIG. 6.

grooves $\frac{3}{8}$in. wide and $\frac{3}{16}$in. deep in the sides at the levels dimensioned in Fig. 1; these grooves of course stop $\frac{1}{2}$in. back from the front edges. At this stage the work should be found

FIG. 4.

fairly rigid when fitted together, and the next step will be to put in two intermediate uprights as at *e* and *f* in Fig. 1; the second of these appears also in Fig. 7, and they should both be 6$\frac{3}{4}$in. or 7in. wide according to whether a back is included or not.

The most economical manner in which to set out the shaped and pierced pediment (*g*, Fig. 1) and valance (*h*) is shown in Fig. 5, which represents a little more than half the entire piece. The lower portion (partially shaded) will enable the reader to accurately set out the valance when the actual work has been divided into a corresponding number of inch squares, and the pediment is cut out of the remainder of the same length of wood, 7in. wide, all the curves being kept long and flowing.

After these parts have been fixed, the one flush with the back and the other $\frac{1}{16}$in. behind the front edges, two arch-pieces may be prepared as at *j* and *k* in Fig. 1, 1$\frac{3}{4}$in. wide and shaped to a curve obtained with a radius of about 18in.

These should also be fixed $\frac{1}{16}$in. back and

will then leave only the doors to complete. The latter can be of mitred picture-moulding with the glass either beaded or puttied in position, and they will require careful fitting in the openings. Little shelves can easily be fitted across the cupboards if desired, and would serve if wide enough instead of the doorstops otherwise required.

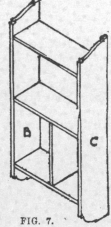

FIG. 7.

Small bullet-catches are the neatest form of fastenings for this class of work, and had best be obtained either direct from Hobbies Ltd. at Dereham, or at one of their branches or agencies, together with the little brass plates for hanging, two of which should be screwed to each of the back edges of the sides.

Fig.   **ILLUSTRATIONS.**

1.—Front view showing alternative cupboard doors.
2.—Section through centre.
3.—Plan through lower cupboard.
4.—Detail of shelf housed into side.
5.—Detail setting out of curved pediment and valance. Each square represents an inch full-size.
6.—Similar detail of sides.
7.—Diagram sketch of main construction.
8.—Scale for Figs. 1 to 3.
9.—Scale for Figs. 4 to 6.

A BOOKREST such as here described is of practical value to those who find it necessary to have at hand a number of volumes for ready reference. It forms a useful part of the equipment of any writing-table for certain year books, the familiar Whittaker, a railway guide, an address book, a dictionary or thesaurus frequently have to be provided with accommodation within reach of the writer. Such a bookrest, while serving a quite prosaic purpose, need be no eyesore, but, made on the lines indicated, becomes an engaging feature well deserving a place on table or shelf by reason of the attractiveness of the design as well as its manifest uses.

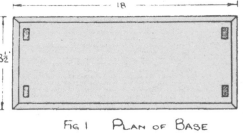

Fig 1   Plan of Base

It is quite easily made by any amateur woodworker, and is one of those jobs that can be taken up and finished in an hour or two, before interest slackens and is a handy way of using up odd ends of hardwood left over from larger jobs.

Suggestions.

Now the kind of wood to be used may be determined by the destined setting. If intended for a gift we would ascertain whether the table on which it was to stand was of walnut, mahogany or oak or any other wood, and see that we matched this if possible. Any of these woods should be eminently suitable and there are even great possibilities in inferior or soft woods such as pine, spruce, sycamore, or birch, especially if we are inclined to paint them in some of the bright enamels that are sold for this purpose. Indeed, a great deal can be said for painted furniture, especially for painted odd articles, for these give joyous splashes of colour here and there in what might otherwise be a drab and uninteresting interior.

Construction.

Now let us look at the essentials of construction. These are quite simple. The ends are merely tenoned into a base that has been prepared to a given size and moulded on the edge. The mortises are marked over, bored out to near the size and pared exactly with a chisel. The ends, whatever shape is decided upon, are fretcut first and cleaned up, and the bottom edge planed square. A gauge is then set to the thickness of the base and this line scribed on both sides of the ends from the bottom edge. The tenons are then marked in their correct positions, cut down, and the outer portions of the shoulders sawn. The portion between the tenons may be partly cut away with a bow-saw or fretsaw, and then pared. The edges of the shoulder should be set in carefully to the scribed line with a chisel and mallet. The tenons are glued and wedged from underneath. Four turned flat balls are fastened

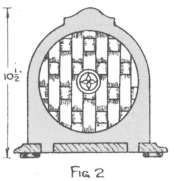

Fig 2

by screws or brads underneath, and if circular pieces of felt are glued to the bottom of these there will be no risk of scratching a polished surface. Approximate sizes are given in the diagrams, but these may be varied according to requirements.

The base is shown in plan at Fig. 1. In Fig. 2 is a design of the end worked with a circular panel that will give scope for a little carving. It is set out carefully and by slight relief an interlaced or basket-work effect is produced. The centre portion is carved as a patera. Fig. 3 will give some scope for those who prefer inlay as a medium for ornamentation. On mahogany, satinwood crossbanding would be used. In oak, black and white chequer board design of inlay would be very effective.

How to Finish.

As to polishing. the most permanent finish for an article of this kind in constant use would be a waxed finish. Carefully scrape and paper all surfaces. Stain, if required, to the desired shade of oak by means of Brunswick black dissolved in turpentine. Darken mahogany by a solution of bichromate of potash. Walnut needs no stain. Oil with raw linseed, fill with some suitable filler and when quite hard clean down with fine paper and give one or two coats of brush polish. This is finally cut down with No. 0 paper and finished with beeswax. Polishing is best done before the final assembling of the parts.

A cutting list for Bookrest to the sizes shown would be as follows :—

				Length. ins.	Width. ins.	Thickness ins.
1	Base	..	..	18	8½	¾
2	Ends	..	..	10½	7	¾
4	Turned Bases.					

An Easily Made Plate Rack.

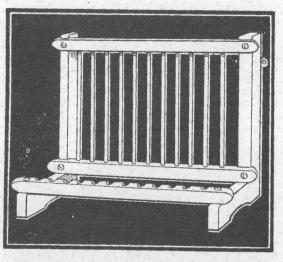

THE plate rack shown at Fig. 1 is of a convenient size for an ordinary family, and it may be easily and quickly made at home by the handyman possessing a few ordinary tools.

It is first made in four portions, consisting of the rack divisions, a front rail, and two ends, which are afterwards assembled by screwing together. Well nigh any kind of wood may be used, and seeing that the parts are in narrow strips, opportunity offers for using up waste pieces in making the rack, only such stuff should be sound and free from knots.

The Rack Divisions.

The divisions are shown at Fig. 2; they are made by preparing two rails 1ft. 8½ins. long by 1in. square, and fitting eleven dowel rods between them. The rails should have recesses 1in. wide by ¼in. deep cut on one edge, and spaced 1ft. 5ins. apart, the ends beyond the recesses being rounded over. The rods are 10½ins. long by about ⅜in. round, holes ½in. deep being bored in the rails so that the rods may be fitted in, as shown at Fig. 2. The holes for the rods should be equally spaced between the inner edges of the recesses in the rails. Screw-holes are bored through the recesses, and the rails and rods are then knocked up to form the complete rack division.

The Front Rail.

Fig. 3 shows this rail complete. It is 1ft. 8½ins. long by 1in. square, no recesses are cut in its ends, but screw-holes are bored to correspond with those in the rails of the rack divisions, and the ends are similarly rounded over. In addition, twelve equally-spaced hollows are cut on one edge of the rail to correspond in position with the spaces in the rack division.

The Ends.

Two of these will be required, each being formed with a back rail 1ft. 2ins. long by 2ins. wide by 1in. thick, and a bottom rail 8½ins. long and of the same section. The rails are half-lapped, glued, and screwed together at right-angles, as shown at Figs. 4 and 5.

Assembling the Parts.

To do this, take the rack divisions and fit the recesses in the rails over the back rails of the ends, and fix in position, as shown at Fig. 4, with long round-head screws. Then fix the front rail to the top edges of the bottom rail of the ends, as shown in the same illustration, using similar screws.

This rack may be hung to the wall or used as a standing rack. If it is hung, strong fixing plates should be screwed to the back edges of the ends, the plates having holes through which nails or screws may be driven into the wall, while the rack will stand much more firmly if the bottom rails of the ends are slightly hollowed.

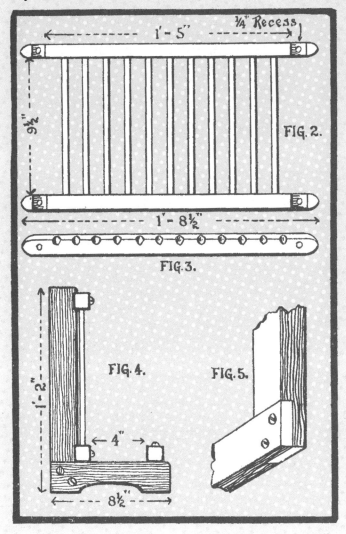

FIG. 2.

FIG. 3.

FIG. 4.   FIG. 5.

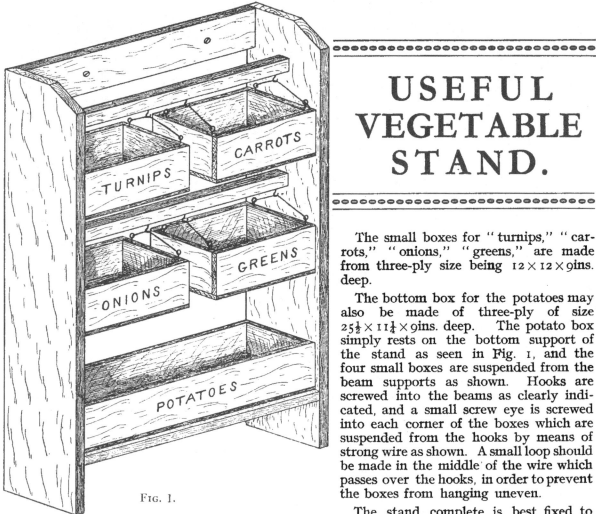

FIG. 1.

USEFUL VEGETABLE STAND.

The small boxes for "turnips," "carrots," "onions," "greens," are made from three-ply size being $12 \times 12 \times 9$ ins. deep.

The bottom box for the potatoes may also be made of three-ply of size $25\frac{1}{2} \times 11\frac{1}{4} \times 9$ ins. deep. The potato box simply rests on the bottom support of the stand as seen in Fig. 1, and the four small boxes are suspended from the beam supports as shown. Hooks are screwed into the beams as clearly indicated, and a small screw eye is screwed into each corner of the boxes which are suspended from the hooks by means of strong wire as shown. A small loop should be made in the middle of the wire which passes over the hooks, in order to prevent the boxes from hanging uneven.

The stand complete is best fixed to the wall in some convenient spot by means of Rawl Plugs, or if there is woodwork to fix to screws alone will, of course, obtain a fixing.

IT is most convenient to arrange vegetables in the home in such a manner that they are easily and readily obtainable at any moment. A suitable position may be found where a stand indicated by Fig. 1 may be fixed, into which the various kinds of vegetables may be kept. The stand may be varied in size if required to take other kinds of vegetables.

Details of the stand are given in Fig. 2, where A is the front view and B the end view. The two side supports should be of strong wood and cut to size given. The two one inch square section pieces for supporting the boxes are cut from strong wood, also the top fixing piece and bottom supports for the potato box. Having cut the pieces, the stand may be built, which is best done by fixing the pieces together with screws, the heads being sunk a little below the surface of the wood, after which they may be filled in with a little putty.

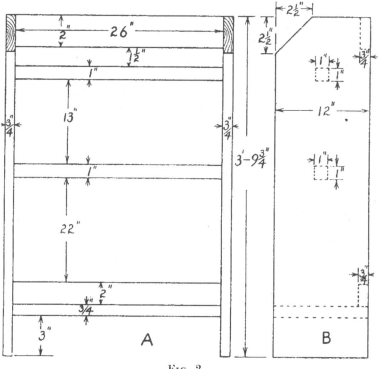

FIG. 2.

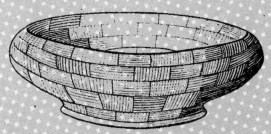

MAKING CHARCOAL AT HOME

Patience, pins and glue are needed for making this
MATCHSTICK VILLA MODEL

Scrap pieces of wood and two methods of making
A TURNED WOODEN BOWL

WASTE NOT
WANT NOT

The use
of
"Bits and Pieces"

TREE-TRUNK
CARPENTRY

SAVE
FOR
VICTORY

You can mystify your friends with this
NOVEL MILITARY MONEY BOX

NOVEL MILITARY MONEY BOX

THE quaint little figure money box herewith should surely be a further incentive to Save for Victory, and at the same time provide a simple piece of work for anyone with a fretsaw and a few odd pieces of wood.

The patterns are provided on Cover 11 of this issue, and can either be traced out on to wood, or actually cut in the paper and pasted down. The novelty is that the actual slot for the money box is hidden behind the face of the soldier.

A Moving Head

As shown in the smaller detail, you lift the head portion and that reveals the slot to take the coins. This head works up and down in a slot which is cut in the front, but is prevented from falling forward by a little disc piece glued on behind.

The back view of the detail of the model herewith (Fig. 1) shows this quite clearly. The various

How the money enters

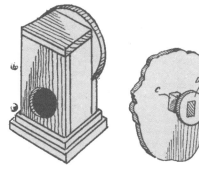
Fig. 1—A rear view   *Fig. 2—Back view of head before cut in two*

parts are cut out from any small pieces of wood, and as most of them is only a plain rectangle, the actual size is given with the patterns.

All are 3/16in. thick, and the grain should run in the direction indicated by the arrow in each instance. The actual construction of the box itself is seen at Fig. 2.

In cutting the parts be sure to get the edges straight so they may be butted up against each other, and there glued securely. Mark the dimension of the various pieces on to the wood, then cut out with a tenon saw or a fretsaw.

Box Construction

The base B is glued centrally on to the top of base A, and then the front and three other sides glued on. The front, in addition to the outline, has the horizontal slot for the money, and the upright slot which accommodates the moving piece C later.

Glue the two sides between the back and the front. Notice in the back there is a 2in. diameter hole cut which is afterwards covered up with stiff brown paper.

For Taking Out

This hole is for the extraction of the money when the paper is removed. The top is a plain piece glued over the back and sides, and so fitted that it does not project over the front itself.

The head portion is cut completely to outline first, then a sawcut is made from side to side through the line of the mouth and put just beneath the ears. This cuts it completely in two.

The lower piece is glued just below the slot on the front where indicated by the dotted lines.

The upper piece is glued to the spindle piece C which passes easily through the upright slot.

To prevent it falling forward, the circular disc piece D is fixed on the other end and glued to form a washer piece as can be seen in Fig. 2. See the head piece moves easily up and down in this slot, and if necessary give a rubbing of graphite to provide this.

The Wording

It is essential, of course, to do all these moving parts before the top is added, so you can easily get to them. The lettering can be cut from ⅛in. wood or painted on, or cut out in some fancy material.

When complete the whole box should be painted up in bright colours of enamel. The face can be left with the paper upon it or you may be able to paint up very carefully in the correct shades.

If you have a friend who wears this type of cap you can easily add his own badge and then follow out the colouring of the whole box with his regimental colours.

A NOVELTY MILITARY MONEY BOX

D

SAVE FOR VICTORY
LETTERING

BACK

2⅝"

4½"

1"

2⅝"

1⅞" TOP

3"

2¼ BASE B

3¼"

2½" BASE A

4½"

SIDES
CUT TWO

C

OVERLAY

FRONT

SAVE
FOR
VICTORY

Patience, pins and glue are needed for making this
MATCHSTICK VILLA MODEL

HAVE you patience and a fondness for making miniature models of things? If so, here is a suggestion on how to make a tiny cottage entirely from used matchsticks. It is, as you can see, a simple, plain affair, complete with a small garden and surrounding railings.

There is no need to finish off the model in colours. You will naturally want people to see that it has been constructed from matches. If you desire a bright and gay little model, however, the roofs could be inked red, with the sides of the house and railing inked green.

Another idea is to whitewash the outside of the cottage and colour the door and windows green. Alternatively, you could ink the roof with blue-black stuff (gives a slate colour), with the outside of the cottage red, the door, railings and base being inked green. A piece of green baize is glued on the base to suggest a patch of grass.

Beginning the Construction

Of course, the first thing you have to do is to collect a lot of used matchsticks. They should,

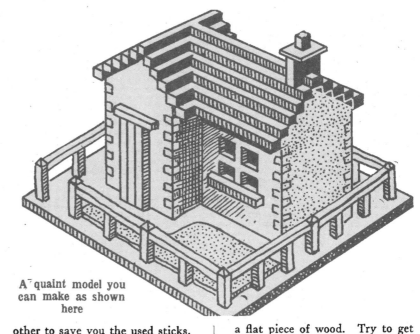

A quaint model you can make as shown here

other to save you the used sticks. In no time, a large number will accumulate, all being the same thickness and length.

With a penknife, or a razor blade, start to build up three end gables in the manner shown at Fig. 4. When you have done that, using tube glue as an adhesive, make a door from three lengths of

a flat piece of wood. Try to get the sticks evenly in length and square at the ends. Don't use bent or twisted matchsticks. They give a lot of unnecessary bother, and don't have the sticks plastered with too much glue. A thin smearing of glue will ensure a stronger and neater job.

The Assembly

To assemble the parts, take the two end gables (with doors) and attach the sides (shown at Fig. 6) to them. Square the work and set aside until dry. Meanwhile, take the other (plain) gable end and attach the gables (at Fig. 4) to it, then square and set aside.

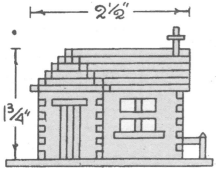

Fig. 1—Front elevation

as much as possible, be all the same length and thickness.

The cottage is made easily from matchsticks 1⅞ins. long by nearly ⅛in. square. When you have collected quite a bundle of them, pick out all the clean, full-length ones. Broken, half-burnt pieces may come in useful in the assembly of the cottage sides or the base, so do not throw them away.

It is imperative that the matchsticks are the same thickness. If your mother or dad uses a particular brand of match, ask one or the

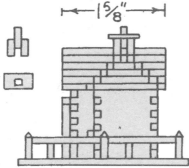

Fig. 2—Side view

matchstick, with a piece affixed on the top to serve as a lintel. You must add a door to two of the end gables only.

Now make two side gables, as shown at Fig. 4. Note how the window aperture is formed. The small upright, central divisions are added lastly, then the window sill. Two more side gables, slightly larger, but constructed in the same way, are required, one being shown at Fig. 6.

By the way, whilst gluing the pieces together have them laid on

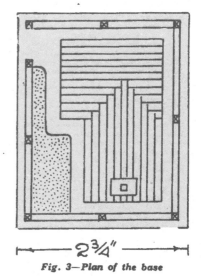

Fig. 3—Plan of the base

You now need a piece of ⅛in. wood for the base, the size being shown at Fig. 3. You can build up a base from matchsticks as detailed at Fig. 5. Build it on a flat surface. Having squared the ends evenly by rubbing with glasspaper held in a block of

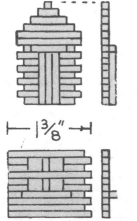

Fig. 4—*End view and side piece*

wood, the surrounding pieces are attached, these serving to make the base stronger.

When the base has been allowed to dry, glasspaper its surface lightly to remove any roughness. The cottage parts are also lightly glasspapered (with fine 1½ grade), then glued together on the base (see top plan at Fig. 3).

The Roofs

The roofs can now be attached.

You need eleven 1⅝in. long pieces, these being attached in formation to the cottage part shown at Fig. 2. Eleven 1⅞in. pieces are attached from this roof to the other end gable, as seen at Figs. 1, 3 and 6.

The chimney is made up from three short lengths as shown at Fig. 2. A thin piece of wood, with a square hole in the centre,

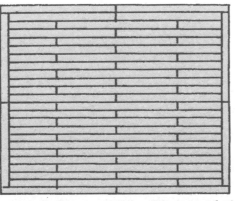

Fig. 5—*How base can be formed from matchsticks*

fits over the projecting central piece to form a ledge. Attach the pot in the position shown.

The thin piece of wood forming the ledge could, by the way, be made up from split matchsticks, or you could use the square sections and reduce the ledge to half thickness by glasspapering, then fit it over the chimney pot.

The Railings

To affix the railings, make holes

for the nine post pieces, the position being shown at Fig. 3. The posts are about ½in. long when sunk in the base, with the tops pointed.

Neatly-fitting lengths of matchstick are glued between the posts. Supporting pieces ¼in. long are glued between the rails and the base. If desired, holes for these

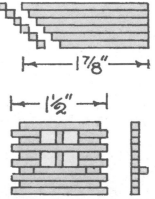

Fig. 6—*Showing shape of roof sticks with another side piece*

could have been made in the base so that the rails rest more firmly on top.

Well, your model cottage is now complete and only remains to be finished in any of the ways stated. It is a distinct novelty in itself and too good as a toy for some little girl who would probably have it broken in pieces in no time.

It is just the thing to exhibit in a War Charity effort.

MAKING CHARCOAL AT HOME

CHARCOAL, is not a very cheap thing to buy, and there are several uses for it. When you are preparing the fibre in which to plant your bulbs, you need charcoal to mix with it, and if you keep fowls, a little charcoal is an excellent thing to put in their food. You cannot make fireworks without charcoal either.

Making charcoal is quite an interesting process. First of all you secure a tin with a lid that fits closely—a syrup tin is just the thing. Bore a hole in the lid, and into this fit a small cork, which has also been holed to take a short length of piping. Almost any sort of piping will do, and if you can fix an old gas burner on to the end of this, all the better.

Firing the Mixture

Now fill your tin with short pieces of dry wood, as tightly as you can, packing it well down, and jamming the lid on. Put it on the fire, made up of red hot coals giving off a nice red glow.

Very soon, steam will commence to filter through the pipe. It will increase in speed until there is quite a strong jet of it, and if you apply a lighted match to it, there will be a faint flicker at first, increasing in strength until it grows to quite a strong flame.

Several Substances Left

Leave the tin on the fire until this gas ceases to come off, then set it on one side to cool. When it is quite cold, you may open the tin, and you will find a mass of black charcoal ready for use.

If you look at the sides and bottom of the tin, you will find a sort of tar, brownish-black in colour. This contains Paraffine, Naphthaline, and several other useful substances.

Marsh Gas and Wood Naphtha is the gas which came off, the latter being the stuff which is added to Methylated Spirits, and which gives it that nasty taste. Scientifically, it is known as Methylic Alcohol.

You can make lots of practical novelties by undertaking
TREE-TRUNK CARPENTRY

THERE is a tremendous lot of pleasure to be had from making furniture and gadgets from timber in its natural state. Tree trunk carpentry, as it is called, is an art that does not appear to be so popular as it deserves. It is possible to make some really useful and artistic articles from odd logs and branches of trees.

The work is not at all difficult and there is great scope for the handyman who will experiment and devise new designs. Much of the wood can be obtained from a timber merchant in the form of surplus offcuts, a bag of fire logs

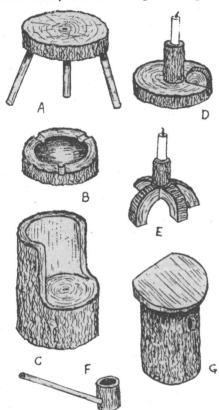

might even yield a few useful specimens; while a visit to the countryside should produce sufficient stock for all ordinary purposes.

The bark may be left on for some articles, or it may be stripped off and the wood polished, stained or varnished. The type of tree and the condition of the bark will generally determine this factor—some logs with a smooth solid bark look quite attractive left in the natural state.

Small Stool

The stool illustrated at (A) is quite an easy piece to start with and can be made from a 2in. slice off an oak, elm or beech tree. A piece 12ins. diameter is a suitable size, although if you intend to make a stool for children 9ins. would be ample. The thickness can be reduced to 1½ins.

Cut the three legs from dowel rod or a piece of broom handle about 1in. diameter and taper one end slightly. Drill holes three quarters of the way through the top so the legs are a tight fit, and tap home, applying a spot of glue if thought necessary.

The legs can be made to fit at right angles to the top, but they are much safer and also look better if they are splayed just a little. If the stool is for use in the garden the bark can be left on, but for indoor use it would be better to peel off the bark, glasspaper smooth and polish.

Table Mats

Table mats can be easily made, but they should not be cut too thick or they will look rather clumsy. Special care will be needed in cutting thin slices, and here a well oiled sharp saw will make the job comparatively easy. For the round mats a good size is about 6ins. Quite novel oval mats can be made by cutting the wood at an angle of about 45 degrees.

Teapot and flowerpot stands are just variations of the table mats made to other sizes. They can be left quite plain or variety can be given by fitting feet of different patterns.

The ash tray shown at (B) is a very useful article to make, and gives good practice in the use of a gouge. About 4ins. diameter and ¾in. to 1in. thick is about right. As the wood is end grain the job will be a little more difficult and the best plan is to drill a number of holes and then cut out the surplus wood with a gouge.

A pin tray is made on similar lines to the ash tray, but is a little smaller and has not got the grooves cut in the rim. It does not matter what wood is used for these two trays, although a hardwood is to be preferred.

A Child's Chair

The 'easy' chair illustrated at (C) is a more difficult job to tackle; not so much in the skill needed but rather as a test of patience. It is, however, well worth the time spent in the making and it is really surprising how comfortable a chair of this type can be. It is an ideal chair for summer days in the garden, and one or two on the lawn are quite attractive. Children are delighted with the miniature ones made specially for them, and will spend many happy hours in them.

A timber merchant will be able to supply a log for the job—probably an odd end of a trunk unsuitable for

cutting up into planks. It does not matter if it is a hardwood or a softwood—the difference will be in the time taken to cut out the wood, so, perhaps, a softwood would be best to start with.

A log 15ins. to 18ins. diameter and about 30ins. long will do for an ordinary size chair, while for a child's chair 12ins. diameter and 21ins. long will be ample. Commence by cutting out a quarter of the log, thus making it the shape of an 'L'. Do this by making a saw cut down through the centre, to be met by another cut halfway through the side of the log.

The Back

Next, the upper half of the log, which will form the curved back must be cut out with a chisel and mallet. A lot of time can be saved by drilling a number of holes with the largest bit you have and as close together as you can get them, and then chipping out with the chisel.

The seat can be left perfectly flat as in the illustration, or it might be thought more comfortable if made slightly curved. Do not cut the back out too thin, the actual thickness will depend somewhat on the kind and condition of the bark. Cut the wood as smooth as you can and give a final finish with glasspaper.

Quaint Candlesticks

The candlesticks illustrated at (D) and (E) are always useful articles to make, and quite easy too. The first one has a slice of about 4ins. diameter and about 1in. thick for its base and a piece of small branch for the stem. This can be any length to suit your fancy, and is either screwed on through the base or a hole can be drilled and the stem made a tight fit. A half circle of a small branch is fitted on the side to act as a handle.

The candlestick (E) is a little more tricky to make. Cut a slice about 1in. thick from a 4ins. to 6ins. diameter log, and cut this in half. Then cut out a semicircular piece from each, leaving the wood about 1in. wide. Join the two at the centre by cutting a slot half way through each—one from the top and the other underneath. The stem is screwed on from underneath, thus holding the two base pieces together tightly. The hole for the candle is bored out with a twist drill of the correct size.

Clock Cases

Clock cases made from small pieces of tree trunk can be very attractive and are easy to make. The one illustrated at (H) is for a small 2¼in. drum timepiece—the type that can be pushed in a hole from the front and secured at the back with two or three nuts.

Choose a piece of wood that will leave a margin of about 1in. round the clock, and slightly flatten the bottom. The semicircular base also has a flattened part or the top to fit on to, which is glued and screwed down tight.

A small hollowed-out trunk is an ideal home for a bird, and a few nesting-boxes in the garden will prove a source of enjoyment to all bird lovers. For the cheeky little blue-tits the internal diameter should be 4ins. and the height about 7ins. Most of the hollowing-out will have to be done with a twist drill and chipping out with a chisel. The bottom can be made fairly level with a red-hot poker.

A sloping roof is fitted which overlaps the trunk by about 1in. The hole for the bird to enter should be near the top and for a blue-tit has a diameter of $1\frac{1}{16}$ins. to $1\frac{1}{8}$ins. The best place for a nesting box is on the trunk of a large tree and where the sun does not shine direct on to the box.

A very simple hanging bird-table can be made from two circular slices of trunk held apart with three chains fixed into screw eyes. If the distance between the two is not more than 5ins. or 6ins., you will keep the larger greedy birds away.

The pipe smoker will revel in the variety of pipes that he can easily make. Cherry wood is the recognised best wood for the purpose, but experiments can be carried out with many other kinds. No definite sizes can be given as each smoker has his own fancies, both as regards size and design. The illustration at (F) shows a favourite pattern.

Only a few of the very many articles that it is possible to make by tree trunk carpentry have been described in this article. The keen handyman will be able to devise many more to adorn the home and garden, and also to form really attractive gifts, the giving of which will afford as much pleasure as the receiving.

Keep your eyes open in the country for suitable odd pieces which may lend themselves to this type of work.

Scrap pieces of wood and two methods of making
A TURNED WOODEN BOWL

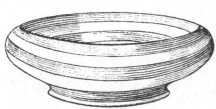

Made by the first method explained

ALTHOUGH at first sight this bowl may appear beyond the scope of the amateur lathe worker, it is not as hard as it seems. There are three methods of doing the job, the method depending both upon the skill and taste of the maker and upon the material available. Throughout the whole process the work is not taken off the wooden faceplate, although the whole may be taken off the headstock, that is metal faceplate with the wooden one still screwed to it as in the sketch.

The first thing to do is to prepare a piece for the base. This must be in one piece (marked C in sketch). Shape this roughly circular before fixing to the wooden face plate, placing a piece of thick paper between it and the face-plate (see sketch). This will enable you to get the work off easily when finished. In all three methods the basepiece is in one.

The Base

The base piece can now be turned to size and at the same time faced up ready for the fixing of the next 'course'. If method (1) is being used, the courses will be already cut and only need gluing in place, each course is faced up before the next one is placed in position and at the same time can be roughed out to the approximate shape.

Gluing

The greatest snag with this 'course' turning is waiting for the glue to set between turning one course and setting the other. This can be speeded up by using one of the synthetic glues that will set in times varying from half an hour to ten minutes. However, the maker will not usually be in such a desperate hurry that he cannot wait a few hours. If good cake glue is used, the next course can be fixed inside of two or three hours.

With method (1) the separate courses should be of different coloured woods. It also means that definite sizes are required to make the 'rings', whereas in the other two methods, any odd pieces

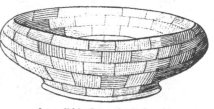

A small block method of making

can be used. Even the courses need not be of the same colour or wood throughout.

Carry on building up the courses and facing up until the required size is reached. Now, with carefully sharpened tools, finish off the bowl inside and outside. Finally finish off with glass-paper from medium to very fine.

Polish

The author finished his with a lump of bees wax held to the work while turning. Then a very coarse piece of sacking is held against the work (still rotating) and with gradually increasing pressure, the heat generated caused by the friction will melt the wax and it will be absorbed into the wood. If the pressure is kept up for a short time it will produce an excellent polish on the surface.

When satisfied with the finish, gently ease the whole job off the wooden face plate with a wide thin chisel. Clean up the under base and glue a piece of felt on to the bottom to prevent marking polished tables, etc.

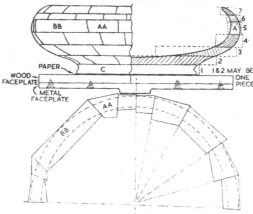

Details of construction with sections through

The Use of "Bits and Pieces"

NO one knows better than the average reader of Hobbies Weekly that it is amazing what can be done with odds and ends and a little mechanical skill. These pages are always full of valuable information on the art of converting the apparently useless into something useful, and although this often applies to small things, there is no reason why we may not embark upon more ambitious schemes.

Not long ago, two cabinetmakers at Ipswich spent their spare time building a steam launch. Now, as everyone knows, boat-building is a craft which requires a good deal of skill, yet these two men, without any expert advice on the matter, built a smart craft thirty-eight feet long, with a saloon that will hold a dozen people. Such a vessel ordered from a builder would cost hundreds of pounds.

A Back-yard Boat

A Cornishman too has built a twenty-foot boat in his back yard at Penzance. This was made from odd pieces of wood, mainly orange boxes. The only cost was that of the nails and fittings. Naturally he thinks nothing of the time he spent on it, because for one thing it was done in the evenings when his day's work was over, and so interested was he in the job, that he was only too pleased to be able to do it. Now he uses it every day for fishing.

A few amateurs at Leek got together recently, and built for themselves an aeroplane of the "Flying Flea" type. They took the engine from an old motor-cycle, bought paint and wing 'dope,' fabric, and some wheels, and now they have a model worth at least £60.

A House Costing £3

From America comes a rather amazing story of a labourer who was tricked into spending all his savings on a plot of land. After the money had been paid over, the man discovered that unless a house was erected on the land within six months, his purchase would be forfeit. The man had no further money with which to build the house demanded in the clause, but being a builder's labourer, he asked his employer if he might pick up the rubbish and odds and ends stored in the yard at the works.

His employer gave him permission, and within three months, the labourer, with the assistance of his two boys, had erected a bungalow twenty-feet square, having several good rooms, with bunks built against the walls, and surrounded by an excellently laid out garden and wooden fence. It had cost the man just £3 !

SEWING BOX MADE FROM CIGAR BOX.

AN ordinary cigar box, preferably one used for holding 50 cigars, provides a good container for reels of thread and other sewing materials. Two long aluminium knitting needles, such as can be obtained for a

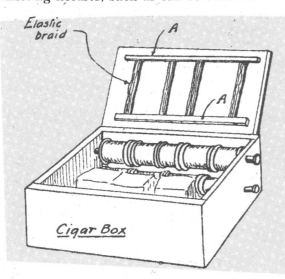

Elastic braid

Cigar Box

few pence, are fitted into holes drilled into the ends of the box. In the end at which the needles are inserted the holes are a loose sliding fit, while at the opposite end they are a little smaller so that the needles are held in place by friction, the spools turn freely on the rods, which need never be removed except when an empty reel is taken out to make room for a new one.

The remaining space in the box can be used for pincushions, scissors and other articles.

Two strips of wood, as shown at AA, may be screwed inside the lid, these two strips previously having bands of braided elastic glued to them. The pressure of the strips, when held by the screws provides a mechanical fixing for the elastic in addition to the grip of the adhesive.

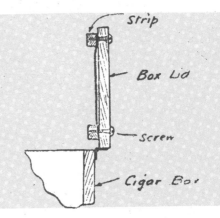

Strip

Box Lid

Screw

Cigar Box

These bands can be employed to hold tape and other light and long articles to be found in the average workbasket.

Novelty Christmas **TUMBLING CLOWN TOY**

"UGLY DUCKLING" TOY CART

BUT WE WANTED A PLAYSTATION!

How to make a **WOODEN SNAKE TOY**

Toy Sand Lorry

SAND AND BALLAST

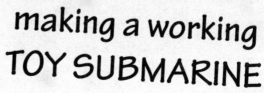

making a working **TOY SUBMARINE**

A TOY RAILWAY ENGINE.

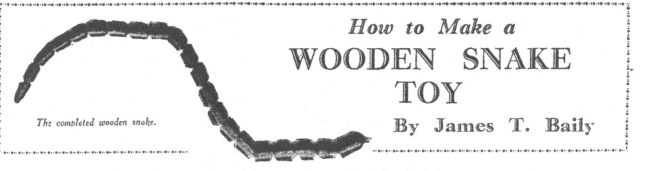

The completed wooden snake.

How to Make a
WOODEN SNAKE TOY

By James T. Baily

A REMARKABLY realistic snake can be made from wood by following the directions below. The snake is a novel toy; it writhes about in a realistic manner. The snake is made from two pieces of strip-wood, ½in. by ½in., which can be anything from 18in. to 24in. long. American yellow pine, canary whitewood, or Virginian red cedar are the best woods to use, because of their capacity to hold glue. Yellow deal, spruce fir, satin walnut, or mahogany are good alternatives. Plane one side of each strip, so that when the strips are placed side by

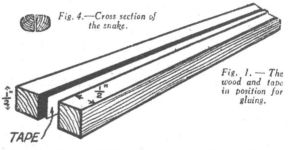

Fig. 5.—The snake held in position for cutting.

side they fit close together. Then get a piece of ½in. tape, and put it between these two planed sides, as shown in Fig. 1. Glue the tape and the strips of wood together and hold them in cramps for about 24 hours until the glue is thoroughly hard and dry. You now have a strip of wood ½in. thick and about an inch wide. With a plane taper one end, and shape the wood to the snake shape, shown in Figs. 2 and 3. Fig. 4 shows a section across the centre of the snake, to indicate how the edges are rounded. Taper the tail and finish with a file and sandpaper. Cut the open mouth with a saw and shape the head with a knife. Glue to the inside of the mouth a piece of tape, fork-shaped to appear like a tongue.

Cutting the Body.

Next, V-shaped pieces of the snake's body have to be cut away, so that he can bend and writhe about.

Figs. 2 and 3.—These diagrams show how the snake is cut from two pieces of wood.

The best way to do this is by using a bench block, as shown in Fig. 5. It is quite an easy job to make a cutting block like this. The two kerfs, or saw cuts, are at 60 degrees to the top of the block and are used to guide the saw when cutting the snake. A strip of wood, B, is fastened on the bottom board, C, to hold the snake secure, and the strip marked D is gripped in a vice. When sawing out the wedges of wood take particular care to avoid quite reaching the tape. The segments of the snake will easily move about even if a fine fibre or two of wood is left on the tape at each joint. In case you go too far, however, and the tape is cut, a repair can be made by sacrificing one segment and splicing.

The snake should be finished in realistic colours.

Fig. 4.—Cross section of the snake.

Fig. 1.—The wood and tape in position for gluing.

TAPE

Shades of yellow and brown paint, mottled and striped, look well. When the paint is dry, brush over with shellac polish.

THOUGHT READING WITH DICE.

THERE is a simple arithmetical trick done with a pair of dice, on the strength of which you can lay claim to powers of thought-reading or magic. Someone throws the dice, and without seeing them, you tell him what he has thrown. Ask the dice-thrower to double the number on the first of the two dice, add five, multiply the result by five, and, finally, add the number on the second die. When he tells you the result, you immediately name the number on each die. This you do by subtracting 25 from the total announced. This gives a two-figure sum, and the first of the two is the number on the first of the dice, and the other is that on the second. For instance, a 3 and a 5 are thrown. The thrower doubles the 3 and adds 5, making 11, multiplies by 5 and adds 5 (the second number thrown). Result, 60. Substract 25 and the answer is 35. If he takes the 5 first and doubles that, etc., the result will be 78, and your answer 53—5 and 3.

A TOY RAILWAY ENGINE.

CHRISTMAS is the time for toys, and most youngsters would revel in the possession of a tiny locomotive such as can be made from the patterns in the centre pages of this issue. This engine, by the way, is the first of a series we are bringing out for a complete model railway. Apart from the toy, therefore, the design should be made up really for the coaches, trucks, station, etc., which will come along later.

The picture above shows the finished engine and tender, whilst the detailed diagram gives the parts numbered as they are on the patterns. It is, therefore, a simple matter to make them up from odd pieces of fretwood always available. No special parcel of wood is made up, but all the parts can be made from $\frac{1}{8}$in. and 3-16in. of waste wood from other designs.

The completed model is just 11in. long, $1\frac{1}{4}$in. wide, and stands $2\frac{7}{8}$in. high. It is a simple matter to make it up from the num-bered details, and, in addition to the $\frac{1}{8}$in. and 3-16in. wood, 11in. of 3-16in. dowelling is required for the axle and a piece of broomstick or similar circular wood is wanted for the boiler, $1\frac{1}{8}$in. in diameter and $4\frac{3}{8}$in. long. These parts are not shown in detail with the patterns, but the sizes are given. The dowelling is cut into 8 pieces, $1\frac{1}{2}$in. long, for the axles, and 4 pieces, $\frac{1}{4}$in. long, for the buffer posts.

The main platform for building upon is numbered Part 1, and this is the main piece (in 3-16in. wood). Under it on each side are Parts 2 (also in 3-16in. wood) with eight holes in each large enough to allow the dowelling axles to revolve. They are glued to the underside 3-16in. inside the edge of No. 1, and support struts (3-16in.) are glued between at each end (Part 3). The eight axles are then put through, and the wheels fixed on with glue. Twelve of the wheels are $\frac{7}{8}$in. diameter, put at the rear of the platform. The four smaller wheels (all are 3-16in. thick) are placed two each side at the front end—as shown by the numbered diagram below.

The two parts 5, cut from $\frac{1}{8}$in. wood, are the support for the front of the boiler, and are glued to the upper side of the platform where shown by the dotted lines. Between them

TOY RAILWAY

Complete Model Railway Series.

—Sheet I.

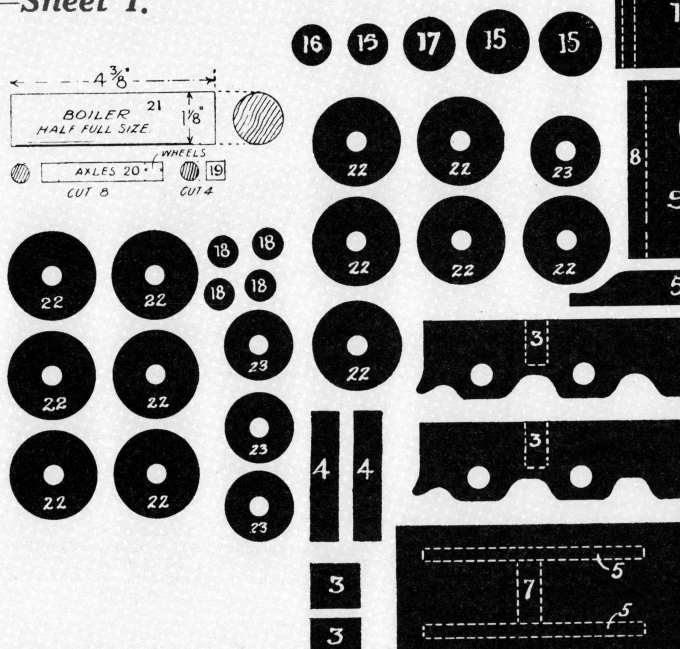

ENGINE & TENDER

is the 3-16in. piece (Part 7), upon which the lowest point of the boiler's diameter should rest. The back end of the boiler is held by the concave curve in part 6, which is glued against the front of the cab (Part 8). This is a rectangular piece, 3-16in. thick, and, on the outside, flush with the edge of the engine base, are the two sides of the cab, (Parts 9). The roof is formed by Part 10, and overlaps slightly the sides of the cab, as shown by the dotted lines.

This completes the actual engine, and only three pieces more are needed to form the tender. These are numbered 11, 12, and

glued between the funnel and the cab, and must be shaped with a circular top, as can be seen in both illustrations. With this, as with the funnel, the lowest piece of wood must be shaped out on the underside to lie evenly on the circular boiler.

Finally, we have to fix the buffers, front and rear. The buffer-plate is made by Part 4, which comes under the engine platform, and on the side of Parts 2. On to these plates is glued $\frac{1}{4}$in. of the 3-16in. dowelling, $\frac{1}{8}$in. from each end. The buffer ends are made of Parts 18, two being required at the front and two at the rear. They are cut from

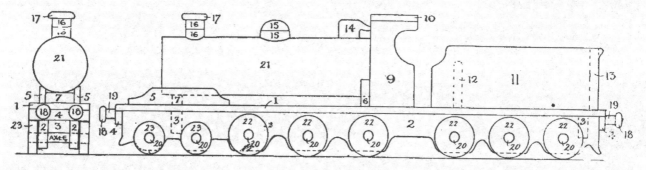

13, and are respectively the sides, the back, and the front. All are glued behind the engine to the top of the base, but whereas the back is put flush with the ends of the sides, the front (Part 12) is glued just $\frac{1}{2}$in. inwards from the other end of the sides.

On the top of the engine boiler are to come the funnel, steam-chest, etc. Part 14 is glued to represent a pipe leading to the cab. The funnel is made up of Parts 16 and 17. Two of No. 16 are required, 3-16in. thick, and are placed over each to hold up the top rim (No. 17). The two circles (No. 15) are

$\frac{1}{8}$ in. thick material, and glued over the dowelling.

As will be seen in the picture of the engine, a matted panel has been put in the side of the tender to relieve the plainness. The edges are chisel-cut straight lines. Those who care can add, either with thin wood or paint, the initials of one of their own district railway companies. The whole article can be given a coat of paint, and here again the particular railway chosen has a definite scheme of colouring which may very well be followed.

"UGLY DUCKLING" TOY CART

Fig. 1—The completed toy—19½ins. long and about 12ins. wide

"MAKE me something to play with, daddy," pipes a small voice, and dad—if he is doing nothing—wonders what new toy he can build easily and cheaply. We show herewith a simple enough pull-along cart—quite a small item as can be judged from the elevation—that should please any toddler. It is an excellent Xmas gift.

The whole thing can be made from scrap wood, even the wheels, if desired, these being eccentric to give the cart a novel "waddling" effect when in motion. Ordinary 3in. rubber-tyred wheels are preferred, however, if you can obtain them locally.

The Construction

The various diagrams provided almost suffice to explain the construction of the cart. You should use ⅞in. hardwood, like oak or birch, for the wheels and axles, with deal for the other parts.

The shaped side pieces are nailed (or screwed) to the end pieces, then the bottom fitted and attached (see Cutting List for sizes). The head of the duck, plotted in 2in. squares at Fig. 4, is cut out with a pad-saw, or bowsaw, and fitted and screwed in position. The axles (plain laths of wood) should be long enough to project about ⅜in. at each side when screwed underneath the bodywork.

Attach the home-made wheels with strong roundhead iron screws. Metal washers should be on each side of the wheels to facilitate movement and prevent undue strain and wear.

Enamelling the Work

The work is enamel-finished. Prepare the surface by glasspapering, then apply the foundation coat. Ducks are usually a mixture of brown and white, so you could paint the whole thing white and add the brown patches here and there, leaving a white patch for the eyes, the pupils of which can be black or brown.

Some ducks are all white, others brown with small patches of black and grey. The latter mixture makes an ideal "ugly duckling" effect. If you prefer bright colours, the cart could be coloured bright green outside and light red inside, the duck itself being a primrose or yellow colour, with the eyes brown and the beak an orange shade.

Suitable Wheels

The wheels could be any of the above colours, but red wheels against the green sides would be ideal, to contrast. When the enamel has dried, obtain a brass screw-eye and drive it into the "breast" of the duck for a cord as in the finished sketch.

Do not forget that a drop of oil applied to the wheels will prevent them squeaking. The axle screws should be fairly long, about 2ins. or 2½ins., so as to be deep sufficiently in the axle ends.

CUTTING LIST

2 body sides—15ins. by 6ins. by ½in.
1 front end—8ins. by 6ins. by ½in.
1 rear end—8ins. by 3ins. by ½in.
1 bottom piece—11ins. by 8ins. by ½in.
2 axles—10ins. by 1½ins. by ⅞in.
1 wheel piece—7ins. by 7ins. by ⅞in.
1 head piece—11ins. by 8ins. by ½in.

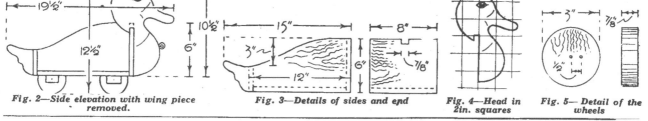

Fig. 2—Side elevation with wing piece removed.

Fig. 3—Details of sides and end

Fig. 4—Head in 2in. squares

Fig. 5—Detail of the wheels

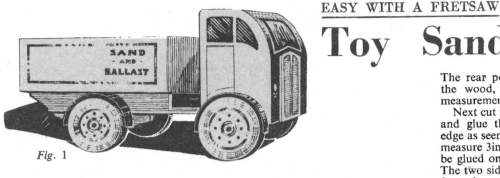

EASY WITH A FRETSAW

Toy Sand Lorry

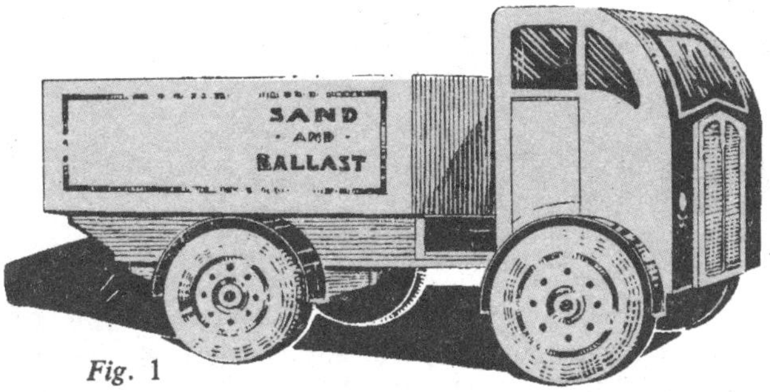

Fig. 1

HERE is a toy lorry made on the lines of those one sees about carrying sand and ballast. The overall length of the toy is 11ins., and the height 6ins., and it is made up in two distinct sections—the cab, with front wheels attached, and the rear box container, with back wheels.

These two sections are pivoted together so as to permit the toy to turn corners and turn about realistically.

The Cab

Commence by making the cab portion. It will be best, perhaps, to first glance at the picture of the finished toy, Fig. 1, to get an idea how it will look when completed and painted up. Wood ¼in. thick is used throughout, and it is so designed that several of the parts may be cut from small odd pieces of wood.

For the cab, look at Fig. 2 which shows, more or less in section form, how it is put together, with the various parts lettered for easy reference. On the inside back cover of this issue we give full-size outlines of those parts, which are shaped, and would, to some workers, be a little difficult to draw on to the wood.

Cut two of part (A), the side of the cab, the window openings at the top being cut out if desired or left solid and afterwards painted in as windows. These two pieces are glued and nailed to the floor (B), measuring 3ins. by 3⅛ins. At a distance of ⅜in. above (B) a second piece (C), the same size exactly as (B), is fixed in, and, through both, a hole 1in. in from the back edge of the pieces is drilled to take the pivot screw, see Fig. 2.

The next piece (D), measuring 3ins. by 2⅝ins. is cut and glued between the sides of the cab, and then the back (E) is cut and fixed similarly, all as seen by the dotted lines on the full-size detail pattern. The piece (E) measures 3⅜ins. by 3ins.

The roof (F) is now cut and shaped from a piece of wood measuring 3ins. by 2½ins., its front and back edge shaping being got by following the edges of the sides at those parts. Piece (G) represents the radiator front of the lorry and is shown with measurements to detail in Fig. 2. It is simply glued to piece (D) centrally, with its lower edge flush with the bottom edge.

Piece (H) is 3ins. by 2ins., and is glued between the two sides and afterwards shaped to the outline of the latter. It may be painted up finally to represent the screen. The axle support (I) is shown full-size on the pattern. Cut two of this piece and glue to the lower edge of the sides (A), see Fig. 2. The hole for the axle screw is shown. The position of this should be pricked into the wood before the pattern is destroyed.

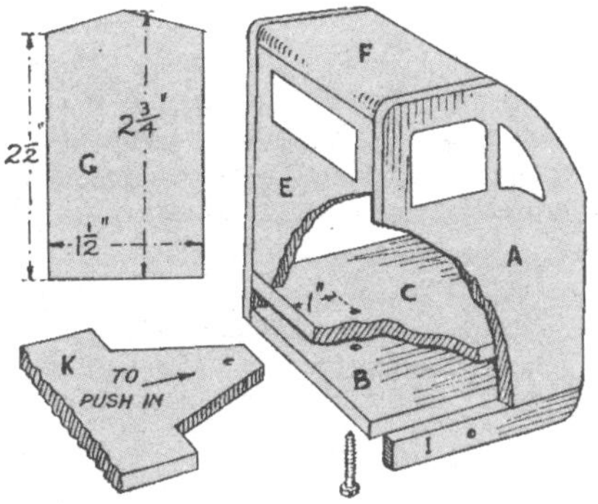

Fig. 2

To the underside of the floor (B) and running crosswise immediately behind and central with the holes in (I), there is an axle bar (J) to take the ends of the wheel screws.

This so far completes the cab, which, when painted will receive the pointed end of the lorry base piece (K). The construction of the lorry is simple, as the diagram Fig. 3 shows. This view shows the underside and the relative position of all the parts. Piece (K) is shown full-size on the pattern sheet. The rear portion, when drawn out on the wood, must be extended to the measurement given.

Next cut two of piece (L), see pattern, and glue them to (K) flush with the edge as seen in Fig. 3. The axle (M) will measure 3ins. long by ¾in. wide and will be glued on to (K) as shown in Fig. 3. The two side supports (N) can be taken from the pattern sheet and glued to (K) with ½in. fine nails added to strengthen the assembly.

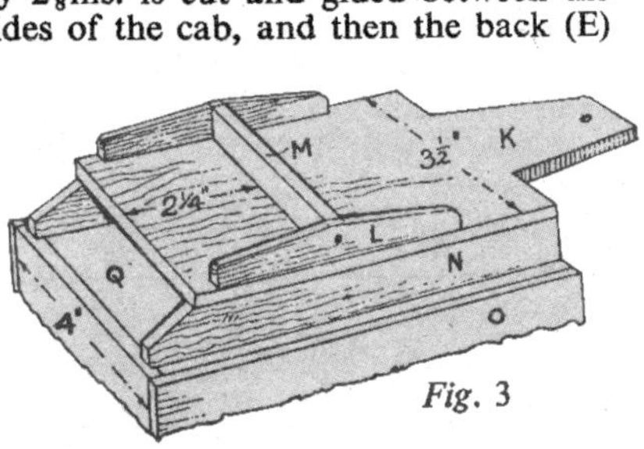

Fig. 3

Making the Body

This completes the chassis, and the box part of the lorry can be easily made up from the sectional diagram Fig. 4. The floor (Q) measures 6ins. long by 4ins. wide, and to its edges are glued and pinned the two sides (O), 6½ins. by 2¼ins., and the two ends (P) 4ins. by 2¼ins. The completed box is simply fixed to the chassis rails (N) in the position shown in Fig. 3. The wheels (2½ins. diameter) may be bought ready-made, nicely turned and painted, or they may be cut with the fretsaw from ½in. wood. Use 1in. roundhead screws for the fixing of the wheels, and place thin metal washers on either side of the wheels.

This latter remark also applies to the cabin wheels.

If mudguards are to be included in the toy, they may be made from tin ¾in. wide, small lugs being left, when cutting their shapes, for the screws which fix them to the sides of the cabin and to the lorry.

The two completed parts of the lorry should be painted up in bright colours before the box portion is pushed into place between the floors (B) and (C) of the cab and pivoted with a 1in. long screw from beneath. It will be understood that the screw must pass loosely through the end hole in piece (K) to allow freedom of movement for the box part of the toy. Thin washers should again be added, one on top and one below the end of piece (K). A cord may be attached to the front of the toy for pulling along. (S.W.C.)

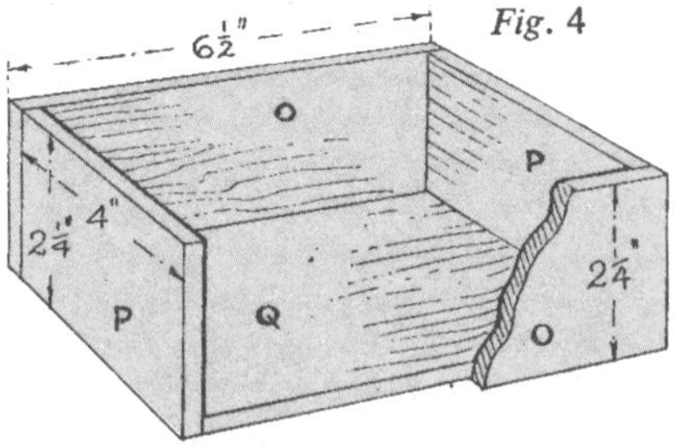

Fig. 4

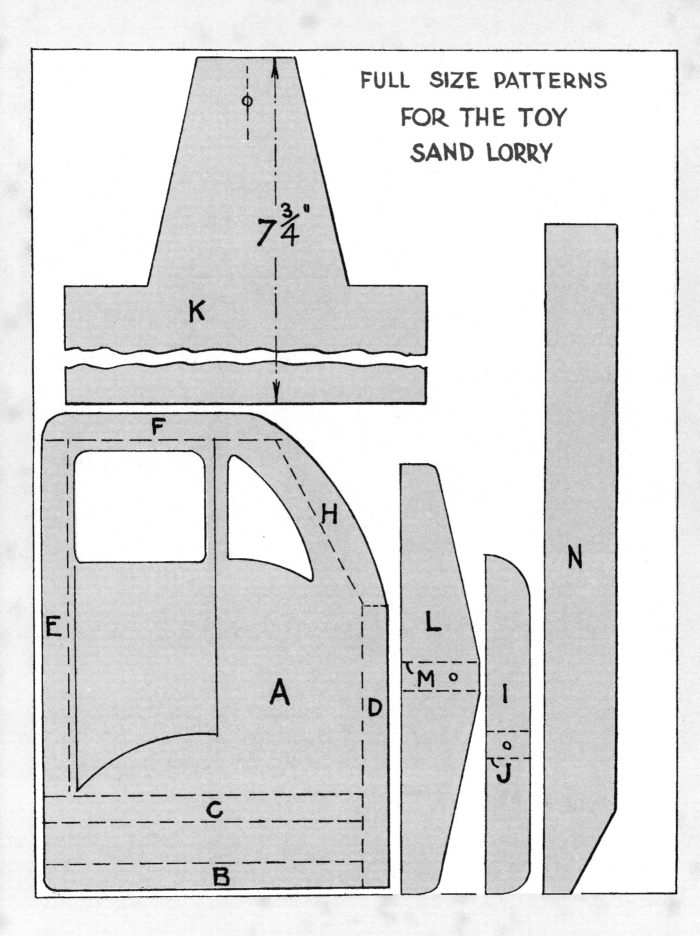

FULL SIZE PATTERNS
FOR THE TOY
SAND LORRY

$7\frac{3}{4}''$

K

F

H

E

A

D

L

M

I

J

N

C

B

A simple novelty to make for Christmas is this
TUMBLING CLOWN TOY

WE have frequently been asked to give details of this toy which appeared in these pages some few years ago. It is quite an old-fashioned novelty, which still has a great claim on the amusement side for the children. It will certainly be a source of entertainment to the modern child, and will probably be quite new to thousands of our boys and girls.

As will be seen from the diagrams, the toy consists of a block of wood representing the clown. He is placed at the top of the ladder and upon being released, he turns over and over, down the ladder, catching on to each rung in turn on his descent.

The Clown Block

The toy is by no means difficult to make, nor will it take long to construct. Fig. 1 shows three stages in making the clown block. A piece of wood of 1¼ins. by 1¼ins. section and 3¾ins. long is

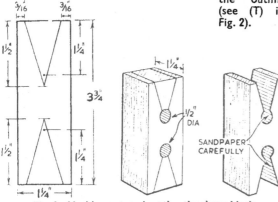

Fig. I—Marking out, and cutting the clown block

marked out, as in Fig. 1 (A). Holes, ½in. diameter, are then bored through, as seen in (B) Fig. 1, and finally the block is gripped in the vice and the wedge-shaped pieces cut out with a tenon saw. It is most important to get these openings quite smooth. Bored holes may be rough, so it will be necessary to get busy with the glasspaper.

In Fig. 2 we see how the clown is painted on the two plain sides of the wood block.

As many workers find it difficult to draw the human figure, the simple comic one shown should not be too difficult. The proportions are easily drawn by putting lines across the illustration and then redrawing them on the wood and using them as guide lines for the finished outline. The paint used should be in bright colours, a good enamel would be best.

If several of these toys are being made for sale, perhaps, there will be no need to mark out each figure separately. Draw one out in outline on metal or cardboard, making this a template for drawing round in pencil direct on to the wood. A strip of the template material may be left on each end to bend over the wood to hold the former in place while pencilling in the outline (see (T) in Fig. 2).

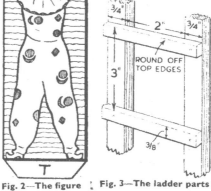

Fig. 2—The figure   Fig. 3—The ladder parts

The actual background round the figure, shown by the hatched lines in Fig. 2, should be painted black. Use a small brush for the clown detail, and if a number of them are being done, keep a brush for each colour while working. This will save time and trouble in cleaning the brush between each colour operation.

The ladder is a simple item to make and it can be of almost any length. In fact, the longer it is, the better the

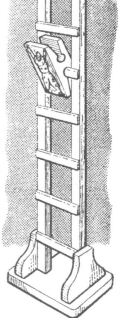

effect when the clown is performing. There must, however, be a limit to the length of the ladder if it is required to stand up on a base, as in our sketch of the finished article.

The size of the base and its side brackets can only be got by trial when the ladder length has been decided upon. The sides of the ladder can be of almost any size in section of wood—say, ¼in. by ⅜in. The edges should be smoothed up with glasspaper and the sharp corners taken off.

The cross steps of the ladder are made from stripwood, ⅜in. wide by about ⅛in. thick. Trim all the pieces to this section accurately, so the figure of the clown falls evenly and smoothly. Also see that the upper edges of the steps are rounded over and made smooth with glasspaper.

Ladder Assembly

Fig. 3 shows exactly how the ladder parts are assembled. Keep the steps quite square with the uprights, and glue and pin them on, using small brass fretpins for the job. Do not forget to prick in the holes beforehand for the pins, to avoid splitting the wood.

The flat base and its side supports should be of ¼in. or ⅜in. wood, firmly nailed and glued together. It must be pointed out here that unless great care is taken to get all the parts accurate, the clown on his descent will occasionally miss his footing and fall off the ladder.

This will also happen if the ladder is not held upright. Follow out the instructions given here, and make any little further adjustments to the steps necessary after testing the clown. Clean the wood thoroughly before applying the paint or enamel

Design for making
THE NODDING TIGER TOY

Full size patterns for making this novelty in wood, are presented on our gift design sheet. The necessary kit of materials (No. 2876) is obtainable from Hobbies Branches and Agents, for 4/5 or post free from Dereham, Norfolk, for 5/3.

OUR BOYS' DEPARTMENT

A MATCH-FIRING GUN.

THE sketch (Fig. 1) shows a simple model that is likely to interest our younger readers. The apparatus consists of a few oddments of wood with a piece of elastic and a pea-shooter or similar form of tube, arranged to form a most effective match-firing gun.

Fig. 2 shows a side view with measurements, a length of tube of about 3½ins. being essential. If this is not available a strip of paper pasted and then wrapped round a lead pencil and allowed to dry will serve admirably. The next part to prepare is the block of wood through which it passes. This measures about 2ins. by ¾in. by 1in., the hole to take the tube being drilled at a slight tilt, a short distance from the top. The hole should be of such a size to fit the tube nicely, this being glued in with a short distance projecting at the back.

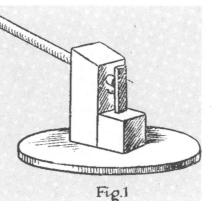

Fig.1

Next is the smaller block to which the projector is attached. This measures 1in. by ¾in., the two blocks being then glued to a circular base of about 3½in. diameter.

It will be best to finally screw them with a couple of tacks entered from underneath so as to make a perfectly strong job.

We now require a small piece of strip-wood about 1in. long and ⅜in. wide by ⅓in. thick. This is fixed by means of a very small hinge to the middle of the lower block. Owing to the softer woods easily splitting, it will be found best to have a piece of very close grained material for this strip, the hinge being attached by means of very small screws. Fix a thin wire tack into the projector on the side facing the barrel and bend it to form a hook, and then enter one similarly on the block facing it, a piece of thin elastic being wound round the two, and the ends secured. If the projector is now drawn back in the position indicated in the illustration, Fig. 3, and let go the elastic will cause it to spring back and hit the barrel with a resounding crack, the ammunition being placed inside the barrel with a short length projecting.

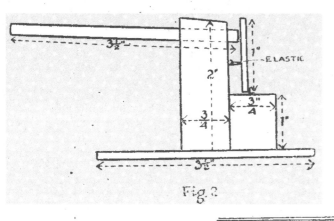

Fig. 2

Fig. 3

A SAND-MOTOR: HOW TO MAKE ONE

THERE is something fascinating to the juvenile mind in a working toy of any description, and the sand motor illustrated at Fig. 1 is a particularly interesting toy.

The motor may be made almost any size, but for ordinary purposes the following dimensions will answer well: Height, 15½ in.; width 8¼ in.; thickness, 2½ in.

It will be as well to commence by making the sides A, these being cut out of one piece, and 15 in. long, 8¼ in. wide and 5-16 in. thick. Next nail on two sides B 12½ in. long 1⅞ in. wide and 5-16 in. thick, these are flush with the top edge of side A. The top C should now be cut out to 7⅝ in. long, 1⅞ in. wide and 5-16 in. thick, with a square hole of 1¼ in. side cut out ¾ in. from the end as shown at D. We may now fit in the partition E, this is a piece of wood 7⅝ in. by 1⅞ in. by 5-16 in., its position being 4½ in. from the top piece C.

There is a slot cut through this piece, the centre being 2⅛ in. away from the end, 1¼ wide and ¼ in. across at the bottom, and ⅜ in. at the top, the bevelled edges being to allow the sand to run freely. Underneath the slot it will be necessary to fix a sliding shutter as shown at Fig. 3, and shown in section at Fig. 4. For this we shall require two runners 3 in. long, 5-16 in. wide and 5-16 in. thick. In each piece cut a rebate 5-32 in. across and ⅛ in. down the edge and then carefully glue these on one end, ½in. past the slot. The shutter should be cut from a piece of hardwood, and be 2 in. long, 1 9-16 in. wide and ⅛ in. thick. A thin French nail may be used as a handle or a better appearance will be given outside if a black headed hat pin is used, the pin may be softened in the fire or gas flame and passed through a hole in the shutter and bent over, the end G being previously passed through a hole in the side.

The Partition.

The partition should now be nailed in position and then the two pieces shown at H and K fitted in. The piece H should be 6¾ in. by 1⅞ in. by 5-16 in., the ends being bevelled to fit, and piece K which is 3¾ in. long by 1⅞ in. by 5-16 in. being bevelled also.

We may now make the two drawers shown at L and M, these should be 4⅝ in. long, 1 ⅞in. wide and 2½ in. deep outside measurements; the ends should be ½ in. wood, the sides to bottoms being 3-16 in. thick.

A length of ½ in. wood should now be cut off about 2 ft. 6 in. long, and planed down to 4½ in. wide, with a chamfer on one edge 1¼ in. along, and ⅜ in. down the edge. Cut off two lengths, each 9¼ in. long, and pare the ends quite smooth, the bevelled edge being continued at each end. One of these pieces should be nailed on to each side flush with the base. Next cut off two 1⅞ in. lengths, and cut off 2½ in. from the width so that they may be nailed on each end just above the drawer fronts, and also nail on the base a piece of ½ in. wood 10 in. by 4 in.

The Wheel.

We have now to make the wheel W, this is 1⅝ in. in width, with a diameter of 7½ in.; first of all get out two circular pieces of 3-16 in. thick wood, exactly 7½in. in diameter, and in each cut a square hole exactly in the middle ½in. side. Next take a length of 1¼ in. thick wood, or two thicknesses glued together and cut a circular piece 7½ in. diameter. Mark off on the edge sixteen points, or at least twelve, draw lines to the centre and mark off 1½ in. from the outside and draw lines from these points to the outside point above. All these notches should now be sawn out and cut smooth with a chisel and then the middle of this piece of wood should be cut away, a hole of at least 3¾ in. being made, the sides should be glued on, clamped down to dry. A sectional view of the wheel is shown at Fig. 5, the elevation showing one circular side removed and the section below a cut through line a a. The next stage is to make the spindle, this is shown at Fig. 6, and if possible it should be turned in a lathe. The length is 4½ in., the square portion being ½ in. side, and the round part 5-16 in. diameter. The length of the square portion should be 1⅝ in., and the shorter round end 1⅛ in. We have now to look around for some large cotton reels, and saw off the ends of three, the end with the short projection being required. Glue two ends together to make the pulley P., the other piece being used to keep the other end of the spindle true. We shall also require two washers, cut out of ⅛ in. thick stuff, these should be glued on the outside of the wheel. The position of spindle and pulley is shown at Fig. 7, and at Fig. 8 is shown the method of securing the reel ends by means of a wedge-shaped pin V, driven in from the side.

The sides of the opening D, made of 5-16 in. stuff as shown enlarged at Fig. 9, should be about 1 in. high, and may be glued in position when nailed or glued up.

To put the motor together, place the wheel in position, thoroughly covering the spindle with black lead, and then screw on the outside. Adjust the pulley and end, putting plenty of black lead wherever any part of the spindle or pulley, &c., touches. The drawers should now be placed in, and the motor is ready.

A coat or two of varnish stain should be applied to the outside.

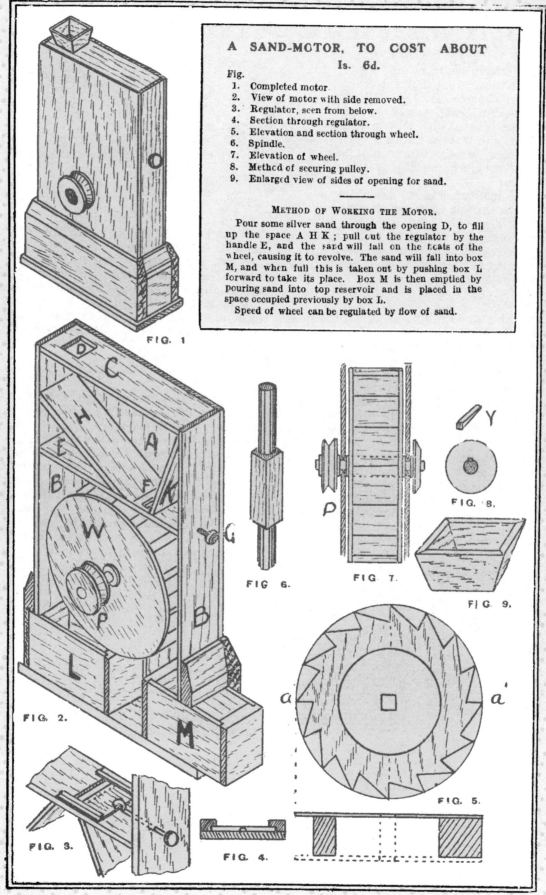

A SAND-MOTOR, TO COST ABOUT
1s. 6d.

Fig.
1. Completed motor.
2. View of motor with side removed.
3. Regulator, seen from below.
4. Section through regulator.
5. Elevation and section through wheel.
6. Spindle.
7. Elevation of wheel.
8. Method of securing pulley.
9. Enlarged view of sides of opening for sand.

METHOD OF WORKING THE MOTOR.

Pour some silver sand through the opening D, to fill up the space A H K; pull out the regulator by the handle E, and the sand will fall on the floats of the wheel, causing it to revolve. The sand will fall into box M, and when full this is taken out by pushing box L forward to take its place. Box M is then emptied by pouring sand into top reservoir and is placed in the space occupied previously by box L.

Speed of wheel can be regulated by flow of sand.

FIG. 1.

FIG. 2.

FIG. 3.

FIG. 4.

FIG. 5.

FIG. 6.

FIG. 7.

FIG. 8.

FIG. 9.

Full details for making a modern
STREAMLINE COACH

WHAT could be more up-to-date than a modern streamlined coach such as the one shown here ? This toy measures 18ins. long, 7ins. wide and 7ins. high, and is fitted with either rubber tyres or plain solid wooden wheels.

These wooden wheels, 2¾ins. in diameter, can be bought from Hobbies at 6d. the set of four. The rubber tyres, for fixing to the wooden discs as described here, costs 1/2 the set, and can also be got from Hobbies.

The construction of the coach is shown in the diagrams. No special tools either are wanted, just the fretsaw, rasp and file and a pot or two of paint to finish the outside, that is all.

Sides and Floor

The first thing to do will be to set out the sides in ⅛in. wood, the shape given in Fig. 1. The exact positions for the axles of the wheels must be carefully set out, too, according to the measurements in Fig. 2. The line for the painted windows can also be got from this figure.

The other side can be got by drawing round the cut-out first, and the holes for the axles should be bored through both pieces at one time to ensure accuracy.

The floor is a plain oblong measuring 17½ins. by 4½ins. by ½in. thick and is of deal and glued and nailed between the sides.

The next stage is the making of the front, back and roof, and as there is some little shaping to be done to these, they will have to be of ¾in. thick deal. Glue between the sides and to the floor so

they can easily be shaped, using the sides as the template for working to.

In Fig. 3 is shown the three pieces glued to one of the sides and the shaping completed. The near side is omitted in this case for sake of clearness.

In making the end pieces, the top and lower edges are first chamfered or planed off to fit between the roof and the floor. Then, after they are glued up, the shaping can be done as described to the curve of the sides.

The Wheels

The next, and fourth stage of construction is the making of the wheel boxes and covers. These are shown fixed in place in Fig. 4.

The shape for cutting is shown in Fig. 5, and the ½in. squares can easily be set out on the wood, and the curve drawn through. The centre for the circle is put in from this. The boxes are cut out of ¾in. deal and glued to the sides of the coach.

The covers are from 3/16in. stuff and put on after the wheels and axles are in place.

Before the wheels are fitted, however, the bonnet should be made and glued on. Wood

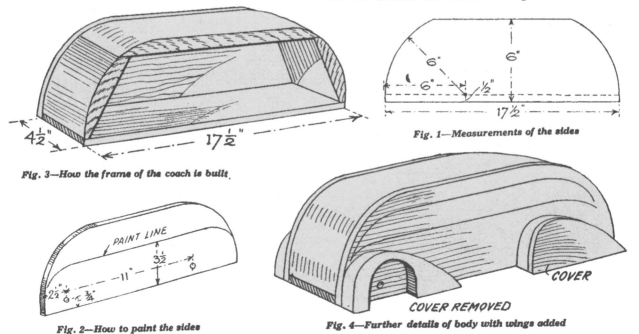

Fig. 3—How the frame of the coach is built

Fig. 1—Measurements of the sides

Fig. 2—How to paint the sides

Fig. 4—Further details of body with wings added

.¼in. thick is again used for this, and the section in Fig. 6 shows how it is to be shaped.

If rubber tyres are to be used with the wheels,

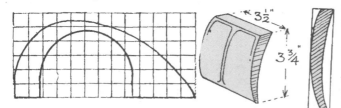

Fig. 6—A side and front view of bonnet

Fig. 5—How to mark out the wings

the discs upon which these are stretched will be made as Fig. 7 shows.

Four plain ¼in. discs are first cut, having a diameter

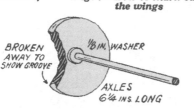

BROKEN AWAY TO SHOW GROOVE

⅛IN. WASHER

AXLES 6¼ INS. LONG

Fig. 7—Details of the axles

of 1¾ins., and round the edges of these is filed a groove deep enough to allow the inside portion of the tyres to bed in. The broken section in Fig. 7 shows one of these wheels with the axle glued in

and the 3/16in. washer which will hold the tyre well away from the sides of the coach.

When threading the axles through the holes, allow a fair clearance before gluing on the wheels, so they revolve freely and do not " bind."

Finish off the toy by painting it in bright colours. The roof and portions of the sides and the tops of the wheel boxes should be painted cream, while the other parts may be a bright green or a red. Hobbies supply tins of enamel very suitable for such toys at 2½d. per tin.

For the windows, either dark blue or black would do, the whole being brightened up with line of white.

The lamps may be represented by small turnings glued on and painted up suitably.

CUTTING LIST

2 Sides	..	..	..	..	17½ins. by 6ins. by ¼in.
1 Floor		..	..	..	17½ins. by 4½ins. by ¼in.
2 Ends	..	..	..	..	3½ins. by 5½ins. by ⅜in.
1 Roof		..	..	..	13½ins. by 3½ins. by ⅜in.
4 Boxes	..	..	..	..	6½ins. by 2½ins. by ¼in.
4 Cover	..	..	..	..	6½ins. by 2½ins. by 3/16in.
1 Front	..	..	..	..	3½ins. by 3½ins. by ⅜in.
4 Discs	..	..	..	..	2ins. by 2ins. by ¼in.
2 Pieces of ¼in. dia. Dowel for Axles, 6½ins. long.					

Making a Working Toy Submarine

THIS little novelty can be made from odd pieces of wood cut with a fretsaw. With the addition of a piece of elastic and home-made propeller, it can be made to dive and surface most realistically.

Cut piece (A) from ½in. wood and two pieces (B) from ¼in. Glue them together with waterproof glue and shape the parts with a penknife. There is no need to be very particular about the actual shape, so long as it is fairly streamlined. Insert a piece of wire to represent the periscope and then give two or three coats of grey paint.

For the propelling mechanism use screweyes and elastic. Cut the propeller itself from tin and shape a shaft from wire as shown. Insert a bead to help it to run smoothly.

Screw the diving fins on each side of the model and tighten the screw in each just sufficiently to allow the fins to be moved for diving. The diving position is shown in the picture on this page.

A weight should be screwed in the slot provided and it should be heavy enough to partially submerge the submarine, leaving just the conning tower and a little of the deck showing.

When the propeller is wound up, by hand, and released, it will dive until the motor runs out, and then slowly surface. (M.p.)

Patterns for the Toy Submarine

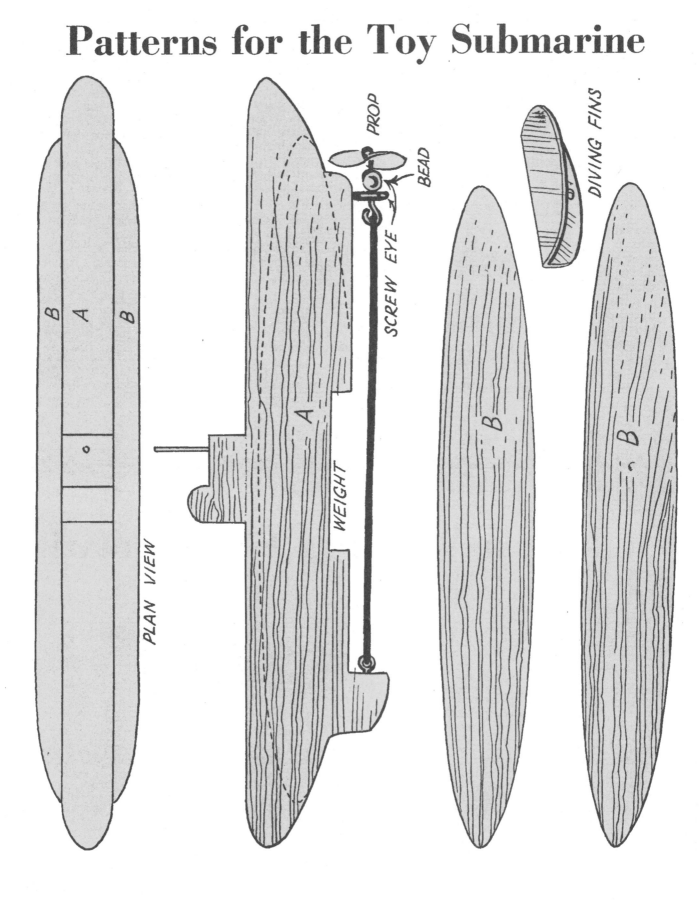

PLAN VIEW

B · A · B

A

WEIGHT

PROP

BEAD

SCREW EYE

DIVING FINS

B

B

How to Make
A CAGE FOR FANCY MICE

SAFE GARDEN TRAPS

NATURE Study

A WALL PIGEON COTE

You get endless
interest if you erect a
BIRD FEEDING STAND

HOW TO MAKE A STANDARD BEEHIVE

MAKING NESTING HOUSES

How to Make
A CAGE FOR FANCY MICE

By H. W. Grimston.

(This Contribution was awarded the First Prize in our recent Competition for the best description of How to Make any Article of either use or ornament.)

FANCY mice have come so much to the fore of late in the animal world, that perhaps a few hints about the building of a simple, but convenient, mouse cage may be welcomed by some of the readers of *Hobbies* who have gone in for the idea.

The cage, of which Fig. 1 is an illustration, can be easily made by anyone possessing a little common sense and a few tools, and is an excellent one for a number of young mice, being very roomy and possessing every convenience as regards cleanliness. The platform, containing the nest boxes, draws out, so that it can be thoroughly scrubbed when required. The nest boxes open at the top, and also at the back, so that they can be swept out daily.

FIG. 1. CAGE FOR FANCY MICE.

To construct the cage, procure an ordinary deal box, such as is used for Parcels Post purposes, measuring about 14½ by 12 inches, or smaller if preferred. The box, placed on its side, forms the body of the cage, the opening, which is afterwards enclosed with a piece of glass, serving as the front, and the lid comes in handy for making the fittings, no other wood being required.

The first thing to be done is to make the platform containing the nest boxes. For this purpose saw off a piece of wood from the lid, about as wide as half the width of the cage. Make a groove with a gouge along each wall inside the cage, at about 3 inches from the top, for the platform to slide into, the edges of the latter being filed down till it fits easily. Next cut a piece of wood 3 inches wide for the front of the nest boxes, drill two large holes in it, one at each end, for the mice to pass in and out,

and nail the front to the platform in an upright position, leaving about an inch margin along the front, as in Fig. 2; then divide the sleeping compartment in two by nailing a wooden partition across the centre at right angles to the front, as B in Fig. 2. This completes the nest boxes, as the remaining sides are formed by the walls of the cage.

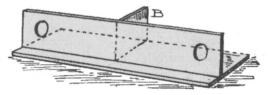

FIG. 2. PLATFORM AND NEST BOXES.

Now we come to the top of the cage, in which four square windows have to be cut, the two in front for ventilation, being afterwards filled in with perforated zinc, and the two at the back, opening with doors into the sleeping boxes, as in Fig. 3. The squares should be cut out with a fretsaw where possible, or else with a sharp penknife; the wood being very soft this will not prove a hard task.

The lids of the nest boxes are made from the wood thus cut out, and open endways as in Fig. 4, the hinges being very simple, just a piece of wire hammered into each side of the lid at one end, and forced into the edges of the cage, the opposite ends when closed resting on the partition between the boxes.

A portion of the back of the cage must now be cut out to make an opening into the nest boxes, as in Fig. 4, leaving only a narrow bar along the top. To do this it is best to force the back of the cage nearly off by inserting a chisel round the edges, and then saw it across where required, afterwards hammering the back firmly down again. The piece of wood thus sawn out must then be hinged on to the lower portion so as to open right back, and when closed it can be secured by a couple of brass buttons screwed on to the upper edge of the cage.

Next turn the cage upside down, and nail a piece of perforated zinc over the roof inside to fill in the open squares. A strip of narrow moulding must then be fastened along the upper and lower edges of the front to form a groove in which the glass can run in and out, the moulding along the upper edge being screwed on with small eyelet screws, as it will have to be removed to allow of the platform being drawn out. A zinc tray for the

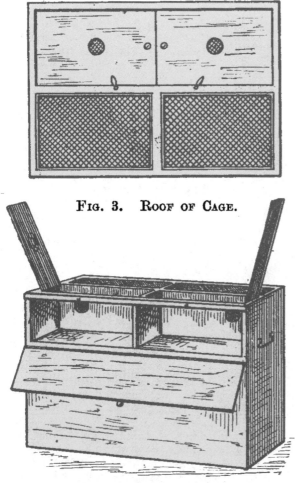

FIG. 3. ROOF OF CAGE.

FIG. 4. BACK OF CAGE.

floor of the cage and a pair of wire ladders can be easily made if the cage maker knows anything of soldering, but if not, any ironmonger will make them for very little. The ends of the ladders must be bent over and run into the edge of the platform beneath the holes so as to hang in a slanting position. The cage is now practically complete, but to give it a more finished appearance the edges and corners of every part should be rounded off with a file and rubbed smooth with fine sandpaper, after which it may be stained or left plain according to taste.

A SIMPLE PLANT-HOLDER.

EVERY housewife counts her home incomplete unless there are one or two "plants" about the house. This is just the opportunity of the woodworker, and the possibility of making a simple Holder, such as illustrated herewith, can easily be turned to good account by the handyman.

It is simple to make, and if turned out in oak, stained or fumed, will form a useful piece of furniture. It is no tiny ornament, but planned to hold a reasonably-sized plant-pot for the floor or a sturdy stool. It is 10¼ ins. high and 11¼ ins. square at the top, tapering downwards to a base occupying a floor space

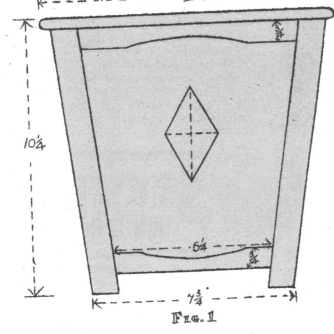

FIG. 1

Fig. 2, as correctly fitted. The illustration at Fig. 3 also gives us details of the cross-strips, but before getting these fixed, we must put in the bottom of the holder a piece of ¼in. or ⅜in. material (3-ply will do for this quite well), which is 6¾ins. square. This must be accurately trued up square, and is then screwed with flat-headed screws driven in flush.

The Cross-Strips.

Now we can prepare and place the bottom strips which cover these screws and serve as ornamentation at the same time. Four pieces of ⅛in. material is wanted, 6¼ins. long and ½in. wide. The ends of each is marked and cut to the shape of the sloping side to sink between the corner uprights. Then we must mark off 1in. from the longer ends and describe an arc as shown at C in the detail of Fig. 3. This can easily be cut with a fretsaw. When the parts are cleaned up, they are glued flush with the bottom edge of the sides and with the ornamental work upwards.

The four strips at the top are similar in shape, but naturally have to be longer. They are 8½ins. long and ½in. wide, cut from ⅛in. wood. In this case also the ends have to be cut to fit the slope of the sides. The curve this time is on the shorter edge, and is marked off 1¾ins. from each end—see B in Fig. 3. These parts are glued along the top, and should be fitted slightly above the upper edges.

of 7¾ins. The actual aperture for the plant is 8¼ins. square at the top, diminishing to 6¾ins. at the bottom.

Make up in Oak.

The wood list is short and inexpensive. Oak is recommended, and besides the four main sides we only require the corner-pieces and the cross-pieces, with the rim round the top to hide the bare edges of the upright parts. Reference to the detail at Fig. 1 will provide most of the dimensions required. Two of the sides are 9¼ins. wide at the top, 6¾ins. at the bottom, and 9ins. long; the other two are 10ins. wide at the top 7½ins. at the bottom. This difference is to allow a plain butt joint at the corner, as can be seen at Fig. 2, which shows by the dotted lines how the top edges appear under the upper rims.

The Corner Strips.

To hide the butt joints at the corners, we have the eight strips cut from pieces of wood 10ins. long, 1in. wide and ¼in. thick. In order to place these along the corner, a small mitre butt has to be made at each end, and by placing the part in position we can mark off on the actual piece the required angle. It is shown also by the dotted lines in A of Fig. 3. The outer edges of these pieces must be planed to an angle of 45 degrees, that they may meet in a single line at the outer corner. They can be seen by the dotted section in

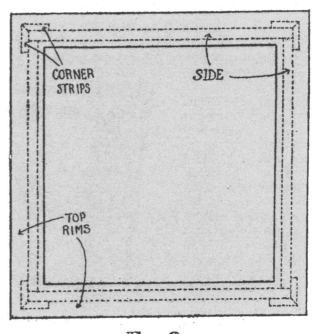

FIG. 2

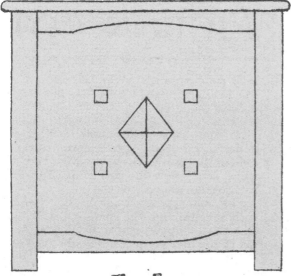

FIG. 5.

diamonds shown are only a suggestion and no doubt readers will find and place some ornament of their own design. Indeed, a small piece of fretwork from a HOBBIES design will add to the charm of the finished Holder.

The lozenge shown in detail and in section (Fig. 6) is suitably made from a piece $3\frac{1}{2}$ins. long, 2ins. wide and $\frac{5}{8}$in. thick. Draw diagonal lines across, and file down from the centre as plainly seen in the diagram.

A Suitable Finish.

As mentioned earlier, the Holder should be finished by staining or fuming, as the owner wishes, or can be polished with Lightning Polish by any amateur.

A shaving may thus be taken off with a plane to bring a flat edge for the top rim to rest upon.

FIG. 4.

The Top Rim.

The four pieces composing the top are laid

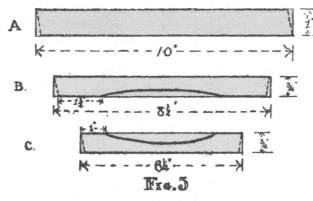

FIG. 3.

An Alternative Design.

An alternative Holder, probably a little more simple can be made with a square container. In this instance the sides will be the same width at the bottom as the top, and the ornamental strips will be all the same length, with square ends. Otherwise, the dimensions are the same, and the shape and detail of Fig. 5 gives an outline of the style if this particular Holder is made up.

on the edges flat, as shown in Fig. 2. They are cut from $\frac{3}{8}$in. wood, and are $11\frac{1}{4}$ins. long and $1\frac{1}{4}$ins. wide. It is necessary to mitre each end to get the corners to fit as shown at Figs. 2 and 4. The outer edge must be rounded with file and sandpaper to the section seen in the latter detail. When the parts are cleaned up they can be glued over the edges of the upright parts, and round-headed brass screws can be added if so desired.

Ornamental Lozenges.

Finally, we have the ornaments on each side. These can, if so thought fit, be added before the panels, or left until now. The

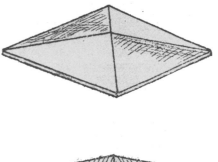

FIG. 6.

A WALL PIGEON COTE

F OR making this cote, planed matchboarding ½in. thick will be as good as anything. This timber will be ⅜in. finished thickness which will be quite strong enough.

As a start, glue together enough pieces of the board to form the front and back pieces. The dimensions are given in Fig. 1. Having cut to shape, draw a line across ⅜in. from the bottom edge, the tenons are cut to this line.

Now draw lines across where the two floors will come, each pair of lines being the thickness of the wood apart—i.e. ⅜in.

The lower portion is divided into three equal parts by the vertical divisional lines, while the middle portion is divided into two by one central division. It is well to repeat these lines on the inside as well, as they form useful guides for fixing the divisions and nailing.

The Openings

The position of the openings will be clear from the drawing. Each opening measures 4ins. by 6ins. and can be cut out with a keyhole saw. Rasp off and sandpaper the rough sawn edges. Now mark out and cut the short tenons along the bottom.

The little end tenons are cut ⅜in. wide, the width of the remainder does not matter within reason as long as the mortises are cut to suit. It is perhaps needless to remark that the back of the cote needs no tenons or openings.

The bottom of the cote, Fig. 2, is made up of matchboarding, glued together. The dotted lines across show the position of the front piece, and the mortises shown should be cut to fit the tenons.

The right angle dotted lines show the position of the lower divisions. For a space of 12ins.

each side, a narrow strip ⅜in. wide is cut away, this is to accommodate the side pieces of the cote.

Glue the front in place, and nail the back to the rear edge of the bottom piece. To keep both front and back pieces quite upright while the divisions are being fixed, nail a strip of wood temporarily across the top. Now turn to Fig. 3, which shows how the cote is fitted up inside, the back being removed for the purpose.

First nail the two lower division pieces in place with nails through the front and back. Take the first floor, nail the centre division to it, lay it on top of the division pieces already fixed and nail it thereto.

The Resting Platforms

Now lay the top floor to the division piece below it and to a fillet of wood nailed across each end. Turn upside down, and drive nails through the bottom into the lower divisions and finish by nailing through the front and back into the floors themselves.

The rest boards across the front, for the pigeons to alight on, are cut 4ins. wide and extend an inch or so each side of the openings. They are supported on small shaped brackets 3ins. by 4ins., and screwed to the front.

These brackets, by the way, are best screwed through from the inside of the front before the latter is fixed itself. The shelves are then glued and nailed to the brackets. Now cut and fit the side pieces and roof.

The boards for the roof are cut to overlap the front 4½ins., and extend below the eaves 2ins. Nail across and where they butt together at the ridge of the roof, plane off the angle to leave a "flat" 1in. wide, to which the capping can be nailed.

Roof Covering

Rubberoid, or roofing felt, is used to cover the roof. Cut to fit each half of the roof, allowing ½in. extra to turn over at the eaves.

Nail across, just against the flat where the capping will come, and also to the edge at the eaves. Along the front and back edges lay a 1in. by ½in. batten, and nail through both batten and felt into the roof boards.

The barge boards are cut from 2in. wide strips of matchboarding. They are shaped up on their inner edges, bevelled to meet together at the ridge, and nailed to the front edges of roof boards and battens.

The capping is a length of 1in. by 2ins. wood, with its top planed to a bevel each side. It is nailed to the "flat" and overhangs the barge boards ½in. Fig. 4 shows all these details. Only the supporting brackets now remain to be dealt with.

These are simple enough (see Fig. 5) and consist of two lengths of 3ins. by 1in. timber tongued and slotted together, and fitted with a strut.

The latter is cut from similar timber, with its ends sawn to an angle of 45 degrees. Screw each end of the struts first by a 2in. screw through the

as in detail, Fig. 7.

Now, through a hole in the wall bracket piece bored directly in front of a line of mortar, not brick, drive in a stout iron nail. This will ensure a sound fixing.

The cote is fixed to the brackets with small iron bolts and nuts, two each side, the holes for same being drilled through brackets and bottom of

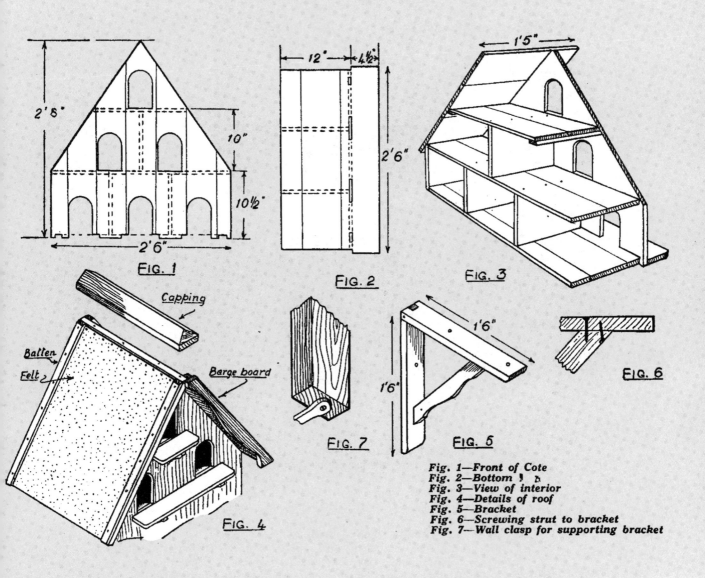

Fig. 1—Front of Cote
Fig. 2—Bottom
Fig. 3—View of interior
Fig. 4—Details of roof
Fig. 5—Bracket
Fig. 6—Screwing strut to bracket
Fig. 7—Wall clasp for supporting bracket

bracket pieces into the strut and then with screws through the struts into the bracket pieces. Fig. 6 explains this point.

The brackets must be secured firmly to the wall. First select the place and also the most convenient height, then drive a stout iron wall clasp into the mortar between the bricks. Use wall clasps with a hole drilled in, raise the bracket to rest on the clasp and drive a screw in to hold it in position,

the cote. Fix the cote to be 2ins. clear of the wall, and paint the lot two coats of best lead paint, preferably white.

Owing to the construction of the cote, a detailed cutting list is not practicable. For general guidance, the following quantities of timber will be necessary. 5½ins. by ½in. P. T. and G. matchboarding, 75ft. run. Planed batten 1in. by 3ins. 11ft. Planed batten 1in. by 2ins. 2ft.

OUR BOYS AND WILD BIRDS.

MAKING NESTING HOUSES.

THE past twenty years or so have seen a great change in the attitude of boys towards wild birds. The time was when nearly every boy stalked the countryside armed with a catapult with the deliberate intention of killing as many birds as he possibly could, and, furthermore, he wantonly robbed their nests in the nesting season. In latter years there has been a great change for the better, possibly owing to better education, and, further, by the passing of laws for the protection of wild birds. At any rate, our boys have taken a greater and kindlier interest in wild birds.

The collection of birds' eggs forms a very interesting hobby, but the wholesale robbery and destruction of nests is quite another matter, and one which any right-minded boy should refrain from doing himself and discourage in others.

The feeding of birds is another healthy sign of this changed attitude. During the past few years numbers of people all over the country have erected bird-feeding tables in their gardens, and have been well repaid for their trouble, especially during the past spells of cold weather, by the numbers of

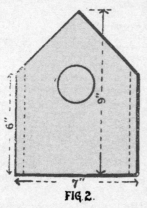

FIG. 2.

birds which have gathered to their feasts, and the interest and amusement they have afforded.

Position.

Our object in the present article, however, is to suggest to our boy readers that it would be a very interesting thing to make one or a number of garden houses for wild birds, and place them in suitable positions in the home garden. It is a simple matter, which any boy may undertake without any outlay other than his time, and will result in interest both to himself and his friends. Such a house is shown fixed to a tree at Fig. 1; this is an ideal spot, as is the wall of a dwelling-house, especially if it is overgrown with ivy or climbers. A pair of birds have been known to use a house similar to this for nesting year after year. In placing the house, care should be taken not to fix it in an exposed position, or where it will be interfered with.

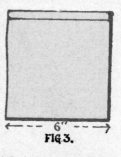

FIG. 3.

Making.

Any odd pieces of wood may be used in making the house, providing it is about $\frac{1}{2}$in. thick; an old grocery box would provide excellent material. The front and back should be shaped as shown at Fig. 2, the front should have an entrance hole about 2in. diameter, as shown in the illustration, but the back should be solid. The sides are shaped as shown at Fig. 3; notice that the top edges are bevelled to correspond with the slope of the roof, and the front and back are nailed to the sides as shown at Fig. 4. The bottom is then cut 9ins. long by 7ins. wide, and nailed to the bottom edges of the sides, back, and front. The roof is in two portions, 9ins. long by 6ins. wide; the joint at the top should be carefully made, so that the roof will be weather-proof,

FIG. 4.

and it is nailed to the top edges of the house. A perch should be fitted to the front, just under the entrance hole, as shown at Figs. 1 and 4.

All that now remains to be done is to paint the house to protect it, hang in a suitable place, and watch results. A very pleasing appearance may be given the house by covering it with strips of bark lightly tacked on to the roof, sides and front, and houses so finished are often occupied more readily.

Fig. 1—A nesting box for tits

Fig. 3—A simple fat-bell

Fig. 5—A wire-bottom peanut feeder

Fig. 7—A seed feeder with glass front

ALTHOUGH a little early to think of the Spring it is not too early to begin construction of these picturesque nesting boxes. The tits, especially the blue-tit and the great-tit are so useful, and so delightfully entertaining in the garden that we should offer them every opportunity to stay and prosper.

Unfortunately the natural nesting sites of the tits are among the first things in nature to disappear when man encroaches with building and urbanisation of land; the hollow and decaying old trees.

Not that all the nesting holes in these trees are ideal—the birds have to make the best of them, and sometimes choose nests that are so deep, and have so narrow an exit, that the young are trampled to death by each other in their attempts to leave the nest.

We can help to remedy this housing shortage, and get a lot of fun in the process, as well as ensuring first-class insect destruction in the garden in return. In the lean time of the year, a little assistance with food too, will keep the tits with us.

These days of wood shortage make prepared timber almost worth its weight in gold—and almost as scarce, but logs can still be obtained fairly reasonably. From these, preferably

oak ones, excellent tit nesting boxes can easily be made, as well as several feeding devices. It has been the writer's experience that the tits seem to prefer these rustic boxes to ones made from boarding.

From a Log

The type of nesting box described here (Fig. 1), evolved by the writer after struggling laboriously for many hours, to hollow out circular nesting holes in logs, is very easily and quickly made; the chief point being to make a good clean plane surface cut.

Briefly, the method is to cut slabs from the bark-covered outside of a good-sized log (of at least 8ins. diameter) to form the four sides of the box (Fig. 2). The front and the back overlap the sides, with two other slabs cut for the bottom and the roof from another log.

Roof and Entrance

The bottom finishes flush with the inner edge of the sides, while the roof overhangs all round by at least two inches. The entrance hole is cut out with a brace and bit near the top of the front.

The component slabs can be nailed together, the heads being punched in a little and the holes filled with putty, as can the spaces there may be between the slabs, to

make the box more weatherproof. The putty is painted over afterwards a suitable colour and the wood should, of course, be well dressed with linseed oil first to prevent the putty cracking away owing to oil absorption from it.

The roof should be hinged to open for inspection and eventual cleaning out purposes, held down by a good catch. A perch may be fitted to one side of the hole, by drilling a small hole and tapering the perch end to fit in tightly.

As regards dimensions, it is best to make the boxes in two sizes, one for blue tits, and a larger one for great tits.

The blue-tits boxes should be no larger than is necessary, otherwise other birds, especially sparrows, will commandeer them. A good size for a blue-tits box is (internal dimensions) 4ins. square with height 5ins. The hole being situated near the top there is a 3in. drop below the hole to the floor. Make the diameter of the hole 1 1/16in., as a larger hole would admit the sparrow.

For Great Tits

For the great-tits the size should be not less than 5½ins. inside, with a drop from the hole of 4ins. to the floor, with 2ins. clearance above the hole, inside. The hole is a little larger, say 1¼ins.

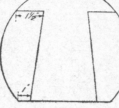

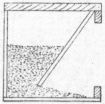

Fig. 2—How to cut the bark sides

Fig. 4—The bell shape cuts

Fig. 6—The peanut feeder and its wire bottom

Fig. 8—Side section of seed hopper

The great-tit is, of course, larger and may have as many as eleven in one brood. It is powerful enough to oust most rivals for its nesting site. being able to pierce a bird's skull with its strong beak.

All nesting boxes should be placed so the entrance hole faces north, to avoid the sun's rays beating into the nest. At the end of the season the nesting material should be removed and baked to remove infestation.

Feeding Devices

Turning to the matter of feeding devices, although it must be admitted that at present we cannot spare the food, or obtain the seed to put in them, there is no reason why economical forms of these gadgets should not be made now against the day when once more we can supply the tits and finches with the foods they especially like.

Two of the types of food holders described here can be made from bark-covered log-slabs cut as mentioned for the nesting box. A fat-bell can be cut out of the solid log as follows.

Tit fat-bell.

Take a 6in. diameter log, 6ins. long, and cut it out as in Fig. 3 where the dotted lines indicate the original log. Commence by marking an inch from the edge, measure across 4ins., then cut the opposite side off. This gives the bottom of the bell

(Fig. 4). Mark off 1½ins. at the top from the edge, and 1in. from the bottom edge and cut as per the dotted lines. Similar cuts on the other sides give the result as in Fig. 3.

Chip out a shallow cupshaped cavity in the bottom, (the inside of the " bell "), say 1½ins. deep, to take melted fat run in and set (in palmier days). The tits soon find the fat if the bell is hung in a suitable position by means of a hook in the " roof," and cling on upside down to eat the fat, to the annoyance of the less acrobatic sparrow and starling.

A Peanut Hopper feeder is shown at Fig. 5. First cut a 6in. square roof slab. Then prepare four slabs so a box measuring 4ins. square inside can be assembled. Before nailing the sides, together, take two opposing sides and drill a row of holes ½in. from the bottom. Make them ½in. apart, and of suitable diameter to take stout wire bars tightly. The wire is fitted after the box is assembled as in Fig 6 which is a bottom end view of the hopper.

Now hinge the roof on and secure with a stout catch on the opposite side. A screw hook should be fitted in the top to hang it up. The nuts are kept pressed down on to the wire bars by means of a loose fitting wooden block 1in. thick.

A Weighty Block

The block must be thick and heavy not only to press the nuts, but also to prevent it jamming higher up in

the box and not falling with the nuts. Increase the weight of the block by scooping out a shallow pit in the top, (like an inlay) then filling it with molten lead run in. First fix in a stout round-head screw so you can lift the block out for re-filling (see Fig. 6). The feeding principle is as in the fat-bell : the tits cling on underneath, and peck upwards.

A Seed Hopper.

This useful feeder is ideal for the finches. Make a box similar to the nut feeder, except that there are only three sides and a floor. One side is an open front, with a wooden crosspiece at the top, and a similar crosspiece at the bottom. The bottom ledge keeps the seed from falling out from the floor. The completed Hopper is clearly shown at Fig. 7.

A piece of glass, for better observation of the hopper's contents, is fitted as (Fig. 8) a side section, being slotted into the sides. This finishes 1in. from the floor at a distance of 1in. from the back.

The method of use is to fill the hopper up from the top with seeds or grain, the food tumbling out on to the floor gradually, to replace that eaten.

These feeding gadgets hung from the bird table, or from rustic work at a height safe from cats, will give the beholder many hours of enjoyment, especially in the winter, apart from the question of the services rendered in return.

You get endless interest if you erect a
BIRD FEEDING STAND

THE Bird Table shown could very easily now be made out-of-doors, and set up ready for the autumn. Well seasoned deal would answer if well painted with wood preservative.

The first piece to prepare is the central post, four feet or so long, 2½ins. square. If it should look at all heavy this can be remedied by planing a chamfer on its four edges as shown.

The foot for the stand consists of pieces (B), (C) and (D). Two pieces of (B) are cut and halved together in the middle so the top and bottom surfaces come flush. These are screwed together and then screwed to the base of the post.

Foundation Parts

On top of these stand the four pieces (C) and trimmed to the same width as the post and nailed to it as shown in Figs. 1 and 2. The four blocks (D) are shaped up from stuff measuring 2½ins. square, and secured by running nails through th sloping surface into the post and screws up through the foot sections (B).

The four brackets E will next be cut and fixed, and —see the detail in Fig. 2. They are ½in. thick and the simple outline can easily be cut with a fretsaw. See the brackets come flush

and square with the top of the post before fixing them by means of nails or screws run through into the post.

The board or floor (F) is a square of ½in. wood nailed through to the brackets from the top. Before this floor is put on however, the upright (G) must be nailed to it, and also the two side brackets (H). In Fig. 3 the shape of the latter is given.

The two gable pieces (I) are next made as given in Fig. 4. Wood ½in. thick is again used. The two pieces are nailed to a cross piece J shown in Fig. 5. In the centre cut a halving slot 1¼ins. wide. by 1in. deep to fit into the top of the post (G) as shown in the ircl ed diagram.

The Roof

The roof covering pieces (L) are prepared and nailed to the gable pieces. These are five boards to each slope lapped ½in. over the piece below as in the diagram at Fig. 6. Commence with the lowest board, then mark the amount of lap upon it and lay on the second board and proceed thus to the top.

The ridge is finished and protected by nailing two boards together—(M) nad (N) and then nailing them thfough to the rail (J) below. While nailing on the

roof boards see that an equal projection is kept at each end beyond the gable boards I.

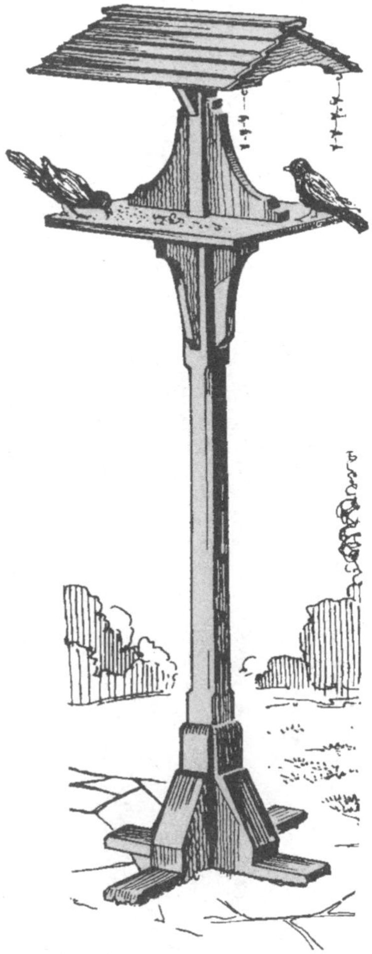

Final Additions

Before fixing the roof to the post the two bracket pieces (K) each side should be cut and nailed on (see Fig. 5). When fixing the ridge (J) to the gable pieces (I), add a couple of stiffening blocks each end and each side of the former as shown. All the woodwork should be painted two coats or creosoted.

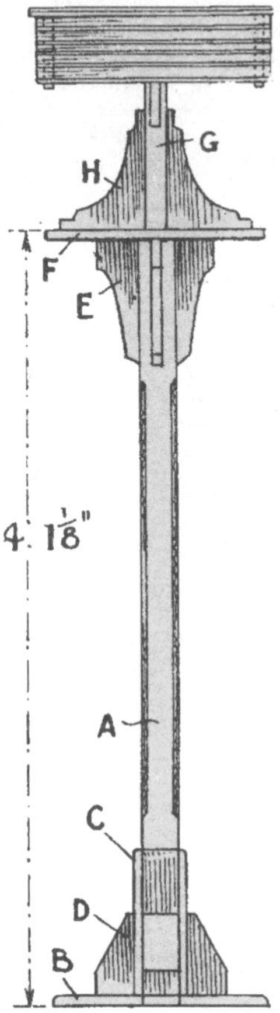

CUTTING LIST

A—1 piece 48 by 2½ins. by 2½ins.
B—2 pieces, 14 by 2½ins. by ⅝in.
C—4 pieces, 9 by 2½ins. by ⅝in.
D—4 pieces, 5 by 2½ins. by 2½ins.
E—4 pieces, 7½ by 2½ins. by ½in.
F—1 piece, 14 by 12ins. by ½in.
G—1 piece, 13 by 1¼ins. by 1¼ins.
H—2 pieces, 7½ by 5½ins. by ½in.
I—2 pieces, 13 by 4½ins. by ½in.
J—1 piece, 13 by 2ins. by ½in.
K—2 pieces, 6 by 3ins. by ½in.
L—10 pieces, 15 by 2ins. by ¼in.
M—1 piece, 15½ by 1¾ins. by ¼in.
N—1 piece, 15½ by 2ins. by ¼in.

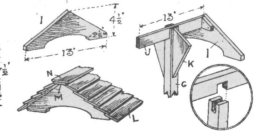

4. 1⅛"

Fig. 1—Section showing parts

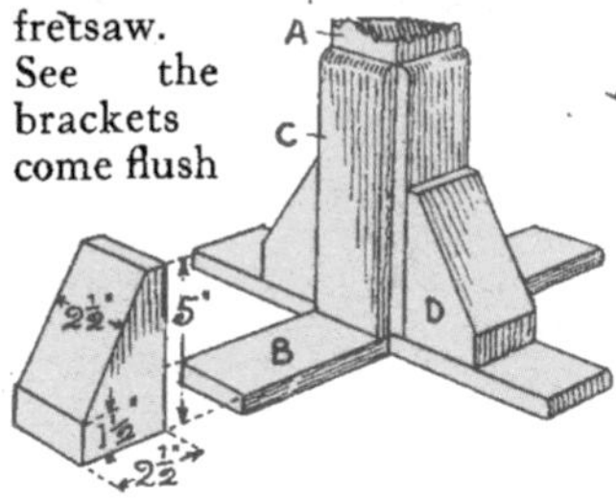

Fig 2—How the base is built

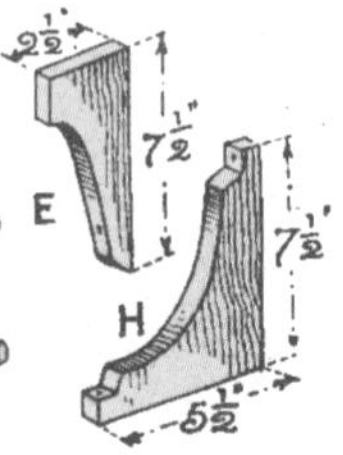

Fig 3— Brackets

Fig. 4—(above) The gables, & Fig. 6—(below) the roofing

Fig. 5—The roof supports

If you are worried by marauding animals make these
SAFE GARDEN TRAPS

MANY people who live in country districts have trouble with rabbits and game coming into their garden in early morn destroying and eating the centres out of young plants. There is no better trap than the steel trap. But the difficulty with it is that one may find his dog in it or the neighbour's cat—which is sure to cause strained relations.

Catch Them Alive

Box traps can be used when one wishes to catch these thieving animals. The box trap has the advantage that small animals can be taken alive so should a harmless animal be caught it can be released unharmed. Box traps can be used to catch rabbits, rats, strayed cats.

The trap shoud be made of old weathered boards if possible. The box consists of the sides and bottom with a partly fixed top as shown at Fig. 1.

at the front and top and may be strengthened with a bracket, Fig. 7. Use at least 1½in. nails in putting together the box and the drop door.

Of course, a great deal depends on the thickness of the material used and if the wood is over ¾in. thick 2in. nails are recommended. The handle is made up of strips of wood 1¾ins. by ¾in. and is raised about 8ins. above the top of the trap.

The Trap Set

The ½in. holes on the top of the handle and trap should be nice and smooth. The centre of the trigger arrangement should come in line with the centre of the hole. Fig. 3 shows how the trigger arrangement looks when it s set.

When apples or carrots are used for bait they can be tied to the trigger which is made from wood 2ins. by ¾in. The front end is reduced somewhat to take away as much of the weight as possible and all the breadth is required when corn or other grain is used.

lower edge level with the top of the box when open. When closed the cord should be slack. Therefore you will have to experiment a little to find out just where to place the screw eye or staple on the top of the door.

A Double Trap

A two-trap door, Fig. 6, which permits animals to enter from either side is sometimes better than a one-trap door. It requires a little more timber and more time to build, but may be worth it.

Both cords are fastened to the same catch thus both doors close at the same moment.

A screen opening is formed on the one side. Of course, one on each side might be better. Then you will know whether or not you have a weasel to deal with. At least you know what you have in the trap.

Wood and Finish

The wood for all these traps should be fairly thick and all joints made strong with glue as well as nails or screws. Remember that the animal may make a wild attempt to get out and if the box is not made strongly it will

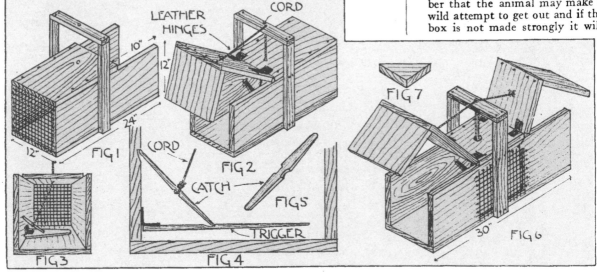

The dimensions given are approximate and may be changed somewhat to suit the timber at hand, but in all examples the drop door should be 10ins. In Fig. 1 the back of the trap is shown with a wire screen to enable one to see what is in the trap.

Fig. 2 shows the front of the trap with the drop door partly open and attached with leather hinges. The door should be a snug fit and be well nailed together

The catch for the trigger is shown at Fig. 5. The catch is fitted into a notch on the side of the box and the top of the trigger, Fig. 4.

The idea is that the downward pressure of the trigger releases the door. If the weight does not hold it up tie a flat stone to the top of the door or undercut the notch, shown at Fig. 4, deeper. The hinge is of leather.

Trap doors should have the

collapse and the animal get free.

There is no real need to paint the boxes, although of course, they would look much nicer and less conspicuous if treated with two coats. They would also naturally be more weatherproof.

Finish off the box nicely and place it in the "run" of the animal concerned. Bait it as necessary, but make sure to visit the catch fairly frequently. Do not leave the trapped animal for days.

slightly bevel the upper edge and nail round sides and back, letting the plinth project beneath ¾in.

Cut the porch sides, C (shown separately at Fig. 5) and nail in front, the bottom coming level with the top of the plinth. The porch roof is of ½in. thick wood, nailed across.

The sliding bars, A, are 10ins. long and cut from ½in. by 1¼in. wood. They are made to slide together so that the entrance can be adjusted in width as desired.

This is effected by either rebating the piece B or, what is simpler, making B of two pieces of ½in. thick wood and nailing them together, as in Fig. 6. Piece B is then nailed to the front of hive, between the porch sides. The brood chamber can now be fitted to the floor section.

The lift, Fig. 7 is the same dimensions and

IN making this standard bee-hive it is important to adhere to the dimensions given, and to use well seasoned timber of the specified thicknesses. The joints can be nailed together, using oval brads, and driving them in at an angle—skew nailing as it is called. Those who feel inclined to make stronger joints can dovetail the corners.

Fig. 1 shows the floor frame, the sides and ends are cut from 1in. thick timber. Leave 18ins. of the sides full width, reduce the width of the rest ½in., then, leaving the reduced portion 4ins. long, bevel the rest off.

The Floor Frame

The legs are 2ins. by 2ins. and are screwed to the frame to splay outwards, as in Fig. 2. The frame should now be covered with ½in. thick boards, as shown in Fig. 3 and blocks of the same thickness and measuring 2ins. sq. are glued and nailed where indicated.

The brood chamber, Fig. 4 comes next. Cut the front and back pieces of ½in. thick wood, and the sides of ⅝in. thick wood. Nail together. Cut lengths of ½in. by 1½ins. wood for the plinth,

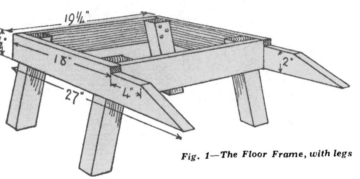

Fig. 1—The Floor Frame, with legs

made of the same thicknesses of wood as the brood chamber, except the height, which is 6½ins. The plinth is fitted the same also, then the lift

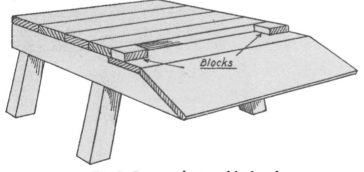

Fig. 3—Framework covered by boards

CUTTING LIST.

Floor Section—
Sides, 1in. by 2½ins. by 4ft. 6ins.
Ends, 1in. by 2½ins. by 3ft. 4ins.
Legs, 2ins. by 2ins. by 2ft. 10ins.
Floor, ½in. by 4½ins. by 9ft. 0ins.

Brood Chamber—
Sides, ⅝in. by 9ins. by 3ft. 2ins.
Ends, ½in. by 9ins. by 3ft. 3ins.
Porch, ½in. by 5ins. by 2ft. 4ins.
Plinth, 1in. by 1½ins. by 5ft. 0ins.
Piece B, ½in. by 1in. by 3ft. 0ins.
Piece A, ½in. by 1¼ins. by 1ft. 8ins.

Lift—
Sides, ⅝in. by 6½ins. by 3ft. 2ins.
Ends, ½in. by 6½ins. by 3ft. 3ins.
Plinth, 1in. by 1½ins. by 7ft. 0ins.

Body Box—
Sides, ⅝in. by 9ins. by 2ft. 11ins.
Ends, ½in. by 8½ins. by 2ft. 8ins.
Piece D, ⅜in. by ⅜in. by 2ft. 8ins.
Piece E, ¼in. by 1¼ins. by 2ft. 9ins.

Roof Section—
Sides, ¾in. by 2½ins. by 3ft. 5ins.
Ends, ¾in. by 3½ins. by 3ft. 7ins.
Roof, ½in. by 12ins. by 4ft. 0ins.
Ridge, 1in. by 2ins. by 2ft. 0ins.

can be dropped over on to the brood chamber.
The body box, which holds the honey sections, is drawn at Fig. 8. Make the sides of ⅜in. wood and the front and back of ⅝in. wood. The latter pieces are ⅜in. less in height as seen, and spaced inwards to leave 14½ins. clear between on the inside.

The roof section, Fig. 9, has sides and ends of ⅞in. thick wood, nailed together. At ½in. above the bottom edge nail ½in. sq. fillets across, back and front where shown. Bore ⅜in. ventilating holes and cover these on the inside with wire gauge to exclude insects.

The roof boards, ½in. thick, are cut large enough to overlap 1in. all round, and nailed on top. At the angle where they meet plane a 1in. flat to bed

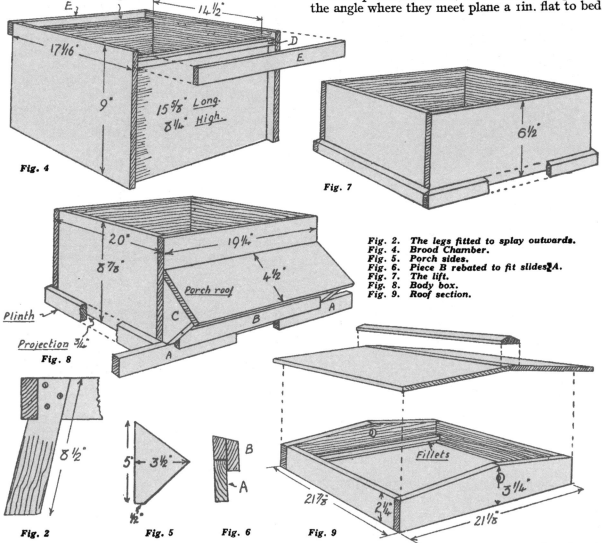

Fig. 2. The legs fitted to splay outwards.
Fig. 4. Brood Chamber.
Fig. 5. Porch sides.
Fig. 6. Piece B rebated to fit slides A.
Fig. 7. The lift.
Fig. 8. Body box.
Fig. 9. Roof section.

At D, nail across pieces of ⅝in. sq. wood, level with the front and back, which will just bring them level with the ends of the sides. To cover the open ends, nail across ¼in. thick strips of wood, E. The body box can now be placed inside the brood chamber.

the ridge capping on. The latter can be planed up from a piece of 1in. by 2in. wood and nailed.
Now drop the roof section on to the lift, the fillets keeping it in place. This completes the bee-hive, which can be painted on the outside to resist the weather.

CORPUS SANUM IN MENTE SANA

How to make a full size
CROSSBOW & ARCHERY BOW

ANGLER'S BOX AND SEAT

Gouges from Scrap

Get more fun at sea
from this simple
SURF BOARD

Prevent likelihood of damage
by making this twin
TENNIS RACKET BRACKET

Get more fun at the sea from this simple
SURF BOARD

HERE'S a recent type of surf board, with original improvements, with which you can bank and turn with ease when skimming along the sea in tow, of course, with a fast launch or motor-boat. The unusual control is due to " wings " attached to the board.

The wings slant about 25 degrees or more and thus enable the rider to " bank " much as a pilot banks his 'plane. Better and infinitely more exciting fun is to be had from this board than any other kind minus the wings. Such " skid " too much so that you easily over-balance.

A few minutes' practice, and you will manage the improved board like an expert. It is light, cheap and simply made, deal shelving being used, plus a few screws and a couple of iron bars (see list).

Construction of Board

The board is made up of three prepared shelving boards, same measuring 6ft. long by 10ins. wide by ⅞in. thick. Obtain the boards from your local timber yard; if they measure 10½ins. across, they will do.

To be strong, the three boards should be jointed together with glue and ⅜in. dowelling. It will prove satisfactory, however, if you prefer to attach them together with the top and rear battens only, same being detailed at Fig. 2.

When the boards are placed evenly together, note that the top batten is affixed on the face side and that the rear one goes to the reverse side. Use glue and 1½in. by 8 flathead iron screws.

MATERIALS

3 shelving boards, 6ft. by 10ins. by ⅞in.
2 wing pieces, Cut from waste of above.
1 rear batten, 30ins. by 10ins. by ⅞in
1 front ditto, 20ins. by 8ins. by ⅞in.
2 iron bars, 38ins. by 1in. by ¼in.
1 piece sash cord, 3ft. long by ⅜in.
1 piece ditto, 6ft. long by ⅜in.
Screws and dowelling as required.

Remove the rear corners from the boards to be flush with those of the batten. With a 6ft. length of wood (or a couple of 3ft. rules), pencil the tapering shape, then remove the waste with a saw, the rough edges being neatly planed.

The Side Wings

The wing boards are cut to size and shape from the waste wood from the surf board itself. When spokeshaved and glasspapered, attach them to the sides of the board about 3ins. from the edges of the latter. The iron bar used is about 38ins. long by 1in. wide by ¼in. thick; it is obtainable from most hardware stores.

Having filed the ends round, drill the number of holes shown on each to suit ¼in. by 6 roundhead iron screws, then bend up the ends to the required angle. Attach the bars to the board prior to adding the wings.

The Rope Holes

It has been assumed that the surf board itself has been rasped, spokeshaved and glasspapered. If so, proceed by boring the holes for the top rope and the rein piece.

If you use ⅜in. sash cord (this is strong enough for the job), the holes are made with a ½in. or ⅜in. bit. Countersink or pare same so the edges will not tend to wear away the rope through use.

The tow rope is not too long—a piece of sash cord about 3ft. will do, whereas the rein piece is about 6ft. long. Before pushing the cord ends through the holes and knotting them as at Fig. 3, the board should be enamelled.

Almost any colour is suitable, but surf boards are often quite bright in order to be easily seen afloat, should the tow ropes break. Apart from this, bright colours are always attractive. Light

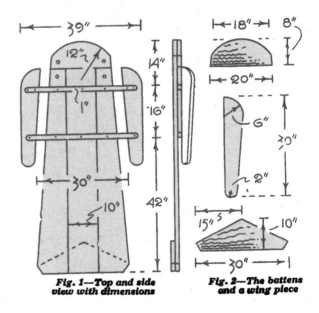

Fig. 1—Top and side view with dimensions

Fig. 2—The battens and a wing piece

green, red and blue are colours you could select, using one only, of course.

In view of dampness, two or three coats of old paint could be applied, after which the finishing colour is added. Be sure one coat is dry before adding another.

A free riding board is a board any swimmer can use without the aid of a motor-boat. It is taken out into the sea some distance from the shore, and is then turned about and "breasted" just in front of the swell or in the trough of a large incoming wave which effectively carries rider and board forward right up to the sands, so that the performance can be repeated again and again.

The surf board just described can be used in this manner, providing it is reversed.

Only swimmers should indulge in these sp[...] To learn the art, kneel first as shown, then st[...] up as you begin to feel confident. Always [...] well back so the board can "skim" over water.

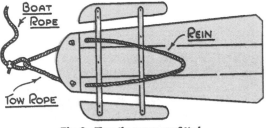

Fig. 3—How the ropes are fitted

SURF-RIDING is a sport that is both exciting and exhilarating and one that can easily be learnt. There are many places around our coasts and in the Channel Islands that are suitable for 'the art of surfing', and for quite a modest sum — about 10/- — an excellent board may be made.

Firstly, obtain from the wood merchants a piece of ¼in. mahogany resin-bonded plywood, 48ins. long and 12ins. wide. It is essential that the ply be resin bonded because this is waterproof. Clean off all edges with a smoothing plane and mark out the curve at the front. Cut near the line with a fretsaw and finish off with a sharp spokeshave. Smooth off the corners and all edges with glasspaper.

Making the bend

So far, the construction of the surf-board has been quite straightforward. The most difficult part is making the bend at the front. This bend upwards should be between 1½ins. and 2ins. from the straight.

HINTS ON SURF-RIDING
1. It is best to surf-ride on an incoming tide, when the waves seem to have more power. In any case only strong swimmers should 'ride' away from the shore.
2. Wade out into the sea until waist deep and then turn to face the beach.
3. Hold the surf-board in front of you, sloping upwards about 45° and held firmly into the body about where the top of your bathing trunks will be. In this position wait for a suitable wave.
4. The best waves for surfing are those that are just about to break or those that have just done so. When a wave approaches, glance behind and leap forward just a fraction of a second before it reaches you. Try to jump forward, keeping the front of the surf-board above water and at about the same speed as the wave.
5. The art of surfing lies in three things:
   (a) Keeping the front of the board above water.
   (b) Jumping forward at about the same speed as the wave.
   (c) Judging the right moment when to leap forward.
These three points will be learnt, on the average, in an afternoon. Of course, the more practice you get, the better you will be, and eventually you will probably get a surf-ride every time.

The surf-board described was easily and successfully bent by using a smooth log about 5ins. in diameter (any similar round and solid object would be suitable). This was held firmly in a vice. The round end of the surf-board was fully immersed in boiling water in a pail and left for about ten minutes, quickly taken out, and bent by hand around the log. Old rags are useful in this operation. Before it was dry the board was firmly held in position and left over-night to allow the curve to set. When dry, the curve will remain in position. On the

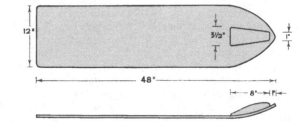

original, the tip of the surf-board was put under the leg of a bench and the back supported in a tilted position by the simple means of placing a chair under it.

The bending operation will have raised the grain of the ply-wood, so it will be necessary to glasspaper smooth again.

Supporting block

A block made from a light wood and shaped on the underneath to the curve on the surf-board will ensure that the board never loses its shape. Make the block from a piece of timber 2ins. by 3½ins. by 8ins. To get the exact curve, it

MATERIALS REQUIRED
One piece ¼in. mahogany resin-bonded plywood.
One piece pine 8ins. by 3½ins. by 2ins.
Brass screws: Two 1in. Number 8.
           Two 1½in. Number 8.
           One 1½in. Number 10.
Half pint yacht varnish (or enamel paint).
Resin glue (optional but advisable).

is a good idea to make a paper template, or pattern, and trace round this on to the wood. Make the top of the block into a streamline shape, rounding off all corners, and secure by means of screwing from the underneath with brass screws. Waterproof resin glue can also be applied.

To finish off the surf-board it is necessary to give it several coats of yacht varnish, glasspapering down in between each coat to ensure a final smooth finish. Of course, the board may be painted, preferably in gay colours, so that it can easily be located if washed out of your hands in the sea.

A surf-board so constructed will give years of service and endless hours of amusement. All that will be required in the way of maintenance is a glass-papering down at the end of the season and a coat of varnish or paint. (A.E.H.)

Gouges from Scrap

THE ribs from an old umbrella can be utilised for making small gouges which are very handy for use in model making or carving. There are usually two sizes of ribs used in umbrellas; these will make ⅟₁₆in. and ⅛in. radius gouges.

With a pair of pliers break off a 5in.

length, after cleaning off the paint, and grind the cutting end to an angle of 30 degrees, taking care not to get the metal too hot when grinding, as it will lose its temper and become very soft. Before sharpening with a slip stone, fasten the tool in a handle made of wood. (J.R.)

How to make a full size
CROSSBOW & ARCHERY BOW

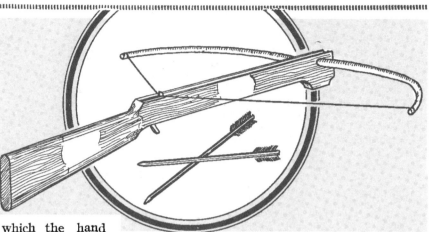

HERE are two ancient weapons of the chase quite capable of affording plenty of sport and amusement now. For the crossbow procure a piece of 1in. thick beech or other hardwood, 30ins. long and 4ins. wide. Divide this into 1in. squares with a soft lead pencil, as in Fig. 1, and copy the shape.

This is quite easy with the squares as a guide. Cut out and shape up, the butt being neatly curved top and bottom and that portion of the stock which the hand grips rounded.

On the top edge, at the distance from the butt end shown by the squares, cut a mortise slot 2ins. long and ¼in. wide, right through and from the slot to the end, work a groove, ½in. wide and ¼in. deep for the arrows to lie in.

Trigger Action

A detail of the trigger catch arrangement is shown at Fig. 2, and should be easy to understand. The trigger catch is shown full size at Fig. 3 and should be cut out of stiff sheet brass, 1/16in. or more in thickness. This is placed in the slot with brass washers each side to centre it, and pivoted by means of a stout wire nail driven through the stock. A small piece of the slot underneath should be chiselled out so that a spring can be fixed therein with a screw.

The other end of the spring is hooked in the small hole drilled in the trigger. A suitable spring is easily made by winding a piece of fine steel wire round a knitting needle. Fine piano wire or a banjo string will do.

To keep the trigger in place and prevent the spring pulling it too far forward a stop is fixed. This is seen in Fig. 2 and is merely a wire staple driven in to bridge the slot and keep the trigger back so that the catch appears just above the slot.

For the bow, get a length of ash, hickory or lancewood, ¾in. sq. and from 24 to 30ins. long. Plane this to round section and taper from the middle to each end to ⅜in.

Let the taper be a gradual one so that the bow can bend evenly. At the muzzle end of the stock bore a hole for the bow and insert.

Sea-fishing line or whipcord will do for the bow string. Cut a notch near each end of the bow and

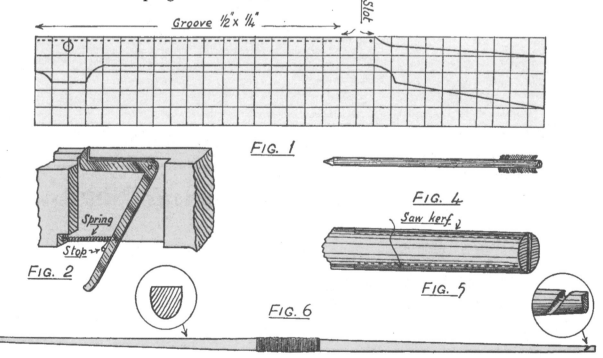

Groove ½" x ¼"

Slot

FIG. 1

FIG. 4

Saw kerf

FIG. 5

Spring

Stop

FIG. 2

FIG. 6

tie the string across, then give the bow a slightly upward turn so that the string lies level across the stock and is not likely to rub against it when released. Fix the bow in position by driving in a thin nail from underneath.

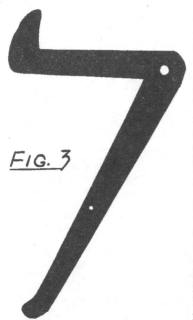

FIG. 3

An illustration of the arrows needed is given in Fig 4. Cut from ½in. dia. wooden rod, about 12ins. long, and taper to a point. To make the flights, run a fine tenon saw down each side to a depth of ⅛in. and a length of 3ins., as in Fig. 5.

Feathers are used for the flights. Trim off one side of each feather to the centre rib, cut to length and glue in the saw kerf. When the glue is hard, and not before, trim the feathers to shape.

Finish the crossbow by varnishing.

To use, draw the cord back by pulling with the first and second fingers until it slips over the catch. Lay an arrow in the groove, with its feathered end against the cord, and release by pulling the trigger.

To make the archery bow shown in Fig. 6, get a length of ash, hickory or lancewood, as for the crossbow. Bows can be made from 3 to 6ft., but a beginner is not advised to start with too powerful a bow. One about 4ft. long and shaped up from a piece of ¾in. sq. wood will do excellently for a start.

Some pains must be taken in the tapering if a well balanced bow is to result. A space of 5ins. in the centre, to be afterwards bound with thread like a cricket bat, should be made round.

From here it is tapered to the ends, the latter being ⅜in. Note the sectional shape it is trimmed to, as seen in Fig. 6, roughly D shape, with the rounded side towards the archer. The ends should be notched, as shown enlarged, for the string.

Trial

Whipcord or sea-fishing line will do for the string. This is provided each end with a small loop, to facilitate stringing, and should be long enough to bend the bow when strung so that it is about 5ins. away from the string at the centre.

Try the bow and if it bends unevenly, then the tapering needs some further attention. When satisfactory, bind the centre with stout thread and varnish the bow.

The middle of the string, for a space of 5ins., is also bound, this time with stout sewing silk, and the exact centre indicated by either a spot of red paint or a red thread tied round.

The arrows are best made from ash, and should be ½in. round and about 30ins. long. They are pointed and provided with feather flights 4 to 6ins. long

Prevent likelihood of damage by making this twin
TENNIS RACKET BRACKET

TENNIS is now a practically all-the-year-round sport although, of course, most is played in the summer months on account of the light evenings and there being less chance of half a gale blowing to deflect the ball.

For a keen tennis 'fan' who always wants his racket ready to hand instead of delving into some dark and crowded cupboard for it, the tennis racket bracket here described should prove very useful.

For Wall Fixing

As the illustration the heads this article shows, the bracket is intended for fixing on the wall, and holds two rackets. For convenience of illustration, one of the rackets is shown without any press or cover, but the other shows how the bracket is so designed to take a racket in a wooden press.

Practically any wood can be used, since if such good wood as oak is used, the bracket can be left in a natural colour, intensified with, say, wax polish,

but if such a common wood as deal is used, the job may afterwards be enamelled in bright colours.

Shaped Back

The back (Fig. 1) is first made from a piece of wood 8ins. by 4ins. by ½in. It is intended that the actual brackets (Fig. 2) be tenoned in, as in Fig. 3, as this

certainly makes the strongest job. It is possible to leave out the mortises and tenons and screw the brackets on with a long screw from behind, but this is not particularly recommended.

The best way to start clearing out the mortise holes is to bore two ½in. diameter holes right through and then clean the corners with a chisel. Whilst the brace and bit is handy, drill the holes for the hanging-up screws. These, incidentally, will be driven into the wall into which proprietary wall plugs have been fitted.

Brackets

The brackets are fully detailed and dimensioned in Fig. 2. At Fig. 3, we see an economical way of setting out the brackets to avoid waste. Naturally we have to cut a bit oversize to allow for trimming.

When the brackets have been cut, they are glued into the back, care being taken that the recesses are in line with each other. This simple job can be done in an evening, particularly if the two bracket pieces are shaped up together.

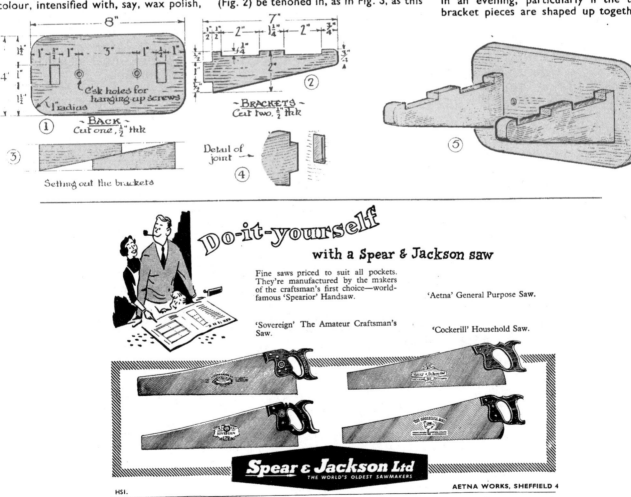

ANGLER'S BOX AND SEAT

THIS roomy tackle box, which can be slung over the shoulder, is ideal for the keen angler. Since it is strong enough to be used as a seat, it saves carrying extra weight in the form of a stool.

There is one large compartment at the top in which you can put items such as pike tackle, ground bait, plastic mac, etc. In the bottom is a drawer for smaller items such as quill floats, hooks, small reels etc. The drawer is held in place, while carrying, by means of a leather or canvas strap which also keeps the lid in position.

Use exterior grade plywood for pre-ference. It will withstand wet conditions and if well painted will last for years. If you can obtain it locally the best grade to use is B.S.1088, which is a marine grade used for boats. It costs a little more but is well worth the extra shilling or two.

The main dimensions are shown in the front and side views in Fig. 1, but of course these may be modified to suit your own particular requirements. Note that the positions of the straps are shown dotted.

Pieces A, B, C, D, and E are cut from $\frac{1}{2}$ in. plywood and are glued and screwed together as indicated in Fig. 2. The dis-tance between pieces C and E is 6 in. as shown in the front view. Use waterproof glue throughout.

The lid F, is now added as seen in Fig. 3. The $1\frac{1}{2}$ in. butt hinges are recessed to give a perfect fit. Reinforce the corners by adding triangular fillet. The drawer guides L are fixed to the ends A later, after the drawer is finished. Make up the drawer as shown in Fig. 4, cutting pieces G, H, and I from $\frac{1}{2}$ in. plywood. The bottom can be of $\frac{1}{8}$ in. hardboard. Secure the pieces with glue and screws. Finish off by adding a front of $\frac{1}{4}$ in. plywood as indicated in Fig. 5.

The Hobbies No. 703 handle is fixed

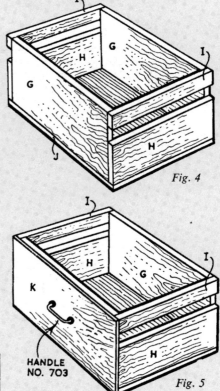

FRONT VIEW
Fig. 1

SIDE VIEW

Fig. 4

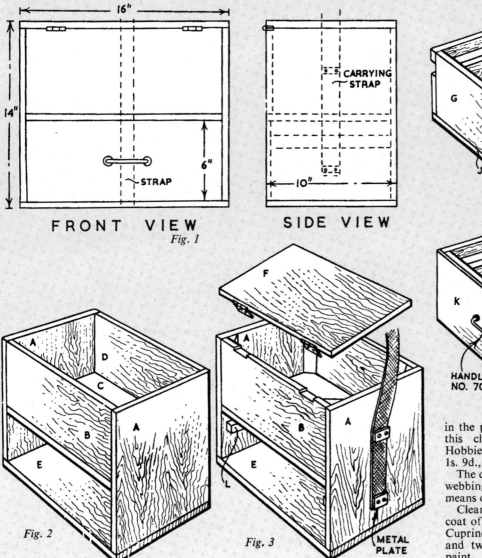

Fig. 2

Fig. 3

HANDLE NO. 703

Fig. 5

in the position shown. You can obtain this chromium plated handle from Hobbies Ltd., Dereham, Norfolk, price 1s. 9d., postage 4½d.

The carrying strap, made from canvas webbing or leather, is fixed to the ends by means of metal plates secured by screws.

Clean up with glasspaper and give a coat of clear wood preservative such as Cuprinol. Finish off with an undercoat and two top coats of exterior grade paint. (Mh.)

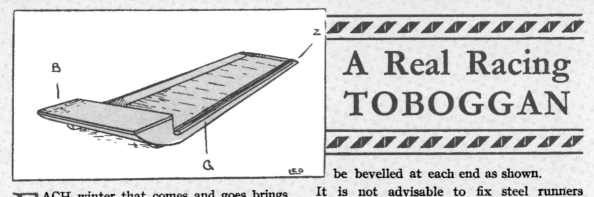

A Real Racing TOBOGGAN

EACH winter that comes and goes brings a small " army " of home-made toboggans; some of them good, some passable : So passable, in fact, that their owners are occasionally filled with disappointment and chargrin at the ease and certainty in which they are overtaken   But from careful observation, the trouble would seem to lie in a mistaken idea of the general principle of construction.

The prevalent design of the wierd and wonderful snow-gliders of the " home-made " variety, is roughly, a plank upon stilt-like " gliders " ; certainly not a pattern conducive to the exhilarating speed associated with the exciting thrill of a racing toboggan.

Without going into scientific details, it is sufficient to know that the runners usually fixed underneath most toboggans are not in the least necessary in the question of speed, and the great, thick contraptions, as used by the novice-constructor, are a positive hindrance. The small runners on a racing toboggan are affixed solely to protect the " floor " from wear by friction, and as a slight assistance in keeping a parallel course.

An Easily-made Racer.

The length of a toboggan varies according to the maker's requirements, of course, but the most favourable length for general English service is round about six feet. Procure two planks, 6ft. × 7in. × ½-in. Mark off 1ft. from the end (after tacking planks together), and slot down 4ins. (Fig. 1). Next, rule off with two parallel markings : one level with the bottom of the slot, and the other in the centre between the first mark and the outer edge of planks (Fig. 2), which, when cut down with a fine saw gives four strips of wood nearly 2ins. in breadth and 5ft. in length. Two of these will be made into runners, and must be bevelled at each end as shown.

It is not advisable to fix steel runners upon your racing toboggan, as these spoil a good " track " when the surface has been hardened into ice. The wooden runners will last quite a long time, even with hard usage, and it is a matter of little trouble to remove the worn runners and replace with new ones at any time that it is found necessary.

Now, mark a point opposite the " step " of the slot already dealt with (A., Fig. 3), and draw a smooth curve to B., Fig. 3. There you have the framework for the toboggan. Strips of wood 2ft. 6ins. are now needed to fill up the " floor " as far as the point " A," which starts the curved front. Almost any odd pieces will do for this, providing they are of equal thickness. For the curve, pieces 2ft. 6ins. are needed, but here, they must be no broader than 1in., so that they will form a fairly even curve, which must be planed smooth when the whole is fastened together.

The runners are now smoothed and fastened 2ft. apart underneath, the nails or screws used being counter-sunk slightly. All that is required to complete the racer is two strips of wood, 2ft. 6ins. × 1ft., and 2ft. 6ins. × 2ins. Cut the planks whilst tacked together with a little backward slant, as at point Z of the illustration of the completed racer, and fix the 2in. strip as shown, the 1ft. piece serving as at point B on sketch.

The two strips left over from the first cut (runners) can be used to advantage as a " grip rail," marked " G." A real racing toboggan ! —LEO.

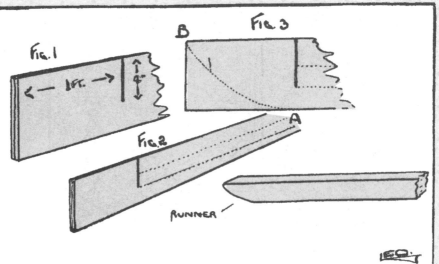

How to make a Cheap Horizontal Bar.

By Norman Lattey.

A SIMPLE but strong horizontal bar can be easily constructed out of five lengths of ordinary bamboo such as may be bought almost anywhere for a couple of shillings, whereas almost the cheapest thing you can buy to serve the same purpose costs over two pounds.

Select four pieces of bamboo about eight feet long and two inches in diameter. These dimensions, it may be said, are suitable for a full-sized apparatus, and would place the bar seven feet above the ground. For a shorter person, or a boy, the bamboos need not be so long. See that they are not too dry. Rather green canes are the best, especially for the cross bar, which has to bear a good weight and must be very tough. This latter should be made from a piece of male bamboo, a variety easily recognised by the smallness of its bore.

Fig. 1.

Having procured the materials, and being provided with four stout pegs about two feet long sharpened at the ends, and a supply of good strong but thin rope, lash the thick bamboos together in pairs as in Fig. 1. In binding the string round them, pass it once or twice *between* the bamboos so as to form a sort of flexible hinge. About a foot from the ends of the thinner bamboo intended for the cross bar, tie the string *tightly*, leaving two loose ends, as shown in Fig. 2. In this sketch also the almost solid form of the male bamboo is apparent. The

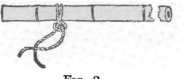

Fig. 2.

use of the loose ends is illustrated in Fig. 3, where they will be seen holding the cross bar to its supports. The necessity of binding these very tightly is obvious, as otherwise the bar is apt to slip round and round in the grip of the hands, which of course is not desirable.

The guy ropes, by which the utmost rigidity is secured, can be well strained or instantly re-

leased by the simple contrivance sketched in Fig. 4. The block A is of rather hard wood some six or eight inches in length, three inches in width, and one inch in thickness; it must have two holes bored in it near the ends *just large enough for the string to pass through.* The

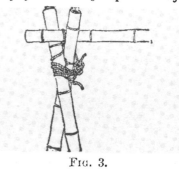

Fig. 3.

method of threading the rope through them is made clear by the sectional sketch B; and the entire contrivance in operation is shown at C.

Fig. 5 is a view of the complete apparatus erected. The guy ropes may occasionally need tightening, according to the energy put into

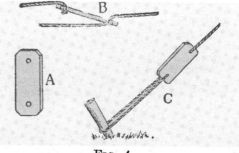

Fig. 4.

the gymnastic exercises; but this will depend on the quality of the rope used. The whole affair can be pulled down and set up again in a few minutes. It will also conveniently pack up into a compact bundle tied together by its own strings. Should the bar exhibit any tendency to curvature, the disposition can be easily overcome by turning the cane round from time to time, in order that the strain may not always be in the same direction. A thin rod of iron

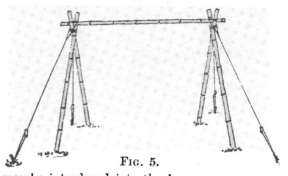

Fig. 5.

may be introduced into the bore as a core to impart additional strength, the internal partitions of the bamboo being removed by heating the end of the rod red hot. But if the bamboo be a sound and young one, not too dry, this extra precaution need not be taken. It will, however, be advisable to subject the bar to a few trials with a weight much in excess of what it will be expected to bear, in order to ensure safety.

FEW ever have the opportunity of visiting continental resorts and taking part in the winter games, chief amongst which is ski-ing. This excellent sport may now, however, be enjoyed in our own land by using wheel-skis in place of the continental kind.

This is a really healthy and enjoyable sport which will become popular in this and other countries, as unlike the older form of ski-ing, there is no need to wait for a heavy fall of snow, but it may be practised all the year round.

The Wheels

Ski-wheels having a flat running board—the smallest size for boys being a little over 2ft. long—with wheels fitted at each end. These should be of the metal disc type, fitted with heavy rubber tyres to absorb shock. A foot rest is fixed on the running board, and leather straps provided for holding the foot securely to the rest.

One of these ski-wheels is shown at Fig. 1, from which it will be seen how simple it is to make. A pair of skis must be provided to enjoy the sport, and also a pair of ski-sticks, but the total cost of the whole outfit is quite nominal.

As the skis will be subject to hard wear and many shocks, it will be necessary to make them strong to prevent accidents. It is therefore advisable to use hardwood for the parts shown at Fig. 2.

Running Board

Each running board is made with three pieces of wood bolted together, and while there is nothing difficult about the construction, the wood must be planed straight and true. For the smallest size ski the two outer pieces of wood should be 2ft. 4ins. long, and the middle piece 1ft. 4ins.

All are required 1in. thick, and when they are finally fixed together the total width should be 3½ins. The object of having three pieces of wood and bolting them together is to form the recesses for the wheels to fit in, as shown at Fig. 1, and the exact width of the various pieces depends upon the thickness of the wheels.

If this is 1in., then the middle piece will be the same thickness, and the two outer pieces 1¼ins. to bring the total width to 3½ins. The positions in which the bolt holes should be drilled are clearly indicated. Four series of holes are required in each running board, two bolts being used to fix the three pieces together, and two for attaching the wheels. The two bolts which fix the pieces together should be fitted and screwed up, iron washers being placed under the nuts to prevent them from cutting into the wood.

Foot Rests

The foot rests are then prepared and fitted, each requiring a piece of wood 9ins. long by 3½ins. wide by 1in. thick.

A piece 2ins. long is recessed at the back for the heel of the boot to fit in, and the front part is hollowed for the sole. Two screws are sufficient to fix the rests to the running boards. The ends of the running boards should be nicely rounded over, as shown at Fig. 3, before the wheels are attached with bolts.

Bolts and Bearings

These bolts should not be screwed so tight that they will prevent the wheels from working freely, the bearings should be well greased, and if there is any fear of the nuts on the bolts working loose, the ends of the bolts could be burred over. As far as the skis are concerned, the only thing remaining is the foot straps.

A pair should be arranged to fit right over the boot, one near the toe, and another as far back on the foot as possible, while a third is arranged to run back around the heel. Fixing could be accomplished with round-head screws, iron washers being placed under their heads, and the ends of the straps doubled back for strength.

It will be necessary to carefully arrange the straps with the buckles outside, and when the correct positions have been ascertained a few stitches could be carried through the heel strap, and each of the others where they meet, to hold them together.

By careful adjustment it will only be necessary to unbuckle the heel strap to remove the foot.

The ski-sticks should be 4ft. 6ins. long by 1in.

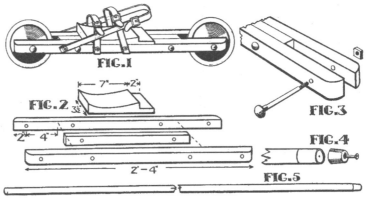

FIG.1 FIG.2 FIG.3 FIG.4 FIG.5

diameter for the smaller size skis. Details have been shown at Figs. 4 and 5 because it will be necessary to tip the bottom ends with metal ferrules, and below them some may care to fit rubber tips, which may be attached with screws. On some surfaces these tips hold better.

Painting a ski-ing outfit is important to its good appearance and it is possible to obtain a striking effect with bright colours.

HOBBIES LTD

Hobbies is still thriving after supplying modelmakers since 1895 and is looking forward to supplying the hobbyist for the next 100 years. Although no longer based in Dereham, it is still located in Norfolk at The Raveningham Centre, just a few miles from Norwich.

Hobbies has a large shop that is crammed full of wonderful craft and modelling ideas.
The mail order side of the business goes from strength to strength, with orders received from around the world.
Why not take a look at the Hobbies website

Contact Hobbies at:
Units 8–11
The Raveningham Centre
Beccles Road
Raveningham
Norfolk
NR14 6NU

Telephone: 01508 549330
Website: www.alwayshobbies.com

To request a full catalogue of Ammonite Press titles, please contact:

**AE Publications Ltd, 166 High Street, Lewes,
East Sussex, BN7 1XU, United Kingdom
Tel: +44 (0)1273 488006 Fax: +44 (0)1273 472418
www.ammonitepress.com**